A
CONNECTICUT
★ Y A N K E E ★
GOES TO WASHINGTON

SENATOR GEORGE P. MCLEAN, BIRDMAN OF THE SENATE

WILL MCLEAN GREELEY

RIT Press
Rochester, NY

Published and distributed by:
RIT Press
90 Lomb Memorial Drive
Rochester, New York 14623
http://ritpress.rit.edu

ISBN 978-1-939125-99-6 (print)
ISBN 978-1-956313-00-0 (e-book)

Printed in the U.S.A.
Cover design: Eric C. Wilder
Cover photo: Alpha Stock / Alamy Stock Photo

Library of Congress Cataloging-in-Publication Data

Names: Greeley, Will McLean, 1956—author.
Title: A Connecticut Yankee goes to Washington : George P. McLean, birdman
 of the Senate / Will McLean Greeley.
Identifiers: LCCN 2022025689 (print) | LCCN 2022025690 (ebook) | ISBN
 9781939125996 (softcover) | ISBN 9781956313000 (ebook)
Subjects: LCSH: McLean, George Payne, 1857–1932. | Legislators—United
 States—Biography. | United States. Congress. Senate—Biography. |
 Governors—Connecticut—Biography. | Statesmen—Connecticut—Biography.
 | Conservationists—Connecticut—Biography. | Hartford
 (Conn.)—Biography.
Classification: LCC E748.M1544 G74 2022 (print) | LCC E748.M1544 (ebook)
 | DDC 328.73/092 [B]—dc23/eng/20220602
LC record available at https://lccn.loc.gov/2022025689
LC ebook record available at https://lccn.loc.gov/2022025690

A Connecticut Yankee Goes to Washington

To my parents

PRAISE FOR *A CONNECTICUT YANKEE GOES TO WASHINGTON: SENATOR GEORGE P. MCLEAN, BIRDMAN OF THE SENATE*

"On one level this is a fascinating, and thoroughly researched, glimpse into the workings of US politics in the early twentieth century. On another level it's an inspiring story of one man's determination and steadfast commitment to securing legal protections for birds. I am glad to know more about George McLean."
—David Sibley, author and illustrator of *The Sibley Guide to Birds*

"This engaging biography reconstructs the career of Senator George P. McLean, highlighting his spirited campaign to protect migratory birds from excessive game-hunting. McLean skillfully shepherded his bill through both Republican and Democratic administrations, overcame strident opposition in Congress, and established an enduring environmental policy."
—Donald A. Ritchie, US Senate Historian Emeritus

"Will Greeley has written a careful scholarly work about an influential politician whom historians have, unfortunately, neglected. This is a thoughtful, and very nicely written, book about people and politics. Not to mention: birds too! And there's a bonus: this book is also a love song to a distant relative. We need more historians who truly care about the people they're writing about, and Greeley does just that."
—Robert D. Johnston, PhD, historian, University of Illinois/Chicago

"This book provides wonderful insights into Connecticut politics from the Civil War to the Roaring Twenties. George P. McLean was a Connecticut powerhouse, serving in its legislature: governor, US attorney, and US senator. Will Greeley does a tremendous job in telling the extraordinary story of this man, his contributions, and his times."
—The Honorable Stanley A. Twardy, Jr., Partner, Day Pitney LLP, former United States Attorney for Connecticut, and chief of staff and aide to Lowell Weicker, governor and US senator for Connecticut

"One of the tragedies of American politics is that we focus so much on presidents and, even then, only the most charismatic. Lost to posterity are the state legislators, governors, and congresspeople who have shaped the American experience. Greeley's biography reminds us of Senator George P. McLean and the politics behind the progressive movements of Roosevelt and LaFollette, the crucible of World War I, and the irrational exuberance of the Roaring Twenties. Greater still is McLean's conservation legacy. A richly painted portrait, no other book does as much to illustrate the life of this Connecticut icon."
—Dr. Michael P. Cullinane, PhD, MA, BA

"I highly recommend *A Connecticut Yankee Goes to Washington: Senator George P. McLean, Birdman of the Senate* to anyone interested in the history of the conservation movement in the United States. For a quarter century, I have taught my ornithology students about the vital importance of the Migratory Bird Treaty Act, but until I read this wonderful book, I had no knowledge of its origins. Will Greeley has done a great service to avian conservation by explaining, in lucid and engaging prose, how political maneuvering and strategies that sound all too familiar to a twenty-first-century ear produced the Weeks-McLean Act, and then the Migratory Bird Treaty Act, which has weathered political challenges for more than one hundred years."
—Dr. Geoffrey Hill, PhD, MS, BS, professor and curator of birds

"The Migratory Bird Treaty Act of 1918 is considered to be one of the most important conservation achievements of the twentieth century, credited for saving millions or even billions of birds, but few of us who value and appreciate this law know the history and sausage-making behind it. During the current era of deep partisan and cultural divide, it is useful and inspiring to be reminded that, historically, both Democrats and Republicans have championed environmental conservation. Senator George McLean was a wealthy, progressive Republican who witnessed declines in bird populations during the course of his lifetime and understood that federal and international laws—with teeth—were necessary to reverse this disturbing and dangerous trajectory."
—Dawn Hewitt, editor of *Bird Watcher's Digest*

"In the process of recovering the story of an esteemed ancestor, Will McLean Greeley has expansively illuminated a significant figure in Connecticut history and the transformative era of industrial growth and reform through which he lived. Greeley's book vividly brings to life his great-great-uncle George P. McLean (1857–1932), Connecticut governor and longtime US senator, showing both his personal side as a well-to-do descendant of colonial Connecticut's Protestant settlers and his career as a Republican Party lawyer and politician who engaged major state and national issues and personalities of his day, secured enactment of the federal Migratory Bird Treaty Act of 1918, and befriended national leaders such as President Calvin Coolidge. In doing so, Greeley has unearthed a wealth of new information about a neglected period of Connecticut history and its Republican side, an accomplishment that should interest professional historians and Connecticut history enthusiasts alike."
—Donald W. Rogers, author of *Making Capitalism Safe: Work Safety and Health Regulation in America, 1880–1940* (2009)

"The Weeks-McLean Act of 1913, one of the great milestones in the history of American bird conservation, has been eclipsed in the popular consciousness by its successor, the Migratory Bird Treaty Act of 1918. George P. McLean was instrumental in the drafting and passage of both laws. This new and comprehensive biography of McLean—senator, governor, and pioneering conservationist—sets those accomplishments in the rich context of a life of public service in an America undergoing some of the most rapid changes in its history. Greeley's gracefully written and thoroughly researched biography is highly recommended to anyone interested in the politics of conservation."
—Rick Wright, Victor Emanuel Nature Tours

"I would highly recommend this wonderful book, which focuses on the important role of George P. McLean in Connecticut and national politics in the late nineteenth and early twentieth centuries. I was fascinated by the role that McLean played in promoting legislation protecting birds; this is a part of environmental history that I knew nothing about. Will Greeley cares deeply about the relative that is his subject matter; I was brought to tears by the epilogue of this book."
—Stephen Armstrong, Social Studies Consultant,
Connecticut State Department of Education

★ CONTENTS ★

★ PREFACE ★

My name is Will McLean Greeley. Middle names sometimes don't seem important, but at a recent family reunion, I noticed that over a quarter of the 150 or so of those attending shared the middle name "McLean." Why had so many people chosen to give their children that middle name?

I remember first asking my parents about my middle name when I was a child, sitting with them in the living room of our home in Kalamazoo, Michigan. "That's your father's great-uncle, I think, George McLean," my mother said. "What did he do?" she asked my father, hopefully, knowing he was generally lukewarm on the subject of genealogy.

"He was a Republican," my father replied disdainfully, shrouded by his newspaper.

"Yes," my mom sighed. She too was a passionate Democrat, so McLean's party affiliation was indeed regrettable. "But wasn't he a governor or something?"

"A *rock-ribbed* Republican," my dad emphasized, ending the conversation.

My mom rose from the couch and moved toward a framed photo on the wall.

"That's George McLean, seated on the steps, holding his hat."

She did her best to describe the other people in the photo, starting with my father, the youngest, sitting on the lap of his uncle William Roger Greeley. George McLean and his wife appeared stern and im-

The Greeleys and the McLeans at Holly House in Simsbury,
1926 (McLean's executive secretary, W.H. Sault, is in the top row, middle)
(source: author's collection)

peccably dressed in the portrait; peeking out between them was a little white bulldog. They looked like the kind of older couple that as a
child I couldn't get away from fast enough. But there was something
interesting, even haunting, about that photo, seeing my dad and his
extended family in their younger days, and George McLean looked
like a serious and substantial man. Someday, I would learn more about
my namesake.

About fifty years later I made good on that vow. Early in my research
on George McLean, I found an intriguing newspaper article about a
speech he made in 1901 to the New England Society of New York.

Newspaper coverage of his speech was extensive, with one leading paper portraying him as an exciting new political star bursting upon the national scene.[1] The young governor of Connecticut dazzled his audience of 500 wealthy New Yorkers, including J.P. Morgan, in an after-dinner speech entitled "Connecticut and the Puritan."

During the speech at New York City's posh Waldorf-Astoria Hotel, McLean was interrupted twenty-seven times by laughter and applause. The *Chicago Inter-Ocean* hailed McLean as "brilliant, witty, charming…unconventional…spontaneous…a fascinating personality."[2] His audience of wealthy financiers and industrialists, wearing tuxedos, smoking cigars and sipping brandy, loved his irreverent barbs lampooning New England's Puritans. The incongruity between the stern man in the family photo and the young governor basking in a standing ovation at the Waldorf captivated me. What else didn't I know about George McLean?

While many former governors and politicians donate their papers to libraries and historical societies, George McLean did not. Why hadn't he given his papers to Yale University, for example, where he received an honorary master's degree in 1904, or to Hartford's Trinity College, where he was given an honorary doctor of laws in 1929? What happened to his papers? Had he wanted them destroyed? McLean died suddenly at the age of seventy-four, so maybe his papers disappeared due to neglect, if they were ever collected in the first place.

A decade or so after George McLean died in 1932, his nephew (and my great-uncle), William Roger Greeley, asked historian Lewis Mumford to write a biography of McLean for $5,000 (which represents around $75,000 in 2020 dollars).[3] This substantial sum would have

---

1   "George P. McLean's Debut," *The Daily Inter-Ocean* (Chicago), December 25, 1901, 7.

2   Ibid.

3   William Roger Greeley, "A Letter to Hugh Payne Greeley from his brother" (unpublished manuscript, 1961).

allowed Mumford to create a thorough account of George McLean's life just fifteen years after his death. Mumford, a college dropout who in later years held teaching posts at Dartmouth, Stanford, and the University of Pennsylvania, was a self-described generalist with broad knowledge of literature, political science, philosophy, religion, economics, and architectural history.[4] It was through his interest in architecture that Mumford met Boston-architect William Roger Greeley in the late 1920s. In 1944, the two men served on the judging panel for the "Boston Contest," an urban renewal initiative conceived by the Boston Society of Architects.[5]

My great-uncle thought Mumford would have written a very interesting biography of his Uncle George. "I got him to agree to do it but Aunt Juliette [McLean's widow] refused to cooperate or finance the project. It appears that it will never be done."[6] One wonders what Mumford, the author of over twenty books and "one of the most original voices of the twentieth century,"[7] would have revealed about George McLean. Mumford wrote a critically acclaimed biography of Herman Melville in 1929, which the *New York Times* described as "the best book on Melville that we have," praising Mumford for placing Melville in his historical context and examining the spiritual aspects of his life.[8]

And why is it that Aunt Juliette "refused to cooperate"? Was it more

---

4   Robert Wojtowicz, "Lewis Mumford: The Architectural Critic as Historian," *Studies in the History of Art*, 35 (1990): 237.

5   Jeffry M Diefendorf, *The Boston Contest of 1944: Prize Winning Programs* (New York: Routledge, 2015), 31. This wartime contest offered a $5,000 prize for a "broad overall master plan to develop postwar Boston." In a speech about the contest in 1944, Greeley said "it is unfortunate that, unlike London, Boston had not suffered bombardments that would open the way to create change in an unhealthy city."

6   William Roger Greeley, "A Letter to Hugh Payne Greeley from his brother" (unpublished manuscript, 1961).

7   Eugene Halton, "A Brief Biography of Lewis Mumford," posted on the website of the University of Notre Dame, https://www3.nd.edu/~ehalton/mumfordbio.html.

8   Herbert Gorman, "That Strange Genius, Melville: Lewis Mumford Writes a Notable Study of *Moby Dick*'s Creator Herman Melville," *New York Times*, March 10, 1929, 4.

Lewis Mumford, (1895–1990) historian, sociologist, and literary critic (source: Lewis Mumford Papers, Kislak Center for Special Collections, Rare Books and Manuscripts, University of Pennsylvania)

than humility and self-effacement that caused her to block the project? Was she reluctant to publish the story of her beloved husband's humble origins, his struggles with political loss, and his frustration with political corruption? Were there secrets she did not want told?

Blazing a new trail on the life of George P. McLean came naturally to me. My career goal in graduate school at the University of Michigan had been to be an archivist at a historical or presidential library. As an intern at the Bentley Historical Library, I found the work slow and stifling: I once cataloged a giant American flag made from thousands of pieces of red, white, and blue elbow macaroni, an unsolicited gift sent to President Gerald R. Ford in honor of the US Bicentennial. My passion for research eventually took me in an unexpected direction, into the world of business and market research. I was indeed blessed, enjoying a thirty-five-year career in a variety of corporate and government settings.

Documenting McLean's life has been something akin to a scavenger hunt, finding documents that became puzzle pieces: newspaper articles, photos, speeches, references to McLean in biographies, scholarly articles, PhD dissertations, and invaluable letters he wrote or received housed in more than a dozen different archives. While George McLean did not write about himself, many of his nephews, nieces, and their children did, and these priceless, unpublished memoirs are an integral part of this narrative as well. Additionally, I have tried to put George McLean into historical context to add meaning and significance to what we do know about him.

Why write a biography about George Payne McLean? McLean's life story is a prototypical rags-to-riches American tale: an obscure farm boy who grew up wearing homespun clothing but later achieved enormous wealth and used his considerable talents to better the world. McLean knew eight US presidents, advised five of them, and hunted and fished with four. He lived a very public life that elucidates three fascinating periods of our nation's history: the Gilded Age, the Progressive Era, and the Roaring Twenties. He lived from 1857 to 1932, a period of massive economic and social change. For instance, the US population increased six-fold during his lifetime, from 23 million in 1850 (about the size of Florida today), to 123 million in 1930.[9] He lived during tremendous technological advances, like the advent of electricity, the internal combustion engine, the telephone, and the airplane. While McLean believed deeply in the value of free enterprise and industrialization, he is remembered most as an environmental conservationist. For nearly seven years as a US senator, he applied his legal acumen, coalition building skills, and the single-minded zeal of a Progressive-Era

---

9   US Census Bureau, "Historical Census Statistics on Population Totals By Race, 1790 to 1990," https://www.census.gov/content/dam/Census/library/working-papers/2002/demo/POP-twps0056.pdf.

reformer to help create meaningful and lasting international protections for migratory birds. His crowning achievement was his bipartisan senate legislative effort resulting in the 1918 Migratory Bird Treaty Act.

In a speech McLean made at the Union League Club of New Haven in 1902, he urged his wealthy listeners to accept the need to reform society and end corruption. "We are living through a time of great societal change," McLean noted in his speech. The industrial world moves faster and farther in one year than it did in an ancient century. They were living in a "billion-dollar age," an age of miracles, a wonderful age, and a very progressive age. But McLean issued a warning—America needed to avoid the fate of Rome. It too grew and prospered, but eventually fell because of "rot at the core" from political corruption, tyranny, instability, and decadence. [10]

McLean was in essence a political reformer who sought to stop America's "rot at the core." The key objectives of the Progressive movement were using government power to solve problems caused by industrialization, urbanization, immigration, and political corruption. While McLean marveled at the wonders of the industrial world, he was not blind to its consequences: the political machines, the urban slums, the lynching of Black people, the unsafe food, the use of child labor, and the environmental destruction so evident in his day.

There were essentially two George Payne McLeans: *Farmer McLean*, anchored in the values of Simsbury and his puritan ancestors, and *Urban George*, living affluently for most of his adult life in Hartford, Connecticut, and Washington, DC. This contrast of archetypes generated tension and struggles in his life, creating many peaks and a few deep valleys. To set things right, George McLean sought to create order out of chaos, both within himself and the world around him. As governor of Connecticut and as a US senator, he was at heart a political reformer

---

10   "McLean Speaks: One More Rule for Convention," *Hartford Daily Courant*, January 16, 1902, 1.

who used compromise to help resolve some of America's greatest social, political, and economic problems.

Born in 1857, bullied by schoolmates for wearing homespun clothing, he became one of the wealthiest men in Connecticut by the turn of the century. As a child, he sat on a pine bench in a one-room schoolhouse, learning about his heroes George Washington, Abraham Lincoln, and senate oratorical giant Daniel Webster. In his sixties, McLean would occupy the very desk Webster used in the senate, rising from it to deliver his own carefully-crafted speeches on such topics as preparing for the Great War, the proper national economic system, and the need for key reforms in the Progressive Era. McLean was a very ambitious man but not without principle. He attained political power so he could use it for the benefit of the people. He trusted them; they trusted him. After all, despite his immense wealth, he knew that he was one of them: a thankful citizen born in an imperfect country that could be improved through good governance, one who dreamed about doing great things in a nation with seemingly unlimited possibilities.

While McLean worked closely with world leaders and witnessed some of history's greatest moments, his life was filled with struggle and disappointment. As governor of Connecticut, his efforts to democratize the Connecticut legislature ended in bitter defeat and political exile. But it will be shown that his political and personal struggles merely set the stage for a successful political comeback in the US Senate. His life story is also an example of how adversity plays a vital role in growth and greatness.

What follows is a reconstruction of George P. McLean's remarkable life, using the best available sources, created by a descendant born nearly one hundred years after his birth, curious to learn about the man who led the fight to save the world's birds.

★ ACKNOWLEDGMENTS ★

Researching and writing a book is a solitary process; but publishing one requires a team of experienced professionals. I am grateful for the support of RIT Press (Rochester, NY), namely Director Bruce Austin, and Interim Managing Editor Steven Bradley, and Managing Editor Alexandra Hoff. I especially appreciated their peer reviews and editorial suggestions, along with the work of copy editor Andrea Valluzzo. Special thanks go to freelance copy editor William Hoelzel for his invaluable editorial assistance and suggestions, and manuscript reviews by Dr. Donald Rogers of Central Connecticut State University. Sincere thanks go to the library and archival staffs at the Connecticut State Library, Connecticut Historical Society, Simsbury Historical Society, Torrington Historical Society, McLean Care Archives, New York Public Library, Yale University, Harvard College, Trinity College in Hartford, and Central Michigan University, among others.

I'm also grateful to my siblings and cousins who encouraged me to write this book, especially Penny Elwell, Carl and Faith Scovel, Brad Greeley, and Robert G. Kaiser. Special thanks go to Ginger Greeley for assembling unpublished family documents about George P. McLean. I would also like to thank Bill and Marylin Cox, who shared many insights on the McLeans.

Many of my aunts and uncles, now deceased, inspired me to write this account of George McLean's life: David and Cynthia Greeley, Mac and Virginia Greeley, Sam and Boo Greeley, and especially Phil and Hannah Kaiser, both keen students of history and government.

Thanks go to my late cousin Dana McLean Greeley, who gave me the rosewood flute that originally belonged to George McLean's father, Dudley Bestor McLean. It was made in New York City by Charles Christman around 1840 and provides me with a unique connection to the McLeans.

I lost my mother Katherine P. Greeley on October 19, 2021. Her encouragement throughout my life to "reach for the stars" provided much of the inspiration for this book. Along with my history-loving father, Roger, my parents spurred my passions and curiosities with their constant love and support.

This book would not have been possible without the love, encouragement, and advice from my wife, Mary. She has stood by me during every phase of this project with caring and loving support.

★ INTRODUCTION ★

A MIDLIFE COMEBACK (1905)

> If the question of the succession to the late US Senator
> Platt were put to a popular vote, Mr. McLean's triumph
> would now be regarded as assured.
> *Springfield (Massachusetts) Republican, May 2, 1905*

It was almost eight o'clock in the evening when the sandwiches and bananas finally arrived at the Capitol in Hartford on a warm evening in early May 1905. Deadlocked on the twelfth ballot, the 247 hungry Connecticut Republican House and Senate caucusers realized that the selection of the next Connecticut Republican candidate for the US Senate was going to take a while. The first ballot had been cast at two o'clock that afternoon, and most of the participants had expected the proceedings to wrap up by six.

Forty-seven-year-old George P. McLean, whom one newspaper had dubbed "The People's Candidate,"[1] was the clear frontrunner, having tallied 103 votes on the first ballot, just twenty-one shy of the 124 votes needed for the Republican nomination to the US Senate. McLean and the other candidates were vying for their party's nomination, but they

---

1   "McLean: The People's Candidate," *Hartford Courant*, April 29, 1905, 8.

knew that the winner would go on to the US Senate, so dominant was the Republican Party in Connecticut in 1905.

During the first ten ballots, the mood had been serious, the caucusers solemnly moving in a line to deposit their slips of paper into a walnut box secured by a shiny brass padlock. They were fulfilling their duty under the US Constitution by which US Senators were elected by state legislatures, not the people.[2] The vacancy occurred with the unexpected death of Orville H. Platt, one of the most influential and distinguished men to serve in the US Senate from Connecticut. Platt had caught a cold while attending the funeral of a senate colleague on a raw March day, which advanced to pneumonia, resulting in his death on April 21, 1905, just thirteen days before.[3]

This sudden US Senate vacancy created an opportunity for Connecticut's state legislators to choose a replacement, and the factions of the majority party–the Republicans–circled around, the way sharks circle chum in the water. The "indirect election" of US Senators follows the procedure the framers of the US Constitution established when they convened in Philadelphia in 1787. At that time, Charles Pinckney of South Carolina introduced the idea that state legislatures should elect US senators; he believed state legislators would choose better US senators—the "elect of the elected." In this way, the upper chamber would be insulated from rash decisions, from "mob rule" of a tyrannical democratic majority. In an apocryphal story, George Washington supposedly compared the activities of the two legislative chambers to making tea: the House boils the water and makes the tea, but the Senate allows it to cool.

Standing about five feet, eight inches tall, McLean was a trim 150 pounds in May 1905, having gained back most of the weight he lost

---

2   *Encyclopedia Britannica*, "Seventeenth Amendment, United States Constitution," retrieved April 11, 2021, https://www.britannica.com/topic/Seventeenth-Amendment.

3   Louis A. Coolidge, *An Old-Fashioned Senator: Orville H. Platt of Connecticut* (New York: G.P. Putnam's Sons, 1910), 585.

during his debilitating term as governor of Connecticut during 1900–1902. As governor, McLean had surprised opponents and supporters alike by demonstrating that he was serious about reforming the state's antiquated and unfair system of representation in the Connecticut legislature. Under the system dating back to the colonial era, each Connecticut town had one or two representatives in the Connecticut General Assembly, irrespective of population, giving the small towns and large cities equal influence. To illustrate the unfairness of this obsolete system, in 1900, the town of Union, with a population of 428, was allotted two representatives, while the city of New Haven, which had 108,000 inhabitants, also had two representatives.[4] In effect, the vote of the smallest town canceled out the vote of the largest. This "town-system" favored the largely Republican small towns over the heavily Democratic large cities, so when McLean, a Republican, pushed for reform, he angered many from his own party. Feeling betrayed, they bitterly fought his reform efforts every step of the way.

Ultimately, McLean's reform proposals were defeated, and the unrelenting attacks on him and grueling pace of life as governor plunged him into a prolonged bout with depression. At his worst, in the summer of 1902, McLean weighed just 125 pounds. His nephew, William Roger Greeley, a twenty-one-year-old architecture student at the Massachusetts Institute of Technology, recalls spending time with him at his office that summer, coaxing him to just sign state papers. Lieutenant Governor Edwin O. Keeler eventually assumed McLean's duties for the last five months of his term.

McLean's opponents for the 1905 Senate seat were determined to keep him in the political wilderness. Members of the Republican Party's "Old Guard" were backing Frank Brandegee for the Senate seat. Brandegee, then a member of the US House of Representatives, was

---

4   Gary L. Rose, *Connecticut Government and Politics: An Introduction* (Fairfield, CT: Sacred Heart Univ. Press, 2007), 39.

viewed as bright and bluntly outspoken with a reputation for laziness. He had also been roundly condemned for being the only Connecticut congressman to have voted for the "mileage grab," or the doubling of mileage reimbursement fees to members of Congress.[5]

For McLean's supporters, the 1905 Senate race was about a much-needed generational change in governance, throwing off the party's "Old Guard" and ending decades of corruption and cronyism. Now was the time to turn the page and elect young men with integrity, courage, and progressive tendencies. McLean was just the right man for the job, wrote the *Hartford Courant*. He had shown courage and independence as governor, standing up to the political machine in his unsuccessful attempt to democratize the Connecticut legislature. He would do more of the same as a Connecticut US Senator.[6]

Around seven o'clock on the night of the 1905 legislative caucus, a messenger brought in two bundles of sandwiches to the fourth-place candidate for the nomination, state Senator Allan W. Paige, who had just twenty-nine votes. Some of the other legislators noticed and a loud clamoring for food spread throughout the chamber.[7] Paige soon announced that he would order another 250 sandwiches. Paige's vote total went from twenty-nine on the thirteenth ballot to thirty-five on the fifteenth, perhaps in appreciation for the sandwiches.

The solemnity of the occasion began to give way around midnight, when the "bulldog tenacity" and seriousness of the caucusers descended to a few practical jokes on the twenty-third ballot: four votes were cast for Joseph Mullin, a *Hartford Courant* reporter covering the event, and one vote for Eli Whitney, the Connecticut inventor of the cotton gin, who died in 1825. When those votes were announced, the Speaker

---

5   "A Whack at 'Em All," *Hartford Daily Courant*, May 1, 1905, 8.

6   Ibid.

7   "Joking and Singing to Pass the Time Away," *Hartford Daily Courant*, May 5, 1905, 1.

of the House, Marcus Holcomb, strode to the podium red-faced and reprimanded the pranksters.[8]

Still deadlocked at one o'clock in the morning, a quartet was somehow assembled from the group of 247 legislators, and they cheered the weary lawmakers by singing "My Old Kentucky Home," and "Nearer My God to Thee." When the quartet launched into "There's no Place Like Home," some of the legislators nodded in agreement and began to sing or whistle along. Others dozed in their high-backed wooden chairs.

Around midnight, "trades and shifts" began between candidates Frank Brandegee and Allan Paige.[9] In exchange for Paige's support, the Brandegee men had offered to give Paige their backing for the upcoming governor's race.[10] The final four ballots took ninety minutes, with Brandegee adding about nine votes per ballot. Finally, at 2 a.m., Brandegee attained 127 votes, surpassing the 124 needed for the nomination.

The Old Guard Republicans had prevailed, vanquishing McLean once again. Was his political career now over at age forty-seven? He could return to practicing law, but McLean loved politics and longed to be a US Senator. Whatever plans he might have had for the future, events beyond his control soon intervened.

Six months after McLean's senate loss, in early January 1906, McLean, already a wealthy attorney, inherited around $3 million (or, in today's dollars, $88 million) from his father's sister, Sarah Abernethy.[11] Mrs. Abernethy was twice widowed; her two husbands have been variously described as New York City dry goods merchants, financiers, and land speculators but whatever they did, they made a fortune. A woman of great charm and sociability, in her teens Sarah attended Miss

---

8   "Ballots in the Early Evening," *Hartford Daily Courant*, May 5, 1905, 1.

9   "Scenes at Midnight," *Hartford Daily Courant*, May 5, 1905, 10.

10   "Brandegee Nominated for U.S. Senator," *Hartford Daily Courant*, May 5, 1905, 1.

11   "$3,000,000 to Relatives: The Will of Mrs. Sarah McLean Abernethy," *New York Times*, January 12, 1906, 2.

Porter's School in Farmington, Connecticut, a prestigious finishing school.[12] During her married life, she lived in a five-story Manhattan brownstone at 39 West 56th Street, where she entertained the city's elite. Mrs. Abernethy was also very active in benevolence and mission work through the Broadway Tabernacle Church in New York City, and helped found the Women's Hospital of New York in 1857, the first of its kind in America.[13]

Inherited wealth can be a mixed blessing. In her 1996 book *The Golden Ghetto,* psychotherapist Jessie O'Neill, describes the damaging consequences that inherited wealth can have.[14] Inheritances can result in "affluenza," expressed by debilitating feelings of guilt, lack of motivation, social isolation, frittering away your life, experimenting with thoughtless relationships, and even descending into debauched living.[15]

At the end of 1906, George McLean had reached a pivotal point in his life. Still working through a prolonged depression that began in 1902, McLean, after his unsuccessful Senate try in 1905, was an ambitious man without a job. A lifelong bachelor, he also lost three vitally important women in his life in 1906: his sister Hannah, then his beloved aunt Sarah, and, the most crushing blow, his mother died in November 1906. And in the midst of this disappointment and grief, he became, very suddenly, one the wealthiest men in Connecticut.

His options for the future were virtually unlimited, but confoundingly unclear.

What would he do now?

---

12 "Miss Porter's School Finishes Socialites, Scholars and a First Lady," New England Historical Society, https://www.newenglandhistoricalsociety.com/miss-porters-school-finishes-socialites-scholars-first-lady/, accessed February 1, 2021. The school is still active today, and among its famous graduates is Jacqueline Bouvier Kennedy Onassis '47, who was the first lady of the United States from 1961 to 1963.

13 Susan Hayes Ward, *The History of the Broadway Tabernacle Church* (New York: Trow Print, 1901), 25.

14 Jessie H. O'Neill, *The Golden Ghetto: The Psychology of Affluence* (Center City, MN: Hazelden Publishing, 1996).

15 Jason Butler, "Will Inherited Wealth Help or Hurt Those You Love?" *Financial Times,* May 9, 2019, https://www.ft.com/content/3122b790-70b3-11e9-bf5c-6eeb837566c5.

PART ONE

SIMSBURY, CONNECTICUT

★ CHAPTER ONE ★

OLD WAYS, OLD DAYS

I like the new ways and the new days
better than the old ways and the old days.
George P. McLean, December 23, 1901[1]

Just as the Apostle Paul referred to himself as a "Hebrew of Hebrews," George McLean could have easily made the case that he was a "Puritan of Puritans." But in a 1901 speech to the New England Society in the City of New York, he displayed a rather irreverent view of his puritan ancestors. The speech was made at the peak of his popularity as governor of Connecticut, at the celebration of the 281st anniversary of the Pilgrims' landing on Plymouth Rock. The speakers preceding him had eulogized the puritans in reverent tones, praising them for their conscientiousness, high courage, and constant activity.

McLean's speech, however, had a different tenor, bordering on sarcasm. His remarks followed a sumptuous dinner that included oysters,

---

1   George P. McLean, "Speech of His Excellency, George P. McLean, Governor of Connecticut," ("Connecticut and the Puritan"), in *Ninety-Sixth Anniversary Celebration of the New England Society in the City of New York* (New York: William Green Co., December 23, 1901), https://babel.hathitrust.org/cgi/pt?id=inu.30000117882187&view=1up&seq=5.

clear green turtle soup,[2] filet of English sole, roasted red head duck, escalope of beef cheron, sweetbreads dreux style, as well as sherbet, fruits, ices, cakes, and coffee. His audience, 500 wealthy New Yorkers, including J.P. Morgan, were satiated and happy, puffing on cigars and sipping port, when McLean rose to make his speech entitled "Connecticut and the Puritan."

They were delightfully surprised when the young governor began: "The Puritans came for individual liberty and got it—for themselves [laughter].... Our forefathers had not been upon that rock more than ten minutes before they claimed title to all the land that might thereafter be found adjoining [laughter], and in good time made that title good."[3]

Later in the speech, he took a jab at one of the puritans' most controversial religious doctrines: predestination. McLean said he had no prowess as a medium to bring back his ancestors from the hereafter. Indeed, he didn't know which way to go to find some of them. He evoked even more laughter when he said he hoped that none of their departed puritan forebears "found their accounts on the exchequer of predestination overdrawn."[4] McLean was, of course, referring to John Calvin's doctrine that God chooses those who will enter heaven based on his omnipotence and grace. Far from idealizing his puritan ancestors, McLean concluded that he liked "the new ways and the new days better than the old ways and the old days." He considered the body of

---

2   Green turtles, now endangered, were once an abundant food source. Turtle soup became something of a craze in nineteenth century England and the United States, and was the highlight of official banquets until the 1920s, when it was phased out due to over-harvesting. Turtle has a delicious meaty, beefy flavor and it is very time-consuming and expensive to prepare. Its unusual taste comes from its shells, bones, and fat. Turtle soup was a great favorite of Winston Churchill. See James Spotila, *Sea Turtles: A Complete Guide to Their Biology, Behavior, and Conservation* (Baltimore: Johns Hopkins Press, 2004), 97.

3   George P. McLean, "Speech of His Excellency, George P. McLean, Governor of Connecticut," ("Connecticut and the Puritan,") in *Ninety-Sixth Anniversary Celebration of the New England Society in the City of New York* (New York: William Green Co., December 23, 1901), https://babel.hathitrust.org/cgi/pt?id=inu.30000117882187&view=1up&seq=5.

4   Ibid.

men listening to him a much better sort, both mentally and morally, than any equal number of their ancestors.

George P. McLean's ancestral inheritance is marked by rigorous religious piety, a strong work ethic, close family relationships, and a remarkable degree of geographic continuity. This continuity of place and culture contributed significantly to McLean's conservativism. As political scientist Andrew Heywood defines it, conservatism is a conventional lifestyle that "seeks to preserve a range of institutions such as religion, government, and property rights, with the aim of emphasizing social stability and continuity."[5] As an adult, McLean would move beyond his conservative roots, becoming more politically moderate with progressive leanings.

McLean's puritan credentials go back to the early 1600s. His maternal ancestors, the Paines (later Paynes), were among the first Europeans in British North America. Emigrant ancestor Thomas Paine, born in Kent, England, came ashore as a boy at Eastham (in modern-day Cape Cod) in 1638, and joined the other religious Separatists there, later known as the Pilgrims. In 1653, Thomas, a cooper (or barrel maker), married Mary Snow, whose mother, Constance Hopkins, was a *Mayflower* passenger. Thomas was praised as a "splendid penman" and a man of more than ordinary education. He lived to be 93, and he contributed in numerous ways to the growth and administration of Eastham as selectman, juryman, surveyor, and mill builder. His wife, Mary, was called a "faithful wife, careful mother, a good and quiet neighbor, and a diligent reader of God's Holy Word."[6]

Key character traits McLean inherited from his Paine/Payne ancestors include self-reliance and independence. Throughout his political career, George McLean exhibited independence, resisting the pressure

---

5   Andrew Heywood, *Political Ideologies: An Introduction* (London: Palgrave Macmillan, 2012), 69.

6   Henry D. Paine, *Paine Family Records: A Journal of Genealogical and Biographical information* Volume 2 (Albany: J. Munsell, 1883), 13.

to conform, to go along, or comply with the wishes of his peers and mentors. McLean's great- great- grandfather Solomon Paine (1698–1754) was a leader in Connecticut's "Separatist Movement," or the revolt against conservatism and rigid ecclesiastical control by the established Congregational church. Swept up by the religious revival that occurred in New England, now called the Great Awakening, in 1746, Solomon Paine was ordained at the age of forty-eight.[7] He preached throughout eastern Connecticut and wrote a widely circulated pamphlet that denounced the established Congregational church.[8] In one sermon, Solomon Paine criticized the "hypocrites in the established church," and its "flat, formal" ministers. His greatest objection was the payment of taxes that funded the salaries of ministers.[9] Solomon's brother Elisha was also active in the Separatist Movement. He refused to pay the mandated assessments to support the established church in their town of Canterbury and was jailed for several months.[10] Solomon and Elisha Paine were among the earliest voices leading to the eventual disestablishment of state churches in New England in 1815.

The other major facet of George McLean's ancestry is his Scottish lineage. An examination of his many speeches yield only a few references to his Scottish roots, like an offhand reference to "my Scotch propensity to preach a little."[11] However, there are clues that he truly valued his Scottish heritage, like the elaborate carving of the McLean Cross on his gravestone. McLean was well aware of his Scottish ancestors as

---

7   Ibid.

8   Ellen D. Larned, *History of Windham County, Connecticut* (Worcester, MA: Charles Hamilton, 1874), 484.

9   John Wilson, *Church and State in American History* (United Kingdom: Routledge, 2019), 50.

10   Silas Leroy Blake, *The Separates: The Strict Congregationalists of New England* (Boston: Pilgrim Press, 1902), 112.

11   George P. McLean, "Speech of His Excellency, George P. McLean, Governor of Connecticut," ("Connecticut and the Puritan"), in *Ninety-Sixth Anniversary Celebration of the New England Society in the City of New York* (New York: William Green Co., December 23, 1901), https:// babel.hathitrust.org/cgi/pt?id=inu.30000117882187&view=1up&seq=5.

he owned a handwritten genealogy written by his immigrant ancestor Allan MacLean (1715–1786) of Kilbride, Isle of Coll.[12] This document traces McLean's ancestors back to 1555, and most of them were "Lairds" (Scottish for "Lord"), or owners of large estates.

The population of the Isle Coll when Allan McLean emigrated to Boston in 1740 numbered about 1,000, and most people farmed, fished, or raised livestock or sheep for wool. Allan was in the Scottish army before he emigrated to Connecticut, accompanied by his brother Neil, a doctor.[13] Allan's decision to emigrate was likely motivated by a desire to find economic opportunities in British North America and move on from chronic warring and political instability. Family writings are very precise on the dates of his voyage to Boston: he departed Glasgow on July 22, 1740, and arrived in Boston on September 17, an eight-week voyage.

Allan stayed in Boston and set up a merchant trading business. But in a short time, his business failed. "The Yankees were too cunning for me," according to McLean family memoirs.[14] Eventually he settled in Vernon, Connecticut, twelve miles northeast of Hartford, with its "Isle of Coll-sized" population of just under 1,000.[15] Allan McLean must have brought money with him because he bought farmland and soon married Susannah Beauchamp in 1741, the daughter of a prominent merchant in Hartford. She died the following year. "I was favored with her good and religious conversation for thirteen months and eight days," he later wrote.[16]

In December of 1744, Allen married for a second time, to Mary

---

12 Mary McLean Hardy, *A Brief History of the Ancestry and Posterity of Allan MacLean* (Marquand, 1905), 34.

13 Alexander Maclean Sinclair, *The Clan Gillean* (Charlottetown: Hazard and Moore, 1899), 412–13.

14 Rev. Allen McLean, *A Genealogical Memorial* of the Connecticut McLean Family.

15 John Hayward, *The New England Gazetteer: Containing Descriptions of All the States* (Concord, NH: I. Boyd and W. White, 1839), 177.

16 Ibid., 8.

Loomis from nearby Bolton, Connecticut. The couple had four children. With his experience in the Scottish Army, Allan turned to soldiering for the British in exchange for a promised land grant for his services. From 1757 to 1762, Allan fought against the Mohawk tribe in New York in the French and Indian War. A Gaelic speaker, he joined the Scottish Highlanders as a lieutenant with the commissary (the supply and transport unit). He never got the promised land grant, even after seeking legal redress; so, after five years in the military, he returned to his farm in Vernon, Connecticut. Allen's grandson—who was McLean's grandfather—wrote extensively about Allan's religious convictions, concluding that "the religion of my grandfather was of high and holy order."[17]

A significant ancestral influence on George McLean was his grandfather, the Reverend Allen McLean (1781–1861). Much is known about Rev. Allen because he was a prolific writer, producing *My Farewell to the World and All It Contains, The Theological Education of the Reverend Allen McLean,* and *A Genealogical Memorial of the Connecticut McLean Family.* That genealogy offers an extensive commentary on the strong religious beliefs of the McLean family through the generations.

George McLean's ancestors were religiously pious and faithful students of the Westminster Catechism, written in 1646 by the Westminster Assembly, a synod of English and Scottish theologians. George McLean's grandfather, the Reverend Allen McLean, said he committed the entire Catechism to memory. The confession is a systematic exposition of Calvinist orthodoxy influenced by puritan theology. There are various forms of the Catechism, but even memorizing the "Shorter Westminster Catechism," which contains 107 questions and answers, totaling over 4,400 words, is an impressive feat.

Allen experienced an intense religious conversion as a teen that led him to pursue the ministry. Not being used to study, Allen spent al-

---

17   Ibid.

most two years at a theological preparatory school run by the Reverend Charles Backus called the "School of the Prophets" in Somers, Connecticut. Charles Backus was a formative influence on Allen McLean (he would later name one of his sons after Rev. Backus); he drove his pupils hard and Allen McLean later wrote that he and the other students studied theology, Greek, and Latin for up to eighteen hours a day. This intense study prepared him for admission to Yale College in 1801. The entrance examination consisted of reciting and translating the four gospels in Greek and the *Orations Against Catiline* in Latin.

After graduating from Yale in 1805, McLean returned to Vernon to farm and occasionally to preach at nearby congregations, hoping for a permanent pastorate. That opportunity came in 1809 when he was called to the Simsbury First Congregational Church, the only church he would ever serve until his death in 1861. For the last ten years of his life, he was totally blind due to an illness, and he was plagued by excruciating headaches. His memoir, *My Farewell to the World,* is a 40,000-word treatise detailing his strong orthodox Calvinist beliefs, providing advice to his children and grandchildren, and sharing his reflections on a variety of topics, including farming, his beloved state of Connecticut, his hometown of Simsbury, and a strong dose of his politics.

"I came from Federalist party stock, then became a Whig," Allen McLean wrote. He then summarized his views of the first fourteen US presidents, from George Washington to Franklin Pierce, providing an interesting glimpse of the man and his political leanings. On Washington: "His name will go down in posterity, covered with the richest honor." On Jefferson: "A professed infidel who much alarmed the good people of New England." On seeing James Monroe during a tour of New England: "He had upon his head the same hat which he wore during the Revolutionary conflict." And on Andrew Jackson's military character: "I am not willing that the Chair of State should be occupied by a warrior." He reserved his harshest words for some of the Democratic presidents whom he no doubt never voted for, such as Martin Van Buren: "A snake in the grass, sly and crafty."

Although George McLean was only four years old when his grandfather Allen McLean died, the Yale-educated minister was a towering influence on George. His grandfather's memoirs show Allen McLean was in a constant state of agitation for the souls of his flock and family. The advice he dispensed to George McLean's father—"Deacon" Dudley Bestor McLean—and his daughter-in-law, Mary Payne, provide insights into the kind of religious instruction and home life that George McLean had as a child.

"Be sober, active followers of Christ," the Reverend Allen McLean wrote to McLean's father, Dudley. "Be on your guard against mere temporary superficial religion. Be friends with your minister. Watch over your conversation and all your conduct. Every year make some improvements to your farm. Every foot of it has been prayed over. Believe in the gospel as it is. Never cease to maintain family religion in all its duties. Be unwearied in your efforts to train your children for Christ and heaven. Pray for them and pray with them. Let your discipline be kind and affectionate. Set your affections on things above, fix your eye on heaven, there may we all meet, and God shall have the glory."[18]

The influence of Reverend Allen McLean is further illustrated by another admonition in the memoir to his son, Dudley (McLean's father) to maintain a strict observance of the Sunday Sabbath. The New England Sabbath traditionally began at sunset on Saturday night and ended at the next sunset, a practice rooted in the Old Testament.[19] The New England Puritans put a very high value on the Bible's Old Testament; they saw themselves as seventeenth-century Israelites fleeing persecution, often naming their children after Old Testament fig-

---

18   Rev. Allen McLean, "My Farewell to the World and All it Contains" (unpublished manuscript, 1861), 85–86. Housed at the Yale University Divinity School Library.

19   George M. Stephenson, *The Puritan Heritage* (New York: MacMillan Co., 1952), 181.

ures like Abraham, Sarah, Isaac, and Rebecca. Throughout his youth, George McLean's family strictly observed the Sabbath, which included two Sunday services, quiet reflection, and fasting except for a simple meal at sunset on Sunday.[20]

The 1846 marriage of George McLean's parents was an arranged affair. The Paynes lived in the small town of Canterbury. Mary Payne's father saw no worthy prospects there for his twenty-five-year-old daughter. When a "Scotch parson"—Rev. Allen McLean—came from Simsbury (some forty miles away) to preach in Canterbury as part of a pulpit exchange, Rev. McLean and Solomon Payne became acquainted. In time, Rev. Allen disclosed he had a "strong and respectable son with pleasing manners" of marriageable age. The two men eventually agreed that Mary Payne and Dudley McLean should be married, and that was that.[21]

George McLean's father, Dudley Bestor McLean, was born in Simsbury in 1821. Several family accounts describe him as unambitious. He was the youngest of a family of five, and that traditionally meant he was expected to take over the farm and look after his aging parents. Dudley played the flute in church, in a rag-tag church orchestra, in lieu of an expensive organ; he also played Scottish and English folk songs on the porch after chores, and hymns from the *Hutchins Hymnal* to accompany family devotions. It was said Dudley could jump a three-rail fence at seventy, but at age seventy-three, he was hooked in the chest by one of their bulls. He died on December 29, 1894, after three days of distressed breathing.[22]

George McLean and his father were quite different. Unlike his father, he was very ambitious, hated farm work, and sought a career in

---

20   William Roger Greeley, "Mary Payne McLean" (unpublished manuscript, ~1965), 34. Housed at the Simsbury (CT) Historical Society.

21   Ibid., 35.

22   Greeley, "Mary Payne McLean," 90.

Hartford as soon as he graduated from high school. His father was very pious and a deacon at his father's Congregational church in Simsbury, whereas McLean in later life became a more liberal Christian, moving beyond what he viewed as the "fear-based" religion of his youth. McLean was a frequent traveler and vacationer, whereas his father is said to have taken just one vacation in his whole life, which he planned to last for a week, but which ended after one day, as he felt like a fish out of water and was anxious to get back to his farm.[23]

While McLean and his father had many differences, they shared an interest in politics and public service. His father held various public offices, including town clerk, judge of probate, and a representative for Simsbury in the Connecticut General Assembly as a Republican in 1870 and 1880. Dudley was also a justice of the peace, performing an occasional marriage. In 1855, Dudley was a state delegate to the Connecticut Temperance Society, the year Connecticut passed a prohibition law, only to have it repealed two years later.[24]

Family memoirs describe McLean's mother, Mary Payne McLean, as industrious, intelligent, resourceful, and a woman in constant motion, providing for others. "Nothing came without effort," it was written—making homespun clothing, and canning home-grown food. She was an "energetic and faithful wife and mother, training her children in the fear of the Lord."[25] One of her diary entries reads that on March 4, 1879, she dipped 30 dozen candles. When her son Charlie, a home-builder and farmer, died of tuberculosis at age thirty-eight on June 11, 1889, her diary entry for June 12 reads: "The saddest day of my life." On March 12, 1899, she recorded that she didn't go to church but read the four gospels through the course of the day.[26]

---

23   William Roger Greeley, "Mary Payne McLean" (unpublished manuscript, ~1965), 40.

24   "Delegates to the Temperance Society," *Hartford Daily Courant*, March 1, 1855, 2.

25   Mary McLean Hardy, *A Brief History of the Ancestry and Posterity of Allan MacLean* (Berkeley, CA: Marquand, 1905), 77.

26   Greeley, "Mary Payne McLean," 92.

Mary and Dudley had seven children (five survived) three sons and two daughters. McLean's sisters, Hannah and Sallie, were both educated at Mount Holyoke College (then known as "Mount Holyoke Female Seminary.") The school, founded in 1837, had rigorous entrance requirements and a demanding curriculum that purposefully avoided teaching home economics and domestic skills. Founder Mary Lyon's vision was to prepare women for teaching careers, educating women to educate other women.[27] Both Hannah and Sallie eventually were active in the women's suffrage movement, which will be discussed in a later chapter.

McLean's sister, Hannah, graduated from Mount Holyoke in 1879 and became a missionary teacher at a Sioux Native American tribal mission in Faribault, Minnesota. She later taught in New Brunswick, Canada, and then for many years at a women's preparatory school in Greenfield, Massachusetts, that was associated with the Unitarian Church. She was considered an original thinker in search of a more liberal religion, having rejected the "ghastly theology" (Calvinism) of her youth.[28]

At the age of thirty-two, she met another Unitarian, likely at a boarding house in Boston, William Henry Greeley, a forty-eight-year-old bachelor and third-generation New England sugar merchant. He married Hannah in 1880; they had three children, but he died nine years into their marriage, leaving Hannah a widow at age forty, with three children under the age of eight. George McLean provided financial support to Hannah throughout her widowhood, and he brought her family to Simsbury for long stretches. One of his Greeley nieces, Hannah, named after McLean's sister, was born at McLean's home in Simsbury in 1913.

---

27   "A Detailed History of Mt. Holyoke College," Trustees of Mount Holyoke College, on the website of Mount Holyoke College, https://www.mtholyoke.edu/about/history/detailed.

28   "Obituary for Hannah McLean Greeley, 1848–1906," Proceedings of Lexington Historical Society and Papers, Volume 4, 1906, 166–69, https://www.google.com/books/edition/Proceedings_of_Lexington_Historical_Soci/agWAAAAYAAJ?hl=en&gbpv=1&dq=Obituary+for+Hannah+McLean+Greeley&pg=PA166&printsec=frontcover.

Mary Payne McLean (1820–1906) (source: author's collection)

George McLean's other sister, Sarah ("Sallie") Pratt McLean (1856–1935), one year older than McLean, also attended Mount Holyoke, though she did not graduate, opting instead to become a novelist, poet, and short story writer. A free spirit throughout her life, she was married briefly and gave birth to twins (named Dudley and Bestor), who tragically died as infants, and then was abandoned by her husband, a gambler and silver-mining speculator. She lived alone in her widowhood, eventually writing twenty novels in the style of Mark Twain. She corresponded with Twain, who praised her writing for its humor and realistic characters. Twain had in his library six of Greene's books: two copies of *Cape Cod Folks, Vesty of the Basins, Stuart and Bamboo, Flood-*

Tide, and *Winslow Plain.*[29] Perhaps it was Sarah who persuaded Twain to lecture in Simsbury. Twain spoke at the McLean Seminary for girls on March 21, 1891, a school founded and run by George McLean's older brother John.[30]

McLean's brother, John Backus McLean (1852–1923), was an ordained Congregational minister who founded and ran the McLean Seminary from 1888 to 1900, then went on to become the state superintendent of schools for Connecticut. He was a man of tremendous energy, physical strength, and broad intellectual interests. He was beloved by his Greeley nephews and nieces, taking them on 100-mile bike trips, encouraging them to do farm chores, and getting them to take part fully in McLean family life while they visited. He wrote poetry, preached at nearby churches, studied theology, botany, ornithology, and geology, and ran the family farm. In later years, George McLean's grandnephew, Dana McLean Greeley, spoke fondly of John, his wife and children, saying they were as fun and informal as George McLean and his wife Juliette were formal and serious. "I was always afraid of breaking the china or spilling my soup when I was around Uncle George," he later said. While the Greeley nephews and grandnephews respected and admired George McLean for his intellectual intensity and accomplishments, he didn't relate especially well to children, though he loved and supported them in his own formal and paternalistic way.

George P. McLean was born at the Simsbury family farm on October 7, 1857, during a period that saw the births of other men who would become leaders in early twentieth- century America: Woodrow Wilson (1856); William Howard Taft (1857); Theodore Roosevelt (1858); and William Jennings Bryan (1860). In 1857, James Buchanan had

---

29   "Sarah Pratt McLean to SLC, 16 December 1881 · Simsbury, CT, (UCLC 40951)," Catalog entry, Mark Twain Project Online (Berkeley, Los Angeles, London: University of California Press, 2016).

30   Mark Twain Stormfield Project, http://twainproject.blogspot.com/2009/10/connecticut-mark-twain-connections.html. Descendants of John McLean recall family stories of smelling Twain's fragrant cigar smoke during the March 21 lecture.

Dudley Bestor McLean (1821–1894) (source: author's collection)

recently begun his ill-fated single term as President, having beaten Senator John Fremont of California, the first-ever Republican Party presidential candidate. In a general way, George McLean and the Republican Party were born at about the same time.

Ever since the American Revolution, Americans have been naming their children after George Washington. By mid-nineteenth-century the name "George" was the fourth most popular Christian name in America, behind James, William, and the most-popular, John.[31] One vivid childhood memory for McLean was the ending of the Civil War, when McLean was seven years old. In 1890, McLean delivered a Memorial Day speech in Bristol, Connecticut, honoring the Sixteenth Connecticut Infantry. He clearly recalled the day the war ended. He was at his one-room schoolhouse, aged seven, "slyly shaping a chestnut twig into a whistle."[32] The sound of church bells and the factory gong was heard, and the schoolmaster dismissed class, saying the war was over. Hurrying home, McLean celebrated by running through the

---

31   "Top Names of the 1880s," Social Security Administration, https://www.ssa.gov/oact/babynames/decades/names1880s.html, retrieved March 1, 2021. Today the name "George" ranks 125th.

32   "Connecticut Soldiers: How Their Memory Was Honored Yesterday," *Hartford Daily Courant*, May 31, 1890, 6.

streets blowing on a tin horn. Coming into view was an old gentleman driving a rickety wagon at a furious pace. His hat fell off as he passed, and McLean stopped to pick it up. McLean never forgot the exultant look on the man's face. "He turned to me and exclaimed, 'Bub, you may get my hat, but don't stop blowing your horn!'"[33]

George McLean grew up working on the 100-acre family farm originally purchased by his grandfather.[34] The farm had six cows, two horses, two oxen, and forty sheep. The horses and oxen pulled plows and other agricultural equipment while the sheep were raised for wool used in making homespun clothing, and sold to local mills. The McLeans grew hay, corn, rye, oats, flax, and tobacco, using the hay as silage for their livestock. Rye was sown in the "Great Field," and ground at a local mill. The miller kept a tenth for his services, and the remaining rye flour was kept to make bread and porridge or sold. Milk from the cows was used for drinking and cooking, of course, and to make cream, butter, and cheese; beef tallow was used to make candles. Pigs and chickens were butchered and salted, and "vegetables galore" were grown and canned. Apples were an important crop, a versatile food providing sauce, dried apples, and cider.[35]

Tobacco was among the crops grown on the McLean farm. Tobacco growing has a long history in Connecticut; it was introduced to the colonists by native Americans in the 1600s. McLean was a lifelong tobacco farmer, tobacco chewer, and cigar smoker. In 1926, a newspaper reported that McLean smoked his own special brand of "low nicotine cigars,"[36] and several political cartoons depict him with a cigar in his mouth.

All these crops and livestock required constant care and effort, but

---

33 "Connecticut Soldiers: How Their Memory Was Honored Yesterday," *Hartford Daily Courant*, May 31, 1890, 6.

34 "George P. McLean Made a Difference Then and Now," *Hartford Courant*, June 16, 1996, 139.

35 Greeley, "Mary Payne McLean," 48.

36 "Farmer McLean," *Watertown News* (Watertown, CT), June 10, 1927, 1.

perhaps the most time-consuming daily chore of George McLean's boyhood was keeping up with the demand for water, not just for people but for livestock. Two to three hours a day of pumping the well and hauling water was required, an especially brutal chore during the cold New England winters.[37] George McLean began each day milking seven cows by lantern light. In later years, he confessed that he hated farming, getting his hands dirty, and from an early age set his mind on leaving the family farm and making something of himself.[38]

George McLean's youth coincided with the steady decline of farming in Connecticut as larger, more productive farms in western states were now connected to eastern cities via railroads. Small subsistence farms in New England simply could not compete with larger and more mechanized western farms. In 1800, ninety-five percent of the Connecticut population lived in rural areas; but by 1900, only forty percent were rural residents.[39] It is easy today to romanticize farm life in the nineteenth century, but for many it was monotonous, exhausting, isolating, and unprofitable, especially when compared to the hustle and bustle of Hartford and New York City, just 130 miles from Simsbury.

The McLean household during George McLean's childhood included his parents, three grandparents, four older siblings, and his father's brother, Uncle Lloyd, who had mental health concerns that required constant care until he died in 1879 at age sixty-five. His grandmother Payne lived with them and was the cause of much "dissension and bitterness."[40] In Rev. Allen McLean's memoir *My Farewell to the World*, he enumerates eleven requests he made of McLean's father, Dudley.

---

37 Greeley, "Mary Payne McLean," 44.

38 Greeley, "Mary Payne McLean," 77.

39 US Census Bureau, *2010 Census of Population and Housing, CPH-2-8*, Connecticut, Table 1: Connecticut Population: Earliest Census to 2010 Washington, DC: US Government Printing Office,) 2012.

40 Ibid.

Item nine was "do not forget to take good care of Lloyd."[41] George McLean showed a special concern for people with mental health conditions throughout his life, serving on several hospital boards and helped establish the nation's first mental health care organization.

As a boy, McLean attended a one-room schoolhouse before matriculating to Hartford Public High School. McLean's two brothers who attended HPHS before him had been bullied for wearing homespun clothing, which led to fistfights with the "townies"—the affluent Hartford-based students who "hectored the farm boys on every occasion." McLean's older brother John didn't back down from the abuse.[42] George McLean, in later life, had a reputation for being impeccably dressed and extremely neat. Was McLean's neatness and fastidious appearance a reaction to the abuse he and his brothers received for being "hicks in homespuns"?

Hartford Public High School is the second oldest public high school in America, behind only Boston Latin. It was established in the 1630s by religious leaders in the Connecticut colony as a school to train young men for the puritan ministry, and it required the study of Latin, Greek, and theology. By the 1800s, the school had added other courses, such as classical studies and English literature. Women were admitted in 1847, though the sexes were separated. During the years McLean attended Hartford Public High School, it enjoyed a national reputation for excellence, and was regarded as one of the top secondary schools in the country.[43] On average, about twenty percent of those seeking entry

---

41   Rev. Allen McLean, "My Farewell to the World and All it Contains" (unpublished manuscript, 1861), 85.

42   William Roger Greeley, "Mary Payne McLean," 65.

43   "A Brief History of HPHS," R.J. Luke Williams, Hartford Public High School Law & Government Academy, https://law.hartfordschools.org/index.php/about-us/a-brief-history-of-hphs, retrieved March 1, 2021.

George P. McLean,
Class Orator, School Editor, c. 1875
(source: author's collection)

to the school did not pass the entrance exam and were denied admission. Once admitted, students were referred to as "scholars."[44]

McLean flourished at HPHS. A fellow student who later became a Catholic priest, the Reverend Father William J. McGurk, said McLean "was considered the brainiest man in the class."[45] There were fifty-three in McLean's 1877 graduating class, twenty-eight women and twenty-five men. Ten of the men went on to college—three to Yale, five to Trinity College in Hartford, and two to Amherst.

McLean, an avid reader throughout his life, discovered such classics as Dante's *Divine Comedy* and Bunyan's *The Pilgrim's Progress* at HPHS, and he developed a love of poetry. There was a touch of the poet in George McLean; perhaps that's what one of his nephews meant when he characterized McLean as a "sentimentalist."[46] In 1904, McLean befriended the poet laureate of North Carolina, John Charles McNeill, during one of his annual golfing trips to Pinehurst, North Carolina. McLean and McNeill had much in common, a love of nature and the

---

44 "H.P.H.S. News and Notions," *Hartford Daily Courant*, May 1, 1875, 1.

45 "Father McGurk of South Manchester Hopes to See McLean Elected," *Hartford Daily Courant*, November 1, 1900, 1.

46 Hugh Payne Geeley, "Memoirs" (unpublished manuscript, ~1970).

outdoors, poetry, and their shared Scottish lineage. One of McLean's favorite poems was McNeill's "Sundown," a poem which portrays the divine beauty of everyday things.[47]

McNeill's "God-and-nature" poetry is suggested in phrases that George McLean penned in his last will and testament, where he describes his vision for the future McLean Game Refuge: a place where trees are "unmolested" by loggers, where fish and animals are safe from sportsmen; a refuge where "the things of God" can be seen and experienced by those who love them; a sanctuary where people can find peace of mind and body just as he had during his sojourns there.

Poetry and poets were wildly popular in the late nineteenth century, especially the New England "Fireside poets" like Henry Wadsworth Longfellow and John Greenleaf Whittier.[48] For McLean, poetry had a spiritual, almost religious dimension. McLean wrote in 1910 that when he got to high school, the poetry of Burns, Kingsley and Whittier revealed a creed of "infinite compassion and love," refreshingly different from the theology of the Congregational pulpit of his youth, which he called "a simple problem of ecclesiastical mathematics." [49]

The immense popularity of poetry after the Civil War has been explained by some historians as a reflection of the growing secularism of the culture, providing its readers with a transformational experience similar to religious conversion so central to the lives of their Puritan forebearers. Poems were read at weddings and funerals, and chiseled onto gravestones.[50]

---

47   "Friendship of George P. McLean and John Charles McNeill," *Hartford Courant*, February 1933, 17.

48   Jill E. Anderson, *"Send Me a Nice Little Letter All to Myself": Henry Wadsworth Longfellow's Fan Mail and Antebellum Poetic Culture* (2007). University Library Faculty Publications, 111, https://scholarworks.gsu.edu/univ_lib_facpub/111. Of the 4,000 letters in the Longfellow archives, half are in response to requests for an autograph.

49   "Golden Jubilee of Dr. Parker," *Hartford Daily Courant*, January 12, 1910, 10.

50   David Haven Blake, "When Readers Become Fans: Nineteenth-Century American Poetry as a Fan Activity," *American Studies*, 52 (January 2012), 99.

In two highlights of McLean's high school experience, he was voted by his classmates as the "class orator" in his junior year, and as the "school editor" as a senior. It is hard for us today to appreciate the importance of oratory in George McLean's youth and the high honor of being named "class orator." One of the standard textbooks on oratory used at schools like HPHS was *Sanders' School Speaker: A Comprehensive Course of Instruction in the Principles of Oratory*, first published in 1857. Oratory was considered an absolute prerequisite for a career in politics, law, and the ministry.[51]

The study of oratory focused on three areas: elocution, gesture, and exercises in declamation. Elocution meant learning and practicing such techniques as articulation, accent and emphasis, inflections, modulation, and the rhetorical pause. Gesture involved the carriage and use of the body for rhetorical effect. The study of oratory also required the extensive memorization of declamations for which students would be judged in oratorical competitions. Declamations were rarely less than 300 words, and many were over 1,000.

McLean's oratorical gifts were extraordinary. Newspaper accounts later noted that his speeches were "delivered with fire" and "impressive power."[52] While his talent for oratory was frequently praised, it was the substance of what he said as much as the way he said it that made its impression.[53] It is not known if he spoke in a tenor, baritone or bass, but in any event, he spoke in a clear, ringing voice heard even in the largest of venues.[54]

There is evidence that public speaking did not come easy for

---

51   C. W. (Charles Walton) Sanders, *Sanders' School Speaker: A Comprehensive Course of Instruction in the Principles of Oratory; With Numerous Exercises for Practice in Declamation* (New York: Ivison & Phinney, 1857).

52   "McLean's Dynamic Speech," *Hartford Courant*, March 14, 1910, 8.

53   "George P. McLean," *Hartford Courant*, June 7, 1932, 10.

54   "McLean's Argument: Addressed a Large Crowd Last Night," *Hartford Daily Courant*, October 3, 1900, 1.

McLean, but required intense preparation and practice. In the latter stages of his two-year term as governor of Connecticut, he repeatedly refused speaking engagements. His speaking schedule was often intense, resulting in the loss of his voice on at least one occasion when he ran for governor in 1900. His oratorical ability improved with time. A writer for the *New York Herald* wrote in 1910 that McLean's public speaking talents had matured; he had mastered the ability to move and inspire his audiences.[55]

McLean's writing ability was similarly recognized when he was named school editor by his classmates in his senior year. Throughout his professional life, McLean wrote his own speeches and labored over them, forever striving for the *mot juste*. McLean's chauffeur, Frank Passini, described McLean's painstaking speechwriting process in an interview in 1971, revealing that McLean would spend weeks writing a single speech, tearing up drafts and rewriting them until he was totally satisfied.[56]

At an 1899 reunion of Hartford Public High School (class of '77), McLean stated that upon graduating he felt he had learned everything that was knowable and was now prepared to either be president of the United States or the editor of the *Hartford Courant* [the city's newspaper].[57] In that same reunion speech, McLean spoke proudly of the rapid development of technology. McLean recalled a demonstration of an electrical spark in a darkened science classroom, and his teacher predicting that someday electricity would be used for lighting purposes. He noted that his grandfather wrote his sermons by the light of a whale oil lamp and worried over what would happen if whales were hunted to extinction.[58]

---

55 "Mr. McLean's Eloquence," *Norwich Bulletin* (Norwich, CT), January 25, 1910, 2.

56 Frank Passini, "Interview with Frank Passini about Senator McLean" (unpublished manuscript at McLean Care Archives).

57 "H.P.H.S. Celebration," *Hartford Daily Courant*, June 10, 1899, 10.

58 Ibid.

McLean did not go on to college, but three of his siblings did, including his two sisters. McLean certainly weighed the option of college, especially law school, and even approached his aunt Sarah for financial help. In the latter part of the nineteenth century, attending college was rare and necessary for only a few professions, like ministers. Only about ten percent of the population in the 1870s even graduated from high school.[59]

George McLean graduated from high school during the Gilded Age, which most historians date from around 1870 to 1900. As historian H.W. Brands describes in his book *American Colossus*, capitalism burst forth during this period with immense energy, transforming America from a nation of farmers into a country of urban workers, managers, and professionals. During the Gilded Age, America was in the grip of a capitalist revolution, Brands writes, exposing a deep tension between capitalism and democracy, a struggle that has characterized American life since its inception. With the advent of industrialization after the Civil War, capitalism was on the ascendency. No areas of life were exempt from this capitalist revolution—it would create unimaginable industrial innovation but also resulted in massive income inequality.[60] The capitalist revolution would prove to be the backdrop and undercurrent of George McLean's life, creating extraordinary opportunities and challenges.

What was next for nineteen-year-old George McLean? He chose Hartford, Connecticut, as the place to stoke his youthful ambitions, leaving the hardscrabble family farm in Simsbury behind. When writer Mark Twain (Samuel Clemens) first visited Hartford in 1868, he called it one of the most beautiful cities in the world. What would it have to offer Hartford High School's class orator and school editor?

59   Michael McGerr, *A Fierce Discontent: The Rise and Fall of the Progressive Movement in America, 1870–1920* (New York: Free Press 2003), 7.

60   H.W. Brands, *American Colossus: the Triumph of Capitalism, 1865–1900* (New York: Doubleday, 2010), 4-6.

★ CHAPTER TWO ★

CLIMBING THE LADDER

The man who learns in his youth to govern himself well has taken a long step toward acquiring a first-class education.
George P. McLean, in a speech at Yale University, 1904[1]

McLean's first job after high school was as a reporter with the *Hartford Post* newspaper from 1877 to 1879, further evidence of his writing ability. McLean humorously reflected on his newspaper career at a speech to the Connecticut Editorial Association in 1910 that his career as a reporter was short but sufficient—"sufficient for me, sufficient for my employer, and sufficient for the public." He was paid seven dollars a week for his services, most of which went to living expenses, leaving about "twenty-five cents a week to spend on riotous living." After two years at the *Post* he "tumbled off the bottom rung of the ladder of journalism." His boss told him that he had been recommended because he was "a bright boy," but his job was to stick to the facts—not indulge in "emerald-hued" commentary. Then he sternly reminded the former school editor of Hartford High that there was only one editor at the *Hartford Post*.[2]

---

1   "Yale's Commencement: Ex-Governor McLean Speaks," *Hartford Daily Courant*, June 30, 1904, 9.

2   "McLean Speaks to the Editors," *Hartford Daily Courant*, April 12, 1910, 16.

While reporting for the *Post*, his efforts were noticed by influential politicians in Hartford who hired him to write speeches, proclamations, correspondence, and drafts of legislation. In addition to freelance writing, beginning in 1880, McLean was employed as a bookkeeper for Hartford's Trinity College, making $300 per year (about $7,500 today). Trinity College, founded in 1823, had around one hundred students when McLean was hired, but it was undergoing a significant growth spurt. By 1900, admissions to the college rose to 500 students, resulting in the construction of a new campus in West Hartford.[3]

Bookkeepers in 1880 provided a wide variety of financial and managerial functions beyond just clerical record keeping, much like modern-day accountants. The job requires attention to detail, reading and math skills, hard work, patience, conscientiousness, logical planning, and good communication skills. Bookkeepers needed to understand the entire scope of an organization's operations and to work closely with other staff, outside suppliers, and customers. In light of all the new construction on campus, the increasing enrollment, the new staff, and the financing needs from 1879 to 1881, McLean's bookkeeping responsibilities must have been considerable.

During this time, Hartford was the most affluent city in America, the home of insurance companies, banks, manufacturers, and many wealthy families, such as the Stowes, Beechers, and the arms-maker Colt.[4] It was the leading city for book publishing, the capital of the insurance industry, and a high percentage of its citizens were college-educated. In 1871, author Mark Twain (Samuel Clemens) moved his family to Hartford, a city he came to love while visiting his pub-

---

3   Hartford (CT) Board of Trade, *Hartford, Conn., As a Manufacturing, Business and Commercial Center: With Brief Sketches of Its History, Attractions, Leading Industries, and Institutions ...*, 1889, 182–87.

4   Charles Hopkins Clark, "The Charter Oak City," *Scribner's Monthly* XIII, n. 1 (November 1876): 2.

lisher, the American Publishing Company. He wrote many of his most famous books in Hartford, including *The Adventures of Tom Sawyer* (1876) and, perhaps his most famous, *Adventures of Huckleberry Finn* (1884).[5]

Hartford was a boom town during the last decades of the nineteenth century, growing from 37,000 people in 1870 to almost 80,000 in 1900 (a 3.5 percentage annual growth rate).[6] Industrialization and the rise in manufacturing were responsible for much of Hartford's growth in population and wealth. It was also a time of massive immigration. In 1850, Connecticut's immigrant population numbered about 38,000, or 10 percent of all state residents; by 1870, immigrants numbered 113,000 or 25 percent of the state; and by 1900, Connecticut had one of the highest percentages of foreign-born residents in the country.[7] This growth caused a myriad of new social and economic problems in terms of safe housing, clean water, waste treatment, and constructing and maintaining streets. City and state political leaders would soon realize that they were ill-equipped to respond.

After George McLean "tumbled off the bottom rung of the ladder of journalism," he soon found a new career ladder to climb—the law and politics. Two things stand out about the path he chose: first, it was a conventional route for a nineteenth century politician, and second, he did not pursue it alone. McLean followed a familiar political career path not unlike his peers—William Howard Taft, Woodrow Wilson, and Calvin Coolidge. They all trained as lawyers, then became active in local and state party politics, served in their state legislatures, and ultimately attained a higher state office. Equally important, an ambitious politician needed the support and assistance of party leaders, and

---

5   Justin Kaplan, *Mr. Clemens and Mark Twain* (New York: Simon & Schuster, 1966), 181.

6   "Hartford's Historical Population," December 14, 2013, ConnecticutHistory.org, https://connecticuthistory.org/over-time-hartfords-historical-population/.

7   "Connecticut," on the website *Immigration to the United States*, https://immigrationtounitedstates.org/446-connecticut.html.

McLean soon began acquiring the political mentors he would need to win elective office. McLean came of age in what has been called the Golden Age of Politics, when voter turnout rates exceeded 80 percent for presidential elections in the 1880s.[8] Still motivated by Civil War era divisions, voters enthusiastically participated in political campaigns, enjoying the nighttime torch light parades, bands, raucous campaign speeches and debates.[9]

In the fall of 1879, armed with one letter of recommendation, possibly from a sympathetic editor at the *Hartford Post*, twenty-two-year-old George McLean went to the law offices of Henry C. Robinson in Hartford's Marble Block building on Central Row. McLean asked if he could apprentice with Robinson. Apprenticing in the office of an established lawyer was a common path for a young man interested in a legal career in the nineteenth century. Apprentices would perform clerical services and routine legal duties for a law firm while studying for admission to the bar. Though dozens of law schools existed, most practicing attorneys in the nineteenth century did not have law school degrees.[10]

Unfortunately, Robinson already had three students, his maximum, but he graciously told McLean he could stay until Robinson could place him at another law office. "[D]aily after that I expected the dreaded change, but it did not come," McLean later wrote.[11] McLean stayed with Robinson for eight years — two years preparing for the bar, and six as an attorney. Robinson became something of a father figure

---

8   Today, turnout rates hover around a dismal fifty percent. *See* "Politics in the Gilded Age," The Khan Academy, https://www.khanacademy.org/humanities/us-history/the-gilded-age/gilded-age/a/politics-in-the-gilded-age.

9   "Torchlight Parades," National Museum of American History, https://americanhistory.si.edu/democracy-exhibition/machinery-democracy/democratic-outfitting/torchlight-parade.

10   Brian J. Moline, "Early American Legal Education," *Washburn Law Journal* 42, n. 4 (Summer 2004): 801.

11   Henry Cornelius Robinson Memorial Tribute (no publisher, 1900), 19, https://archive.org/details/henrycorneliusro00slsn/page/n7/mode/2up, retrieved July 12, 2020.

to McLean, encouraging him to participate in local and state politics, helping him improve his public speaking, expanding McLean's worldview, and significantly impacting his spiritual development.

Henry Cornelius Robinson was born in Hartford in 1832 and graduated from Yale in 1853. He apprenticed as a lawyer with his older brother and eventually took over the firm, serving business, philanthropic, religious, and educational interests in Hartford. For many years Robinson was counsel and a director of the New York, New Haven and Hartford Railroad Company. A Republican from the formation of the party, Robinson held several political offices, including mayor of Hartford in 1872 and member of the general assembly in 1879. In 1880, he was a member of the National Republican Convention, which nominated James Garfield and Chester Arthur for their national ticket. Robinson drafted a considerable part of its platform.[12]

Henry Robinson played an important role guiding McLean's early professional and personal life. Later in life, McLean spoke fondly of Robinson's generosity and strong guiding hand. Robinson gave him unconditional support and instilled confidence in the aspiring lawyer's development. McLean wistfully concluded that Robinson "did for me what my father could not do."[13] Robinson appears to have helped him forge a new identity differing from his rural upbringing, giving his intense ambitions focus and direction.

McLean admired Robinson's intellectual brilliance, cultured manners, and consistency of character—he was the same at work as he was in civic, political, and other personal and social settings. The two also shared an interest in hunting and fishing. Robinson encouraged McLean in May 1886 to form the Simsbury Game Club for the protection

12   "Introduction to Henry C. Robinson Papers," Yale University Archives, https://archives.yale.edu/repositories/12/resources/4367.

13   Henry Cornelius Robinson Memorial Tribute (no publisher, 1900), 19 https://archive.org/details/henrycorneliusro00slsn/page/n7/mode/2up.

of game and fish.[14] While McLean had a lifelong interest in hunting and fishing and a love of the outdoors, this was his first effort to put legal and organizational structure to it.

Robinson also significantly influenced McLean's religious views. On Christmas Day 1884, Robinson gave McLean the book *The Life of Horace Bushnell,* which McLean later says helped free him from the fear-based religion of his youth and led him to "a new Christian creed of compassion, love, and kindness." In 1910, McLean stated that the book was a turning point in his spiritual development. The religion of his boyhood was based on fear, McLean later said. "Boys were afraid of the girls, girls were afraid of the boys, boys and girls were afraid of their parents, parents were afraid of the minister, the minister was afraid of [S]atan, and all [were] afraid of Jehovah."[15]

Horace Bushnell (1802–1876) was a Congregational minister and Yale-educated theologian who today is viewed as the "father of American Christian Liberalism."[16] Bushnell urged his followers to turn away from polarizing dogmatism and the calcified legalism of puritan theologians, and to instead emphasize the grace, joy, and light of the Christian life. Bushnell also urged parents and teachers to nurture faith in children through positive relationships and modeling, not harsh catechizing and memorization.[17]

In September 1881, McLean passed the examination for admission to the bar.[18] His early law career involved preparing and filing legal documents, appeals, wills, contracts, deeds, handling probate cases, and some criminal work, including a murder case. McLean prosecuted

---

14   "The Simsbury Game Club," *Morning Journal-Courier* (New Haven, CT), May 1, 1886, 3.

15   "Golden Jubilee of Dr. Parker," *Hartford Daily Courant,* January 12, 1910, 10.

16   *Britannica,* The Editors of Encyclopedia, "Horace Bushnell," Encyclopedia Britannica, February 13, 2021, https://www.britannica.com/biography/Horace-Bushnell, accessed February 24, 2021.

17   Ibid.

18   "Local Matters," *Hartford Daily Courant,* September 28, 1881, 3.

four individuals for violating the "no liquor license law" in Kensington, Connecticut—a borough in a "dry town." Another early case was representing several heirs in a probate case who were challenging the mental competence of their deceased mother, Philomena Goddard, who had given the local Methodist church $25,000, leaving them nothing.[19] The heirs lost the case; Mrs. Goddard's gift helped fund a new building for the Simsbury United Methodist Church in 1908.[20]

For an ambitious young man coming of age in the 1870s, a career in Republican Party politics in a rapidly industrializing state like Connecticut provided ample opportunities. In November of 1882, George McLean ran for his first political office, winning a seat in the Connecticut General Assembly representing Simsbury. McLean ran as a Republican in a state that was almost evenly split between the Republican and Democratic parties. The split was keenly felt during the years leading to the American Civil War.

At the outset of the Civil War, nearly half of Connecticut's population was steadfastly opposed to fighting the South.[21] McLean spoke about this political division in Connecticut in a speech in 1910, noting that at war's end in 1865, he attended a victory rally at the town hall. The following day a school mate called him a "Black Republican."[22] McLean called his accuser a "Copperhead," referring to a faction of Democrats in the North who opposed the Civil War and sought a negotiated settlement with the Confederates, often blaming Northern abolitionists for the conflict. Historians have long debated whether their motive was a principled dedication to state's rights, or business alliances with Southern cotton growers, or even white supremacist views.

---

19   "In General," *Hartford Daily Courant*, August 9, 1883, 1.

20   "Cornerstone Laid for New Methodist Church in Simsbury," *Hartford Daily Courant*, June 24, 1908, 12.

21   Matthew Warshauer, *Connecticut in the American Civil War: Slavery, Sacrifice, and Survival* (Middletown, CT: Wesleyan University Press, 2011), 6.

22   "Ex-Governor McLean: Subject was Representative Democracy," *Norwich Bulletin* (Norwich, CT), January 29, 1910, 5.

After the Civil War, Republicans, as the party of Lincoln, were viewed as the party that had saved the Union, quashed the rebellious Southern states, freed the slaves, and had a positive vision for a rising, industrial nation. Republicans enjoyed solid support among the growing Northern industrial and financial interests, newly enfranchised Blacks, and shares of the farm, immigrant, and laborer vote. The Democratic Party, which had largely supported slavery before the Civil War, continued to oppose postwar efforts to integrate African Americans into society after they were freed. While the Democrats picked up support from some immigrants and labor, their continued alignment with segregationists' Southern states was largely disastrous in national elections.[23]

State assemblies in nineteenth century America were rough-and-tumble affairs, legislators were paid little, and they came from all walks of life. When McLean was elected to the Connecticut General Assembly at age twenty-four, he was among the youngest, where the average age of a representative was forty-seven. The two-hundred forty-nine members of the Connecticut Assembly in 1883 consisted of all kinds of people—Yale graduates, men with common school educations, immigrants from Ireland, Scotland, and Germany, farmers, Civil War veterans, and a few who traced their lineage back to the *Mayflower*.[24]

McLean's career in the Connecticut Assembly roughly parallels that of Theodore Roosevelt, who was elected to the New York Assembly in 1882 at the age of twenty-three—the youngest member of that State Assembly. Roosevelt was appalled at the blatant corruption of some of the assemblymen. He was frequently teased for his dressy clothing,

---

23   Allan Peskin, "Who Were the Stalwarts? Who Were Their Rivals? Republican Factions in the Gilded Age," *Political Science Quarterly* 99, no. 4 (1984): 703–16, accessed August 9, 2021, doi:10.2307/2150708.

24   Evening Post Association, *Evening Post Annual: Biographical Sketches (with Portraits) of the State Officers, Representatives in Congress, Governor's Staff, and Senators and Members of the General Assembly of the State of Connecticut* (1882).

called a "dude" and a "fop."[25] Since McLean was also an impeccable dresser, one wonders if he, like Roosevelt, was taunted by his peers in the Connecticut General Assembly.

McLean's most notable accomplishment as a Connecticut assemblyman was helping establish the Connecticut Board of Pardons. As chairman of the Committee on State Prisons, McLean was credited with preparing the Board of Pardons bill and overcoming the power of special interests (like trial lawyers and politicians) who opposed it. "No member of the House took a more intelligent interest in this subject—his earnest and convincing argument in favor of the bill had much to do with its successful passage," wrote the *Hartford Courant* in May of 1883.[26]

The new State Board of Pardons consisted of the governor, a doctor, a state supreme court justice, three laymen appointed by the legislature, and a secretary. The board was authorized to grant pardons for any crime, and to commute the death penalty. McLean acted as secretary for seventeen years, from 1884 to 1901, at a salary of $300 per year. His responsibilities on the board included screening pardon applications, organizing meetings, and acting much like a court reporter during hearings. McLean was a meticulous note taker, recording witness testimony (for example, "I was sick and had debts to repay. I had to steal.")[27] Some of the testimony was gruesome and graphic, like the murder and rape cases the board heard. Pardons required a unanimous vote, and McLean was a voting member. The board met twice each year, in December and June. During their first year, 1884, they reviewed over thirty requests for pardons.

The history of the pardoning power in Connecticut is worth noting.

---

25 Edmund Morris, "The Cyclone Assemblyman," *American Heritage Magazine* 30 (February/March 1979)

26 "Legislative Notes," *Hartford Daily Courant*, May 1, 1883, 2.

27 Board of Pardons records, RG 025, Connecticut State Library, https://cslarchives.ctstatelibrary.org/repositories/2/resources.

Suspicious of royalty and executive authority, Connecticut's early co-lonial leaders chose to place the pardoning power in the hands of the state legislature, but over time, this process proved ineffective and sub-ject to corruption. Decrying this scandalous history, reformers argued that the main requirements for obtaining a pardon from the legislature in Connecticut were influence and money. A *Hartford Courant* exposé detailed several suspicious pardons, like some express train robbers who looted a train in western Connecticut, and were later granted pardons by the legislature.[28] The low-paid, part-time state legislators were ac-cused of taking bribes or trading pardons for favorable votes on bills or other considerations. Lengthy hearings for pardons were conducted in a circus-like atmosphere, attracting raucous spectators from surround-ing towns, crowding the chamber beyond its capacity.[29]

The failures of Connecticut's legislative pardoning system are best illustrated by the pardon request of John Robert Johnson in 1875, a Swedish immigrant convicted of first-degree murder in 1872. Johnson had gained the sympathies of his fellow inmates at Wethersfield State Prison, convincing them that at the time of his crime he had been un-able to pay his rent due to a work injury, and was heartlessly evicted by an unsympathetic landlady. Returning to his lodgings to get his cloth-ing, Johnson claimed he was attacked by the woman "as soon as she set eyes on him." Johnson asserted he was merely acting in self-defense when he struck and killed the woman.[30]

Johnson's story was eventually heard by John C. Taylor, secretary of the Connecticut Prison Association. Taylor, a Civil War veteran who had experienced the cruelty of prison camps firsthand, was generally sympathetic toward the imprisoned, and he would "go to great lengths

---

28   "Board of Pardons: Twentieth Anniversary," *Hartford Daily Courant*, December 10, 1903, 12.

29   Ibid.

30   Ratcliffe Hicks and Cornelius Gardiner, ed. *The Johnson Trial, Speeches and Public Correspondence of Ratcliffe Hicks* (United States: The University Press, 1896), 266.

to help anyone who was open to the offer of friendship."[31] Taylor persuaded his friends in the legislature to reduce Johnson's murder sentence from death by hanging to life in prison.

Johnson subsequently became a nurse at the Wethersfield State Prison hospital and soon earned the trust of the prison doctors. With access to the prison infirmary, Johnson began ingesting large amounts of chalk and vinegar, giving him a pale and sickly pallor. His ghastly appearance and histrionic groanings convinced prison doctors that Johnson was dying. Armed with the doctor's certified reports of ill-health, Prison Association Secretary John C. Taylor and several prominent Hartford attorneys returned to the legislature, this time asking for commutation of Johnson's murder conviction and deportation back to Sweden. Convinced, the legislators voted to pardon Johnson.[32]

On the day of his release, Johnson was escorted to the floor of the Connecticut General Assembly by Secretary Taylor, whereupon an "elated" Johnson "ridiculed and guffawed the very men who had granted him his pardon." They were "a nice lot of dupes," he roared from the floor of the House. There was nothing wrong with his health, and he would go back to Sweden "when he got good and ready."[33] Newspapers said the legislators were rendered speechless by the scene. This "shameful event," wrote a reporter from the *Hartford Courant*, had an important bearing on the decision to reform the present Board of Pardons.[34]

The Connecticut Board of Pardons was a major improvement over the previous legislative pardon system. Pardons were now granted sparingly, like one for a horse thief dying of consumption, or for a

---

31 Gordon Bates, *The Connecticut Prison Association and the Search for Reformatory Justice, 1875–2015* (Middletown, CT: Wesleyan University Press, 2017), 4–5.

32 "Board of Pardons: Twentieth Anniversary," *Hartford Daily Courant*, December 10, 1903, 12.

33 "Board of Pardons: Twenty Years in Existence," *Morning Journal-Courier* (New Haven, CT), December 10, 1903, 12.

34 Ibid.

man who had been imprisoned for writing a bad check, signing it as a German count, now judged to be insane. In 1892, the board refused to pardon a convicted murderer even after a letter-writing campaign from well-connected politicians, including then-Governor William McKinley of Ohio. On the twentieth anniversary of the board in 1903, the *Hartford Times* wrote that financial and political factors no longer influenced the board. "All prisoners, rich or poor, friendless or powerful, will receive what the just man hopes for—justice tempered with mercy."[35]

In 1884, McLean showed considerable independence and courage on another important issue facing the legislature—his support for the so-called "short haul" rate bill, which sought to prevent railroads from charging higher freight rates for short distances. McLean believed that the current system of charging higher rates for short distances discriminated against shipments originating in Connecticut and favored those who were shipping long distances, namely the popular New York to Boston "long-haul" trade route. Higher rates for short distances hurt Connecticut farmers and businesses who frequently used the railroads to move products locally.

McLean supported the bill to reduce "short haul" rates. One newspaper reported that "Mr. McLean of Simsbury gave some instances of unjust discrimination in freight rates," in a March 1884 speech to the Connecticut House.[36] Backing the bill put him at odds with his mentor and employer Henry Robinson, a director of the New York, New Haven, and Hartford Railroad Company, known as the New Haven Railroad.[37] This is a clear example of McLean resisting the pressure to

---

35   Ibid.

36   "The Short Hall Bill Passes the House," *Meriden Daily Republican* (Meriden, CT), March 27, 1.

37   "George P. McLean," *Commemorative Biographical Record of Hartford County, Connecticut, Volume 1* (Hartford: J.H. Beers & Co, 1901), 80.

blindly favor the corporate stance of the New Haven Railroad; instead, he opted to support the needs of his constituents, even risking his relationship with mentor Henry Robinson. He later praised Robinson for not interfering and encouraging him to vote as he wanted. McLean never forgot the unconditional support and friendship he shared with his mentor.[38] Ultimately the short-haul bill passed in the Connecticut House (with McLean voting in the affirmative) but was voted down in the State Senate.[39]

McLean made an excellent first impression after his first year of elective office. *The Meriden Daily Republican* wrote in May of 1883: "Mr. McLean of Simsbury was an interesting talker, and always commanded attention. He might be called brilliant for a young man."[40]

After serving in the Connecticut House from 1883 to 1884, McLean won a seat in the Connecticut State Senate from 1886 to 1887. According to a *Hartford Courant* editorial, McLean was known for his thoroughness of preparation and "showed remarkable aptitude for his duties."[41] While a state senator, he advocated lowering the taxation of estates, reforming insurance rates, conducting tubercular testing of livestock, and abolishing the prison contract labor system used by businesses. During his last year in the state senate, McLean was named executive secretary for Connecticut Governor Phineas Lounsbury, who served as governor from 1887–1889.[42] The role of executive secretary then was much like today's chief of staff—managing appointments, correspondence, speech writing, and providing advice and counsel during an era when government staffs were very lean. McLean's appointment is further evidence that, just ten years removed from high

---

38   Henry Cornelius Robinson Memorial Tribute (no publisher, 1900), 19, https://archive.org/details/henrycorneliusro00slsn/page/n7/mode/2up.

39   "Connecticut Matters," *Hartford Daily Courant,* April 21, 1883, 4.

40   "The Final Adjournment," *Meriden Daily Republican* (Meriden, CT), May 3, 1883, 2.

41   "Legislative Notes," *Hartford Daily Courant,* January 21, 1886, 3.

42   "[McLean] to be Executive Secretary," *Meriden* (CT) *Journal,* January 12, 1887, 3.

school, he had caught the eye of powerful Republican Party officials. One newspaper said about the appointment that McLean was a "coming man in the hands of his friends. Mr. McLean has occupied a seat in both branches of the legislature and has therefore acquired a sufficient knowledge of practical politics."[43]

While McLean was in the state senate, he was appointed to a five-member commission charged with the revision of the Connecticut state general statutes.[44] This two-year project involved a thorough review of over four thousand sections of the state's general statutes. States periodically revise their statutes to incorporate amendments and repeals, make consolidations, and eliminate obsolete laws. The revisions are not changes to the law, but they make the body of statutes more accessible and consistent. This thorough revision of the statutes required an in-depth understanding of the law and law-making process, and his appointment indicates the depth of McLean's legal acumen and indefatigable work ethic. McLean was paid $4,500 for his work on the commission (about $120,000 in 2020 dollars).

In addition to his service on the revision commission, McLean continued to work throughout the 1880s as a lawyer for Henry C. Robinson until he started his own law firm, Sperry, McLean & Brainard in 1897. In later years, McLean's political opponents accused him of being the "chief lobbyist at Hartford for the New Haven Railroad" in the 1880s and 1890s.[45] McLean did perform a considerable amount of legal work for the New Haven Railroad, but many lawyers worked for railroads because the size and scope of the rail industry in America in the nineteenth century was immense. In the 1880s, railroads accounted for about ten percent of the American economy, employed

---

43   "[McLean] to be Executive Secretary," *Meriden* (CT) *Journal*, January 12, 1887, 3.

44   "The Revision Completed," *New York Times*, August 21, 1887, 5.

45   "Railway Lobbyist After Position in U.S. Senate," *Oakland* (CA) *Tribune*, July 27, 1909, 16.

tens of thousands, and transported both goods and passengers through-out the country. [46]

Some of McLean's work for the New Haven Railroad involved help-ing the company acquire rival lines. The 1880s and 1890s were decades of consolidation for America's railroads, and the larger, more efficient companies like the New Haven bought out their smaller rivals. In fact, the New Haven Railroad so aggressively bought or leased nearly all its competition that it earned the nickname "The Consolidator."[47] The re-lationship between the railroads and the government was fraught with challenges and complexities, particularly over the question of jurisdic-tion. Who should regulate the railroads—local, state, or the federal government? To curry favor with government officials, the railroads engaged in the widespread practice of giving free passes to members of the state legislatures, to members of Congress, and to other public officials, even the president of the United States.

One example of McLean's legal work on behalf of the railroads in-volved the safety of railroad crossings. Horrific accidents were all too common at crossings. The key question facing governments and the railroads was who would pay to make these crossings safe? It was costly to make safety improvements, such as constructing bridges or under-passes, or re-routing tracks. In the early 1890s, a bill in the Connecti-cut General Assembly sought to compel the railroad companies to pay for all crossing improvements. Representing the New Haven Railroad as an attorney for Robinson, McLean helped craft a compromise that was passed on June 19, 1893.

The compromise centered around who was there first—the railroad or the public highway. If a new rail line crossed an existing highway, the rail-

---

46   Herbert Hovenkamp, "Regulatory Conflict in the Gilded Age: Federalism and the Railroad Problem," *The Yale Law Journal* 97 (January 1987): 1018.

47   "History of New York, New Haven & Hartford Railroad," New York, New Haven & Hartford Railroad Abandoned Structures Collection, Archives & Special Collections at the Thomas J. Dodd Research Center, University of Connecticut Libraries.

road would pay three-fourths of the costs for the crossing improvements. If a new highway crossed an existing railroad, the government and the railroad would each pay half for the safety improvements. In addition, state tax money would be used for the government's share, taking local governments out of the picture.[48]

After the law was passed in 1893, many local governments sought redress for the payments they had made for road grade improvements in the past. On March 7, 1894, McLean represented the city of East Haven in a lawsuit demanding that the state reimburse the city for its earlier crossing grade improvement. The court awarded the city $2,850, less McLean's legal fee of $500.[49] McLean was criticized for this "lobby matter," but he brushed it off, saying he was only helping the town get redress under the new law.[50]

George McLean's involvement with pardons did not end when he left the board in 1901. In 1909, he appeared before the board on behalf of one of the longest-serving prisoners in Connecticut history, John Warren. Warren had been convicted in 1859 for the second-degree murder of his wife when he was twenty-one years old; he had been imprisoned for fifty years. McLean urged the board to free Warren, citing the fact that he had been a model prisoner who had already paid a terrible price and no longer posed a threat to society. He characterized Warren's crime as a "brainstorm" (crime of passion), a condition that had not been recognized by the court fifty years before.[51] Ridiculed by the public and the press, the brainstorm defense was supported by persuasive

---

48   Brent D. Ogden, *Railroad-Highway Grade Crossing Handbook*, Federal Highway Administration, Office of Safety Design, August 2007, 11. In 1893, the Supreme Court, in New York and N. E. Railroad v. Town of Bristol, upheld the statute.

49   "Another Charge Brought Against the Lobby," *Hartford Daily Courant*, March 7, 1894, 1.

50   "The Lobby Matter," *Morning-Journal Courier* (New Haven, CT), March 8, 1894, 2.

51   "Will Not Pardon Oldest Prisoner," *Star-Gazette* (Elmira, NY), December 14, 1909, 1.

testimony at the trial from five past presidents of the American Psychiatric Association and the American Neurological Association.[52] Despite McLean's arguments, John Warren's request for a pardon was rejected.

McLean's first major foray into the national political scene came in support of Republican James G. Blaine for president in 1884. Despite the Republican Party's dominance, an emerging ideological split emerged in the 1880s between the older conservatives and a group of younger Republicans looking for reform. Blaine represented a faction called "Half-Breeds," or "half-Republican," mainly reform-minded Republicans in favor of civil service testing and a merit system for government jobs. Against them were the Republican Party's conservatives, the so-called "Stalwarts," who generally favored the spoils system of patronage. Notable Stalwarts include Chester Arthur, Roscoe Conking, and other conservative Republicans who had supported Ulysses S. Grant for president and even sought his political comeback.[53]

Twenty-seven-year-old George McLean actively campaigned for Blaine in 1884.[54] Blaine is a largely obscure figure today, but he "was America's most able and popular political leader in the late nineteenth century," according to biographer Edward P. Crapol.[55] Blaine sought the Republican nomination for president in 1876, 1880, and 1884 and later served as US Secretary of State under Republican President Benjamin Harrison from 1888–1892.[56] While Blaine narrowly lost the presidency to Democrat Grover Cleveland in 1884, his reform "Half

---

52   Emil R. Pinta, "Examining Harry Thaw's "Brainstorm" Defense: APA and ANA Presidents as Expert Witnesses in a 1907 Trial," *Psychiatric Quarterly* 79 (July 2008): 83–89.

53   Allan Peskin, "Who Were the Stalwarts? Who Were Their Rivals? Republican Factions in the Gilded Age," *Political Science Quarterly* 99, no. 4 (1984): 703–16, accessed March 11, 2021, doi:10.2307/2150708.

54   "Two Enthusiastic Rallies," *Hartford Daily Courant*, October 2, 1884, 2.

55   Edward P. Crapol, *James G. Blaine: Architect of Empire* (Wilmington, DE: Scholarly Resources, 2000), xiv.

56   Ibid., 81.

Breed" movement prevailed in 1888 with the election of Benjamin Harrison, whom McLean also supported.[57]

In 1890, McLean ran unsuccessfully for Connecticut's Secretary of the State, the only popular election he ever lost. The bizarre Connecticut state elections of 1890 have taken on mythic status, much like the controversial national election of 2000, where George Bush beat Al Gore, but only after the US Supreme Court settled the electoral deadlock. The 1890 election was different. According to a provision of the Connecticut Constitution of 1818, if a candidate for state office did not receive a majority of the total votes cast, the election would be decided by the state legislature, where the Republicans almost always had a majority. Now in 1890, in the race for governor, secretary of the state, and other key state offices, none of the candidates won a majority, but the legislature could not resolve the deadlock. The incumbents held onto their offices as if the 1890 election had never been held.[58]

This meant that Governor Morgan Bulkeley, the Republican elected in 1888, refused to recognize his 1890 successor. Opponents of Bulkeley attempted to bar his entry into the governor's office, but Bulkeley gained entry to the padlocked office with a crowbar, earning him the nickname the "Crowbar Governor." Bulkeley, who was president of Aetna Insurance from 1879–1920, borrowed money from Aetna to pay the state's bills when the legislature refused to appropriate funds for the government.[59] McLean's law firm, Henry C. Robinson & Company, provided legal representation for Bulkeley during his disputed second term as governor. Bulkeley became an important mentor to McLean, backing his run for governor in 1900.[60]

---

57   "The Republican Convention," *Hartford Daily Courant,* May 17, 1888, 2.

58   Frederick Morrison Heath, 1931–"Politics and Steady Habits: Issues and Elections in Connecticut, 1894–1914," PhD diss. (Columbia University, 1965), 3.

59   Kevin Murphy, *Crowbar Governor: The Life and Times of Morgan Gardner Bulkeley* (Middletown, CT: Wesleyan University Press 2010), 122.

60   "See Chapter 1 – The Comeback" about the McLean-Bulkeley Senate race in 1904.

After McLean's loss for secretary of state in the deadlocked election of 1890, he continued to work as an attorney for Henry Robinson. He drafted wills, managed trusts, and performed complex litigation work for the railroad industry. The *Hartford Courant* provides glimpses of some of his other casework, such as defending drunkards, enforcing county dry laws, and resolving boundary disputes between farmers. It may have been a bit mundane for the ambitious McLean. He soon set his sights on a new target.

In January of 1891, according to the *New York Sun*, McLean began a year-long campaign for the position of United States Attorney for Connecticut. The four-year term of George G. Sill (a Cleveland appointee) was set to expire in January of 1892, so to obtain the appointment from President Benjamin Harrison, McLean sought endorsements from the Connecticut Republican State Central Committee and the entire Connecticut congressional delegation. McLean may have overstepped in soliciting support, so much so that Connecticut's senior US Senator, Orville Platte, mildly protested the way McLean secured his signature to the petition.[61] Despite his naked ambition, McLean was appointed by President Harrison on February 10, 1892, and was confirmed by the US Senate on March 15, 1892.

The Office of the United States Attorney is one of the oldest positions in the federal government, created by the Judiciary Act of 1789. The role of a US Attorney is to prosecute criminal cases brought by the federal government as well as prosecute or defend civil cases where the United States is a party. US Attorneys also initiate, and direct criminal investigations, and recommend the sentencing of offenders.[62]

---

61 "Politics in Connecticut: A Lively Scramble for the U.S. Attorney," *The Sun* (New York), January 3, 1892, 10.

62 United States, Department of Justice, *The United States Attorneys' Manual,* April 2018, https://www.justice.gov/jm/justice-manual.

According to his campaign biographies, McLean never lost a criminal case as a US Attorney, and he lost only one civil suit.[63]

Early in his career as the federal attorney, McLean led a crackdown on opium dens operating in Hartford, where the drug was manufactured, sold, and smoked. These dens were common in large cities, often run by newly arrived Chinese immigrants. In November of 1892, McLean prosecuted his first case against an opium manufacturer. Again in 1895, he prosecuted three Chinese nationals charged with manufacturing and selling opium and with the attempted bribery of the arresting officer.[64] McLean also prosecuted a counterfeiting case against Henry "Big" Oliver of Bridgeport. Laying out captured evidence, including molds, ladles, and counterfeit coins, McLean questioned an array of witnesses including Secret Service agents and a US Marshall. Oliver pleaded guilty to counterfeiting silver dollars and half-dollar coins.[65]

The civil suit that McLean lost was a high-profile case between Yale University and Storrs (Connecticut) Agricultural College over federal money awarded to Connecticut colleges as a result of the Land Grant Act of 1862, also known as the Morrill Act. Starting in 1862, Yale was the recipient of Land Grant Act funds, but the college had only a small agriculture curriculum. In 1892, after the creation of Storrs Agricultural College (which became the University of Connecticut), the money was diverted from Yale to Storrs. Universities rarely like to see funding withdrawn, so in July 1895 Yale sued for the withheld funds plus damages.

McLean, "of counsel of the state of Connecticut," reasoned that the federal government had granted the money to the state, not to any

---

63 "George P. McLean," in Norton, Frederick Calvin, *The Governors of Connecticut: Biographies of the Chief Executives of the Commonwealth that Gave to the World the First Written Constitution Known to History* (United States: Connecticut Magazine Company, 1905), 368.

64 "Chinamen Held for Trial," *Morning Journal-Courier* (New Haven, CT), May 1, 1895, 7.

65 "Trial of a Counterfeiter," *Morning Journal-Courier* (New Haven, CT), March 23, 1895, 2.

specific university.[66] The land-grant money, he argued, never did have any business at Yale. "It is as out of place there as bare feet and patches would be at a junior promenade,"[67] McLean argued. Yale had received more than $300,000 from the Morrill Act over a thirty-three year period but had graduated only thirteen people "now found on farms."[68] Ultimately the court awarded Yale $154,604 in damages, but ruled that federal land grants were made to states and not to specific institutions. The state of Connecticut in the future could do what it wished with its land grant money.[69]

In a curious detour from his legal work, in August of 1892, McLean was named president of the newly organized Scherer Manufacturing Company, producer of an automated burial apparatus.[70] The company made a device for lowering caskets into graves, consisting of a metal frame placed around the open mouth of a grave: "A touch of a spring and the casket is lowered noiselessly into the grave."[71] Perhaps McLean was swept away with the entrepreneurial fever of the age, like Mark Twain, who lost large sums on a typesetting machine, an engraving process, the magnetic telegraph, a steam pulley, and the Fredonia Watch Company.[72] Scherer Manufacturing made twenty of the burial devices, putting them on trial at various cemeteries, but McLean later said the expected boom in demand never came. Despite reducing the

---

66   "Hearing in the Suit of Yale University Against the State," *Hartford Daily Courant*, July 12, 1895, 4.

67   "Yale-Storrs Controversy," *New York Times*, September 25, 1895, 4.

68   Ibid.

69   Mark J. Roy, "Land Grant Status Acquired After 'Yale-Storrs Controversy,'" *UConn Today*, University of Connecticut Communications Department, September 26, 2012, https://today.uconn.edu/2012/09/land-grant-status-acquired-after-yale-storrs-controversy/.

70   "Connecticut Notes," *The New Hartford Tribune*, August 26, 1892, 2.

71   R. J. (Rufus J.) Haight, "Literature Received," *The Modern Cemetery*, The Association of American Cemetery Superintendents Volume 3, No. 7 (September 1893), 84.

72   Richard Zacks, "The Nineteenth-Century Start-Ups That Cost Mark Twain His Fortune," *Time*, April 19, 2016, https://time.com/4297572/mark-twain-bad-business/, accessed May 7, 2020.

weight of the frame from 400 to 150 pounds so it could be carried by one man, the company failed, and the patent was eventually sold at a loss to an investor, who later reneged on the note. The experience "hurt my pride," McLean confessed in a speech to a group of businessmen in 1901.[73]

One year after McLean's term as a US Attorney expired in 1896, he formed his own law firm, Sperry, McLean & Brainard. The firm's location in the Aetna Building at 218 Main Street in Hartford was no accident as the firm was primarily in-house counsel for Aetna Insurance Company. Aetna President Morgan Bulkeley chose McLean's firm for its counsel because of their long friendship and McLean's political influence and connections. For example, in June of 1897, the *Hartford Courant* reported that an examination of Aetna's tax returns revealed the company had been getting certain tax exemptions which other insurance companies did not seem to get. From 1887 to 1896, these special tax exemptions amounted to $2.9 million.[74] A subsequent investigation by the state board of equalization decided that the exemptions were proper.[75]

Another key client for Sperry, McLean & Brainard was the newly formed American Telephone & Telegraph Company. McLean represented them in multiple suits where they sought permits to erect telephone poles throughout Connecticut. In addition to getting court orders to lift injunctions prohibiting the poles, he pressed for the prosecution of individuals who had cut them down, including a $5,000 fine for one perpetrator.[76]

McLean's reputation as a tough interrogator is illustrated in an 1897

---

73   "Governor's Advice Before Group of Businessmen," *Hartford Daily Courant*, April 20, 1901, 2

74   "More Tax Exemptions: Good Luck of the Aetna Life in Making Its List," *Hartford Daily Courant*, June 5, 1897, 2.

75   Ibid.

76   "Those Windsor Locks Poles," *Hartford Daily Courant*, March 2, 1898, 6.

case concerning the spread of disease among livestock.[77] McLean was defending a state law permitting officials to kill tubercular cows and not compensating the owners for the slaughtered livestock. The trial hinged on the actions of a veterinary surgeon, F.G. Atwood, who had a reputation for declaring diseased cows healthy, thereby allowing herd owners to avoid the killing of their diseased stock.

McLean began his questioning of Atwood with a discussion of scientific terms relating to diseases in cows, which "thoroughly exposed the ignorance of the veterinary surgeon."[78] McLean then brought forward some letters and asked if Atwood had written them. After a long scrutiny, Atwood admitted that he wrote them. McLean read one of them aloud, calling attention to all the grammatical errors and mistakes. Then McLean leaned in and pointedly asked Atwood:

McLean: "How many species of bacteria are there?"

Atwood: [the question was evaded].

McLean: "There are four, are there not?"

Atwood: "No, there are twelve."

McLean: "Twelve! Don't you know there are 30,000?"

Atwood: "I wasn't going that high."

"A general burst of laughter greeted this and Atwood was dismissed.[79]

McLean's term as US Attorney expired in March 1896, just in time for him to participate in the presidential election that year, widely acknowledged as one of only a few that brought about fundamental realignments in American politics.[80] The election of William McKinley over Democrat William Jennings Bryan solidified the Republican Party

---

77   "Tuberculosis Hearing," *Hartford Daily Courant*, April 8, 1897, 5.

78   Ibid.

79   There are indeed about 30,000 formally named species of bacteria; see Daniel Delhaize, "Species Numbers in Bacteria," *Proceedings of the California Academy of Science*, June 3, 2005, 56(6 Suppl 1): 62–71.

80   Richard Hal Williams, *Realigning America: McKinley, Bryan, and the Remarkable Election of 1896* (Lawrence: University Press of Kansas, 2010).

as the party of urban voters, business, industry, Blacks, Union veterans, and the aspiring middle-class (including a share of labor and immigrants). It ushered in an era of Republican dominance of the presidency (seven presidents of the next nine were Republicans) and of both houses of Congress (seventeen of the next twenty sessions were Republican.) Meanwhile, the Democrats carried on in defeat as the sectional party of the South, advocating state's rights, limited government, the interests of western farmers, and opposition to the protective tariff; they were generally viewed as out-of-step with industrialization and the Republican Party's growing internationalist approach to foreign policy.

One other important facet of the election of 1896 was the dissolution of the Populist Party, which had emerged in the early 1890s as an important force in the South and the West. Many former Populists joined the Republican Party, planting the seeds of a party division that would emerge in 1912 when Theodore Roosevelt split from the Republican Party to form the Progressive (Bull Moose) Party.[81]

McLean was given the honor of being named temporary chairman of the State Republican Party at the state convention in Hartford on September 2, 1896, enabling him to make the nominating speech for William McKinley to several thousand delegates and spectators. McLean assured his audience that he was confident of a Republican victory in 1896, but the party needed to reach out to the millions of Democratic voters who were being deceived by their cunning leaders by inciting class and sectional jealousies. These Democratic leaders' advice has been as beneficial to the industrial well-being of the nation "as was the advice of Eve to the dietary experiments of Adam."[82]

But the heart of McLean's speech hinged on repudiating the Democrats' "free silver policy"—their advocacy of an expansionary monetary

---

81 Gary Miller, and Norman Schofield, "Activists and Partisan Realignment in the United States," *The American Political Science Review* 97, no. 2 (2003): 245–60, http://www.jstor.org/stable/3118207.

82 "Speech by Temporary Chairman McLean," *Hartford Daily Courant*, September 2, 1896, 1.

policy to allow the unlimited coinage of silver. Republicans supported a strict adherence to the more carefully fixed money supply implicit in the gold standard. The Democrats believed that the US government would promote prosperity to farmers and laborers by inflating the money supply through the increased minting of silver. (That policy was strongly supported by western silver miners). The Republicans steadfastly opposed free silver, arguing that the best way to national prosperity was "sound money," or gold, the benchmark for international trade.

There were vastly different worldviews behind the silver versus gold debate, with the Democrats looking out for "the little guy" and rural interests, while the Republicans were promoting the urban eastern "moneyed interests," who valued the stability of the gold standard. McLean spoke about the importance of the gold standard, stating that "economic panic would follow Mr. Bryan's election." He also articulated Republican Party fears that the Democrats desired nationalization of industry: "first the railroads, telegraph and telephone lines, then the income tax, and the single land tax, then a small portion of fortunes of the rich, then a larger portion, then—everything."[83] McLean advocated economic liberty and individualism and warned that Bryan's predilection for "government paternalism" was akin to socialism and a portent of anarchism. "Tell the boy that he can build no more castles in the air and he will build a hovel on the earth," McLean warned.[84]

McKinley won the 1896 election with 7.1 million votes to Bryan's 6.5 million. The electoral vote was not as close: 271 for McKinley, 176 for Bryan. Bryan ran again for president in 1900 and lost to McKinley, and Bryan lost again to William Howard Taft in 1908. However, as one of the most progressive members of the Democratic party, Bryan would see many of his ideas and reforms adopted later by Republicans,

---

83   "Speech by Temporary Chairman McLean," *Hartford Daily Courant,* September 2, 1896, 2.

84   Ibid.

Holly House, built in 1896 (Source: author's collection)

including Theodore Roosevelt, and even George McLean, though to a lesser degree than Roosevelt.[85]

McLean made a major personal achievement in 1896 with the construction of his new home at 75 Great Pond Road in Simsbury, just north of the McLean homestead that was built in 1808 by his grandfather, the Rev. Allen McLean. The Colonial-style mansion—with three-stories and twenty-two rooms—had shingled and gabled roofs, columned porches, clapboard siding, and a large mahogany entrance door. There was an office, a library, a sitting-room, a dining hall, six bedrooms, a billiard room, seven fireplaces, and an octagon-shaped veranda.

McLean named it "Holly House" because there were several beautiful holly trees nearby. He lived there with his mother and other members of his extended family, and there were occasional visits from his sister, the novelist Sarah Pratt McLean; and his aunt Sarah Abernethy, the widow who had lived in New York City. In later years, McLean's staff of six servants lived there as well.

McLean's income during the period from 1880 to 1900 appears to have been considerable. His salaries as a public servant were modest,

---

85   Richard Hal Williams, *Realigning America*, 122.

but his fees as a lawyer with Henry Robinson, and later as a partner in Sperry, McLean & Brainard, were likely substantial since he could afford to build Holly House and to make extensive land purchases. By 1900, McLean had acquired several hundred more acres of land surrounding Holly House, a practice he continued throughout his lifetime. His earnings as a US Attorney could also have been significant, since until 1896, US Attorneys were paid on a fee-system based on the cases they prosecuted. In one example, a US Attorney in 1804 reportedly earned an annual income of $100,000 (about $2.1 million in 2020 dollars) through fees on cases he handled. [86]

After McLean died in 1932, several of his nephews speculated that as a young man McLean was "married to his work" and put his personal life on hold. One nephew believed that McLean may have had an unrequited love, a woman who spurned him. McLean occasionally appeared as part of the city's social life in the society pages of the *Hartford Courant* in the 1880s and 1890s. He attended whist and bridge parties in the 1880s, and at least one costume masquerade in 1883, where McLean dressed in a "handsome court costume." [87]

McLean took many lengthy vacations during his young adulthood. In 1890, he took a two-month trip to Europe with his friends Dr. and Mrs. George H. Knight. Knight was the superintendent of a state-run mental health facility, and a life-long friend. The three left New York City on July 4, 1890, for Hamburg, Germany, sailing on the new passenger ship S.S. *Normannia*, known for its comfort and elegance. On board were 480 cabin passengers and 460 steerage passengers.

McLean went on another major trip in August 1899, this time across the continent to the Pacific coast, with stops in Vancouver, San Francisco, Salt Lake City, and Yellowstone National Park. He was among

---

86 Robert Longley, "About the United States Attorneys," ThoughtCo., https://www.thoughtco.com/the-united-states-attorneys-3322420

87 "The Masquerade," *The New Hartford Tribune*, February 9, 1883, 3.

the park's 9,579 visitors in 1899 (which compares with over four million visitors to Yellowstone in 2018).[88] In fact, because the park had opened in 1872, McLean was among the first 100,000 visitors to see Yellowstone. Most visitors to Yellowstone before 1900 were members of the upper class, staying at the exclusive park lodges, and taking the five-day stagecoach tours, which included a stop at Old Faithful geyser. Stagecoach drivers based at the park hotels drove large carriages called "tally-hos" and were colorful in both dress and personality.[89]

His traveling companion on this cross-country trip was Andrew F. Gates, a Yale-educated lawyer and close political confidant of McLean. Gates was the chairman of the state's Republican Central Committee from 1901 to 1902, and later served as chairman of the state railroad commission. Married in 1893, Gates was the father of two young children at the time of this trip, during which he and McLean spent two weeks hunting in Idaho.

When McLean returned from his trip in September of 1899, "he was well browned and in excellent health,"[90] ready for the biggest challenge of his life—running for governor of Connecticut in 1900. In June of 1899, one newspaper speculated on the upcoming election and who would likely run. McLean was among the five potential Republican candidates it listed, saying he was the most ambitious and aggressive of the lot, a "hustler" with strong friends in the Republican Central Committee who were "pulling wires, laying pipe and engaging steerers" on his behalf.[91] The forecasters differed on who would prevail, but they all expected it to be a lively affair. "There will be no kindergarten performances. The struggle is likely to be decidedly spicy, for

---

88   John William Uhler, "Yellowstone National Park Visitor Statistics," *Yellowstone Up Close and Personal,* https://www.yellowstone.co/stats.htm.

89   Lee H. Whittlesey, *Storytelling in Yellowstone: Horse and Buggy Tour Guides* (Albuquerque: University of New Mexico Press, 2007), 170.

90   "Messrs. McLean and Gates Reach Home," *Hartford Daily Courant,* September 25, 1899, 9.

91   "For the Governorship," *Naugatuck Daily News,* June 15, 1899, 2.

if appearances are not misleading powerful influencers will be pitted against each other."[92]

With the century ending, George McLean, age forty-two, was at the peak of his powers and well positioned for a new challenge, having patiently climbed the political ladder for two decades. The end of a century often prompts introspection, even fear and trepidation about the future. As the calendar approached 1900, one Connecticut newspaper wrote anxiously about "the old order ending and a new, unpredictable order beginning."[93] The French call this *fin de siècle*, or the end of the century—the conclusion of one era and the start of another.

Beginning in the late 1890s, there were signs that the nation's economic prosperity and technological innovation were breeding feelings of cynicism, pessimism, ennui, and a belief that rising urbanization and wealth would lead to decadence and a loss of traditional morality. People were learning of new ideas about human evolution, psychology, and the unconscious mind, often expressed in the arts and sciences. Books like the *Strange Case of Dr Jekyll and Mr. Hyde*, in which Robert Louis Stevenson suggested that grotesque conflicts and dualities exist within people.[94] H.G. Wells, a socialist, touched on themes of social unrest and disorder in groundbreaking books like the *Time Machine* and *War of the Worlds*, promoting the notion that prosperity and progress were carrying seeds of doom and destruction to a society blinded by materialism and greed.[95]

Historian H.W. Brands writes in his epic study of the Gilded Age

---

92   "Events in New England States," *Standard Union*, November 25, 1899, 3.

93   Betina Entzminger, "Fin de Siècle Anxieties and Cave Endings: Mark Twain's A Connecticut Yankee in King Arthur's Court," *Mark Twain Journal* 55, n. 1/2 (Spring/Fall 2017): 100–112.

94   Greg Buzwell, "Man is not truly one, but truly two: duality in Robert Louis Stevenson's Strange Case of Dr Jekyll and Mr. Hyde," *British Library Newsletter,* British Library Trust, May 15, 2014, https://www.bl.uk/romantics-and-victorians/articles/duality-in-robert-louis-stevensons-strange-case-of-dr-jekyll-and-mr-hyde.

95   Iain Sinclair, "An introduction to The War of the Worlds," *British Library Newsletter*, British Library Trust, May 15, 2014, https://www.bl.uk/romantics-and-victorians/articles/an-introduction-to-the-war-of-the-worlds, accessed September 4, 2020.

that the lives of ordinary people greatly improved from 1870 to 1900. The nation's output increased three-fold, and average per capita income doubled. Much of this productivity came from the advent of electricity, which improved the quality of life for many ordinary Americans in countless ways. According to Brands, infant mortality declined by a third during these decades, and average life expectancy increased. Freight and passenger train travel had proliferated throughout the nation, including the innovation of refrigerated train cars to improve the distribution of food. Housing and public services improved and kept up with booming demand. US population increased by 40 million between 1870 and 1900, with one-third coming from immigration. Education at all levels became more widely available during the final decades of the nineteenth century.[96]

Yet for all these advances in material and cultural life, Brands writes, "there remained a feeling that things had gone wrong." Income inequality, economic volatility, labor unrest, institutional racism, and the increasing concentrated power of large corporations were among the pressing political and social ills that needed to be addressed by the nation's leaders. A key characteristic of the Gilded Age, according to Brands, is the ongoing struggle between capitalism and democracy. As 1900 neared, "capitalism had never enjoyed such a formidable advantage," Brands concludes.[97] America's political leaders would be called upon to address this tension between democracy and capitalism in the coming century.

In a January 1902 speech to the Union League Club of New Haven, McLean expressed his alarm over how fast the industrial world was moving, and urged his listeners to embrace needed change and reform. Throughout McLean's life, he encountered the need to change laws

---

96   H.W. Brands, *American Colossus: the Triumph of Capitalism, 1865–1900* (New York: Doubleday, 2010), 542–45.

97   Ibid., 545.

that had been set up with the best of intentions by previous generations but were now obsolete, ineffective, or subject to corruption. What is fair today may be unfair tomorrow, and what is cherished today may be properly discarded tomorrow, McLean argued.[98] What once had made sense, like entrusting the pardoning power to Connecticut's (small) seventeenth-century General Assembly, no longer worked in the industrialized Connecticut of the 1890s. Preserving old laws and customs out of reverence to the past, McLean argued, is wrong. "Age does not strengthen an unjust law any more than whitewash strengthens a weak wall," McLean stated in a 1902 speech.[99]

Social and political reform would not come easily. Change required courageous leaders willing to pay the price of standing up to entrenched interests. McLean was clearly ambitious and driven, keen to be one of those leaders in this coming age of reform. He had carefully and patiently carved out a path to the 1900 governor's race, from his admission to the bar in 1882, to his two terms in the state legislature, to his seven years as clerk of the Board of Pardons, and to his four years as US Attorney. Along the way, McLean had made many political friends and gained a few important mentors who viewed him as intelligent, hard-working, principled, loyal, and a strong public speaker with a promising political future.

The newspaper that predicted in June of 1899 that "there will be no kindergarten performances" in the race for governor in 1900 would be proven right. The struggle for the governor's office would indeed be "spicy," and "powerful influencers" would be bitterly "pitted against each other." The candidates vying to be Connecticut's fifty-ninth governor, elected at the beginning of a promising yet turbulent new century, were in for the fight of their lives.

98　"McLean Speaks," *Hartford Daily Courant*, January 16, 1902, 1.

99　Ibid.

★ CHAPTER THREE ★

A LITTLE HELP FROM HIS FRIENDS

"This New World of ours is rising above the Old World.
We have raised the red, white, and blue above all other
colors on earth in a tidal wave of prosperity."
*George P. McLean, campaign speech for Governor,
October 2, 1900*[1]

The race for governor of Connecticut in 1900 was on one level a titanic intra-party battle between two bitter factions, a power struggle between two Republican party kingmakers who viscerally disliked each other. But the 1900 governor's race was about much more: it was also a battle of competing visions of democracy at the dawn of the twentieth century. One side, led by Sam Fessenden, wanted to preserve Connecticut's nineteenth century "town-system" of representation in the state legislature that heavily favored rural interests. The other side, led by McLean, sought to empower Connecticut's growing cities, giving urban voters more say in the state legislature, and in the election of Connecticut's US senators. Though Sam Fessenden

---

1   "McLean's Argument," *Hartford Courant*, October 3, 1900, 1.

backed Donald Warner for the nomination, it was rumored that what he most wanted was a deadlocked nominating convention, and then emerge as a "dark horse" candidate to gain the nomination himself.[2]

No one was more important to McLean's run for governor than his closest friend and mentor, Orsamus Fyler. The two men first met at the 1880 Republican state convention, when McLean was a twenty-three-year-old reporter for the *Hartford Post*, and Fyler, forty, was a Republican Party leader, decorated Civil War veteran, prominent businessman, and civil servant. Fyler was impressed with McLean's friendliness, ambition, intelligence, and public-speaking ability. McLean was immediately taken by Fyler's honesty, fearlessness, and keen political insights. Sharing a love for the stir and clash of politics, their friendship lasted for over twenty years. McLean was forever in Fyler's debt, believing that Fyler rescued his career from "utter failure and defeat" on multiple occasions.[3]

Orsamus Fyler was born in Torrington, Connecticut, in 1840, and enlisted in the Nineteenth Connecticut Volunteer Infantry Regiment in 1862. He fought in several major Civil War battles, including Cold Harbor, Petersburg, and Winchester, where he was severely wounded in 1864. Fyler returned to Torrington after the war, married and had a family, carrying with him scars from the war that would never heal. His left tibia was shattered by an artillery shell, requiring him to walk with a crutch, causing excruciating pain. Fyler resumed farming and grain dealing, and he invested in real estate, and prospered. Like many other disabled veterans, he obtained well-paying government appointments—postmaster of Torrington from 1866 to 1885, state insurance commissioner from 1886 to 1892, and state railroad commissioner from 1887 to 1902.

---

2   "Fessenden's Fate Will Be Decided Today," *Boston Globe*, September 5, 1900, 7.

3   "Eulogy by McLean at Fyler Funeral," *Hartford Daily Courant*, November 23, 1909, 6

Orsamus R. Fyler, 1840–1909 (collection of the Torrington Historical Society)

In mid-1899, McLean was far from a "sure thing" to be the next governor of Connecticut. He was but one of six gubernatorial candidates that the *Naugatuck* (Conn.) *Daily News* had identified as contenders. So, when Orsamus Fyler, chairman of the Republican Central State Committee, announced in July 1899 that George McLean was his pick for governor, some of Fyler's Republican colleagues strongly objected.[4] When asked about McLean's reputation as a machine politician and lobbyist, Fyler expressed total faith in McLean, saying McLean was "sound and clean," no matter what his rivals were claiming in the newspapers.[5]

McLean scored an early victory for the nomination when the

---

4   "A Tribute to the Character of Senator McLean," *The Nebraska State Journal*, March 5, 1911, 7.

5   Ibid.

Republican Party Central Committee in May 1900 chose delegates for the Republican convention in September: two-thirds of the delegates were aligned with Fyler, and one-third with Fessenden.[6] During the summer, it was rumored that the Fessenden forces would unite behind McLean, but when the September convention arrived, the Fessenden forces vowed for a fight to the finish.[7]

On September 4–5, 1900, the Republicans held their state convention at the 2,000-seat Hyperion Theater in New Haven. The theater was a bit undersized, and soon filled way beyond capacity as the 502 delegates and many more enthusiastic spectators arrived.[8] McLean's chances were boosted when the former governor, Morgan Bulkeley, endorsed McLean for the nomination. Bulkeley was a longtime friend and McLean supporter, but the newspapers speculated that his support was equally driven by a desire to crush his old foe, Sam Fessenden.[9] Joseph L. Barbour, the former speaker of the Connecticut House, gave McLean's nominating speech, recapping McLean's career as a legislator, attorney, US Attorney, and founder of the Board of Pardons. Barbour said McLean was a "farmer's son" but sympathetic to the needs of Connecticut's growing cities.

Former state senator Randolph Chandler then nominated McLean's rival, Donald Warner. There were many things he did not like about George McLean, Chandler began. He pounded the podium for emphasis after each phrase: "We want a governor, not a lobbyist! We want a man, not a boy! We want a churchman, not a clubman! We want a man who was educated under the influence of that great emancipator Abraham Lincoln!" Hearing this, the McLean delegates jumped onto their seats and yelled at Chandler until "peacemakers came forward" to

---

6   "Out for McLean: The Coming Man," *Hartford Daily Courant*, May 1900, 10.

7   Heath, "Politics and Steady Habits," 61–64.

8   Fessenden's Fate," *Boston Globe*, September 5, 1900, 7.

9   Ibid.

lead Chandler off the stage.[10] No sooner had order returned when another McLean rival, Frank Brandegee, seconded Warner's nomination. Perspiring heavily in the unseasonably warm auditorium, Brandegee removed his coat and denounced McLean's candidacy as a dangerous experiment, a flirtation with the forces of disorder and anarchy. This set off another round of booing, ending in a call for voting.[11]

The voting took an hour and half. At two-thirty in the afternoon, the tellers announced that McLean received 275 votes to 225 for Warner, a narrow but decisive win. McLean was escorted to the platform to great bursts of applause and cheering, while others threw their hats in the air.[12] McLean was greatly touched by the victory, and called for unity. Then he stressed the need to reach out to Democrats in the November election.[13] McLean knew that the reform of the Connecticut legislature had long been popular among Democrats, and his openness to reform would give him the edge he needed to win. At that point, the convention made the vote for McLean's nomination unanimous, thus ending what the *Buffalo Review* called "the longest and most bitter fight that has ever taken place in Connecticut political history."[14]

Having secured the nomination, McLean now faced Democrat Samuel L. Bronson in the November election for governor. One leading newspaper said that the Republicans were fatally split after the contentious nominating convention in September, opening the door for a Democratic victory. McLean made his first campaign speech for governor at the Hartford Auditorium on October 2, 1900, to a standing-room-only crowd. He praised the accomplishments of the popular Republican President William McKinley, like the annexation

10   "McLean Nominated for Governor," *Hartford Daily Courant*, September 6, 1900, 1.

11   Ibid.

12   Ibid.

13   "Fessenden Was Beaten," *Buffalo Review*, September 1900, 1.

14   Ibid.

McLean Campaign Button for Governor, 1900 (with President McKinley) (from the collection of Dr. Kenneth Florey)

of the Philippines, Guam, and Puerto Rico after the recently concluded Spanish-American war. He pointed out that these new territories, along with the 1898 annexation of Hawaii, provided coaling stations and naval bases for American merchant and military ships, which were vitally needed as the nation increased its worldwide trade. He derided the Democrats for their opposition to McKinley's foreign policy successes and moribund economic policies.

McLean credited McKinley for the resurgent economy that had brought about new jobs, lower prices, and higher wages for workers, and reminded his audience of the disastrous economic depression of 1893 under Democratic President Grover Cleveland. "The only thing that had a boom under [Cleveland] were soup plates for three million honest, laboring men out of employment."[15] Cleveland's tariff reductions to boost free trade had been a failure, McLean argued, and his imposition of the nation's first income tax was a disaster, too. (It was ultimately declared unconstitutional by the Supreme Court in 1895).[16]

---

15   "McLean's Argument," *Hartford Daily Courant*, October 3, 1900, 8.

16   Pollock v. Farmers' Loan & Trust Company, 157, U.S. 429 (1895), affirmed on rehearing, 158, U.S. 601 (1895).

McLean made a special appeal to urban workers: "This nation belongs to laborers. The government is their servant. Industrial liberty is their polar star." The Republican Party offered them "peace and plenty" over the "poverty and contention" of the Cleveland years.

McLean had good reason to believe that many of Connecticut's moderate Democrats might vote for him. Four years earlier in the 1896 presidential election, McKinley's Democratic opponent, William Jennings Bryan, was viewed as too radical for many Democrats; some feared that Bryan might nationalize the railroads and other industries. It has been estimated that as much as 25 percent of Democrats switched sides over fears that Bryan's reform agenda would kill manufacturing jobs in Connecticut.[17]

McLean then highlighted the need for constitutional reform in Connecticut. The current system of allocating representatives in the legislature was "wrong in principle," and he was "ready to join hands" with Democrats to reform that system.[18] While the right method to solve the problem had not yet been discovered, he was committed to finding the best possible way of meaningfully resolving this "unsatisfactory situation."[19]

McLean won the November election for governor with fifty-four percent of the vote, taking seven of Connecticut's eight counties, losing only New Haven county, his opponent's home base. McLean benefited from the fact that his Democratic opponent, Samuel Bronson, was virtually unknown outside of New Haven County. Bronson was a popular local judge who had inherited a fortune from his father's publishing empire, but his millionaire status was out-of-step with many Democratic Party voters.

---

17   David Rhinelander, "The Presidential Election of 1896 Was Nasty and Expensive," *Hartford Daily Courant*, October 6, 2000, B1, B3.

18   "McLean's Argument," *Hartford Daily Courant*, October 6, 1900, 8.

19   "A Lost Issue," *Hartford Daily Courant*, October 24, 1900, 10.

On November 9, 1900, the *Courant* reported that McLean was headed for a month-long rest in the South, run down from the grueling campaign.[20] Just before he left, on Saturday night, November 11, the town of Simsbury had a "jollification" to celebrate McLean's victory: a one-thousand-person parade, four bands and a drum corps, streets illuminated with Chinese lanterns, bonfires in profusion, and all the buildings in town "gaily decorated with flags and buntings."[21] During the parade, a cannon from the state arsenal was fired from a nearby hill, the bell from Westminster School pealed, and a slow-moving train from the Central New England railway passing by blew its steam whistle for several minutes.

At the conclusion of the parade, several thousand people gathered around McLean's home, Holly House, where the word "Welcome" was spelled out in red, white, and blue Chinese lanterns hanging from the veranda. Among the celebrants were Orsamus Fyler, Morgan Bulkeley, and McLean's law partner, Lewis Sperry. After the playing of "America" by Colt's Armory Band, McLean advanced to the front of the veranda and congratulated the nation for reelecting William McKinley president of the United States. He also paid tribute to McKinley's "intrepid associate, Teddy Roosevelt of New York," the hero of San Juan Hill.[22]

McLean then quoted Shakespeare: "There is a tide in the affairs of men. Which, taken at the flood, leads on to fortune."[23] McLean was referring to the ebb and flow of power, that one must "go with the flow" and not miss the opportunity at hand. "This is the flood tide for

---

20   "McLean Will Take a Rest," *Hartford Daily Courant*, November 9, 1900, 8.

21   "Simsbury's Greeting for Governor-Elect McLean," *Hartford Daily Courant*, November 12, 1900, 3.

22   Ibid.

23   William Shakespeare, *Julius Caesar*, Act 4, Scene 3, Line 249, taken from the Folger Shakespeare Library, https://shakespeare.folger.edu/shakespeares-works/julius-caesar/act-4-scene3/?search=tide%20in%20the%20affairs%20of%20men/#line-4.3.244.

the Republican Party," McLean declared, and will lead to "better hope and fortune for us all."

Then Colt's Armory Band struck up "Hail to the Chief" to great applause. McLean singled out his indispensable mentor Orsamus Fyler, who hobbled up the porch steps. Overcome by emotion, Fyler said this was the proudest night of his life. He spoke movingly about how he had watched McLean progress and mature over the past twenty years. They were both born on farms, Fyler noted. It was a wonderful thing to see a farmer rise to chief executive of the state. Then former Governor Morgan Bulkeley spoke briefly, saying he looked forward to seeing McLean's portrait as governor displayed alongside his own. After three cheers were given for McLean's mother who was in attendance, a procession of horse-drawn carriages took the governor-elect and his friends on a victory tour, passing by various homes in Simsbury, ending with refreshments at the Simsbury Casino.[24]

January 19, 1901, inauguration day, was a red-letter day in the life of George P. McLean, beginning with his inaugural procession to the state Capitol in Hartford at one o'clock in the afternoon. For a Connecticut January day, it was mild, around forty-five degrees with periods of sunshine. The parade featured the Governor's Foot Guard, soldiers in bright red, white, and black colonial infantry uniforms, followed by ten, black, glossy four-horse-drawn carriages filled with dignitaries and guests. Governor-elect McLean and current Governor Lounsbury rode in the lead carriage, followed by the foot guard as they marched to fife and drum music up Trumbull Street "upon clean asphalt pavements with the jauntiness of spring itself."[25] Spectators lining the street applauded continuously, and the governor-elect periodically saluted as his carriage followed the parade route.

---

24   "Simsbury's Greeting for Governor-Elect McLean," *Hartford Daily Courant*, November 12, 1900, 3.

25   "McLean's Message," *Hartford Daily Courant*, January 10, 1901, 3.

Arriving at the north entrance of the state Capitol, McLean was escorted to the floor of the General Assembly, where he was sworn-in by Chief Justice Charles B. Andrews. McLean's inaugural address to the General Assembly began about three o'clock and lasted forty-five minutes. He had to stop delivering his address for a moment when the gas lights had to be lit.[26] He spoke in an "earnest and eloquent style" without interruption by any applause. "The listeners were watching closely," said one newspaper account. "No message ever held its hearers more attentively."

McLean's inaugural address shows that he was a proponent of reform in the nascent Progressive Era. Historian Stanley Milkis defines this somewhat amorphous era this way: "The Progressive movement accommodated a diverse array of reformers with the common objective of strengthening the national government and making it more responsive to popular economic, social, and political demands."[27] Fundamentally progressives sought to improve and transform other people through government intervention, end class conflict, and correct social and economic disparities brought about by industrialization and income inequality.[28] Most progressives were drawn from the educated middle class, who sought to inculcate their values upon others, but depended upon an emerging number of courageous political elites for leadership, namely Theodore Roosevelt, and in Connecticut, George McLean.

The hallmark of McLean's inaugural address (and his subsequent term as governor) was democratizing the antiquated and unfair system

---

26   "A Defect at the Capitol," *Hartford Daily Courant*, January 10, 1901, 10.

27   Sidney M. Milkis, "Progressivism" Encyclopedia Britannica, 2007, https://www.britannica.com/topic/progressivism.

28   Michael E. McGerr, *A Fierce Discontent: the Rise and Fall of the Progressive Movement in America, 1870–1920* (New York: Free Press, 2003), xv.

of representation in the Connecticut legislature.[29] It was time, McLean stated in his inaugural address, to end the town-based system (which strongly favored Republican interests) by reapportioning representation based on population.[30] Fully one-third of his address dealt with reforming the state legislature, showing his sense of urgency and support for serious change.

The implications of McLean's quest for change were sweeping. Such reform, if implemented, would diminish the control of political machines in the legislature. And since members of the US Senate were elected by state legislatures, McLean's reform efforts had national as well as state implications. A system of representation based on population would empower the growing urban areas of Connecticut, giving immigrants and urban workers a greater say in state government and the election of US Senators.

McLean also spoke out against political corruption and the buying and selling of votes, another progressive concern. In addition to better enforcement of laws against bribery, McLean called for finding "true remedies" that might fundamentally root out the ignorance and selfishness behind political corruption. He challenged teachers in high schools and common schools to help in making "men honest before they become dishonest."

Other progressive elements of his address include advocating for free textbooks in the public schools, a growing practice in other New England states. McLean also urged the legislature to pass new laws enabling women's suffrage in local and municipal elections. While fall-

---

29 *Public Documents of the State of Connecticut,* Vol. I, Hartford: Printed by Order of the General Assembly, "Message of His Excellency George P. McLean, to the Connecticut General Assembly, January 1901," https://babel.hathitrust.org/cgi/pt?id=ucw.ark:/13960/t6c25xs8s&view=1up&seq=13&skin=2021&q1=mclean, accessed May 1, 2020.

30 McLean's final recommendation was one representative for each town, two for those with at least twenty-five thousand people, and one additional representative for each twenty thousand over the latter figure. See "The Governor's Message," *Hartford Daily Courant,* January 10, 1901, 10.

·ing short of calling for suffrage in state and national elections, it was a small step in emancipating women and moving beyond fixed, Gilded-Age roles for the sexes.

In a further nod to progressives, McLean urged the adoption of indeterminate prison sentencing for certain criminal offenses, giving inmates a chance to be released sooner if they made progress under a program of training. McLean singled out the vital importance of the state board of health, and the importance of preventing disease, including expanding the new Sewage and Wastewater Commission in Connecticut, further measures aimed at improving the lives of the state's teeming and struggling urban citizens.

Another characteristic of the Progressive Era was improving the efficiency of government through modern management systems. A leading proponent of these reforms was Frederick Winslow Taylor (1856–1915), a mechanical engineer widely known for his methods to improve organizational efficiency.[31] In his inaugural address, McLean called for the creation of a new government post, a state tax commissioner, who would professionalize property assessments and modernize fiscal policy. This new commissioner would be charged with improving the tax assessment process and rooting out scofflaws who failed to register their taxable properties. McLean thought it odd that a person could be fined for neglecting to obtain a dog license but not concealing taxable property.

McLean then called for a new tax on "moneyed corporations." This proposal spoke to the concerns of many progressives over the increasing wealth and power of large corporations. Tax revenue in Connecticut was fundamentally based on property values, so heavy manufacturers had straightforward assessments based on the value of plant and equipment. But banks, insurance companies, and other services had less "real property," and therefore generally had lower tax

---

31   McGerr, *A Fierce Discontent*, 128–29.

assessments. McLean now urged that the legislature classify corporate stock as taxable, thus increasing the tax burden on "moneyed corporations" and creating a broader tax base for the state. These proposed reforms, McLean believed, would help reform the state's "unequal and unjust" taxation system.

Other government improvements McLean endorsed in his inaugural address included advancements in "scientific agriculture," for growing fruits, vegetables, and sheep herding, and he supported a new technique of growing tobacco under cloth, so-called "shade tobacco." McLean also called for the "intelligent treatment" of fish and game management in the state, and warned against the "extermination of our trout and game birds from our brooks and woodlands."

McLean concluded his address by paying tribute to the working class, pledging to make their lives better. "Our first concern," McLean stated, "should be to educate and elevate the man who works for his daily bread, for upon his industry, economy, intelligence, and honesty depends the future of the Republic."

His inaugural day ended with a gala ball at the Foot Guard Armory Hall in downtown Hartford. Built in 1888 as an armory and drill hall, the square, red-bricked building housed one of the largest auditoriums in Hartford and was used for musical performances, variety shows, and large social gatherings. The hall would be jammed with guests, making it difficult to get from one to the other throughout the evening.[32]

The hall was "tastefully decorated" in white, green, and cerise (a deep reddish pink) buntings. All the roof supports and ceiling posts were entwined with smilax, or vine-like green boughs. Four areas for box seats had been constructed on the north end of the hall, one of which was reserved for the governor's closest staff and friends. Among the special guests at the Governor's Box were his brother John and his wife,

---

32   "Governor's Reception," *Hartford Daily Courant*, January 10, 1901, 9.

as well as thirty-six-year-old Juliette Goodrich, a Simsbury native, who six years later would marry George McLean.

At nine-fifteen in the evening, Governor McLean entered the hall to great applause, followed by an hour-long reception where the new governor shook hands with hundreds of guests. After the reception, the dancing began, featuring waltzes and two-steps. Dancing commenced with the "Coronation March" by Meyerbeer, with the bachelor governor dancing with Mrs. W.C. Skinner, a family friend. Other music included Johann Strauss Jr.'s waltz "Wine, Women and Song," and John Philip Sousa's two-step "Spirit of Liberty." It is not known how much the new governor danced. The celebration lasted until three o'clock in the morning,

Many at McLean's inaugural ball were people he had known for decades, who had helped him slowly climb the political ladder, now sharing in this crowning achievement of his early political career. A cadre of newspaper reporters were there detailing the day's events and preparing adulatory commentary about his inaugural address for publication in the next day's editions. There may have been job seekers at the gala, seeking "just a minute" of his time, and other friends and fellow politicians wanting just one minute more. Maybe he danced with Juliette Goodrich, his future wife, or maybe they just made eye contact across the room.

Also seated in the Governor's box was John McLean, his older brother who provided valued advice and counsel throughout McLean's life. It was John who twenty-five years earlier had been bullied for wearing homespun clothing to Hartford Public High School. Humility is knowing where we come from and who our people are. For the McLean brothers, humility came from milking cows before school by the light of whale oil lanterns each day, hauling heavy buckets of water to the livestock, and bringing in the harvest each summer and fall when city kids weren't worrying about such things. Perhaps the new governor and his brother took a moment to share a smile, a knowing look, maybe a congratulatory handshake. In that handshake was an unspoken acknowledgment that they had both come a long, long way from spreading manure on the rye field using their horse-drawn wagon.

★ CHAPTER FOUR ★

REFORM GOVERNOR

The people of Connecticut today are
dissatisfied with the unequal distribution
of power in their law-making body.
*George P. McLean, in his inaugural address
as governor, January 19, 1901*[1]

Speaking at a dinner on December 4, 1914, for his friend and
Connecticut Governor-elect Marcus Holcomb, George McLean
joked about how Holcomb's life was about to change. McLean
was, in effect, summarizing his two years as Connecticut governor. He
recalled that at first most everyone will be nice to a newly-elected governor. Holcomb could look forward to his ride to the inaugural in a
sleek carriage driven by four beautiful horses. He'll be watched closely
at the inaugural ball, and his dancing will be critiqued in the newspapers. But ultimately the pomp and ceremony will give way to the
reality of governing: "Hail to the Chief" will soon be replaced by "to
Hell with the Chief," McLean quipped.[2]

---

1   "McLean's Witty Sallies," *Hartford Daily Courant*, December 4, 1914, 8.

2   Ibid.

Governor McLean, 1901
(source: Simsbury Historical
Society)

McLean's first year as governor of Connecticut was something of an extended honeymoon. He had good reason to feel that he had reached the summit of his "first mountain," or the achievement of an early life ambition, as sociologist/historian David Brooks describes it in his book *The Second Mountain: The Quest for a Moral Life*.[3] For forty-three years, McLean had been striving ever upward, diligently, single-mindedly, forgoing marriage and children in favor of advancing his political career. Now, he had reached the goal.

The *Hartford Courant's* reaction to his inaugural address was complimentary, calling it courageous, wise, visionary, brilliant, and full of ideas, especially praising his bold plan to address the inequitable system of representation in the General Assembly.[4] They called his compromise solution to improve representation sensibly thought out. And it wasn't just the pro-McLean *Courant* that gave him positive reviews; the Democratic-leaning *New Haven Journal-Courier* praised the newness

---

3 David Brooks, *The Second Mountain: The Quest for a Moral Life* (New York: Random House, 2019).

4 "The Governor's Message," *Hartford Daily Courant,* January 10, 1901, 10.

of his message, especially his proposal to reform the legislature.[5] The *Journal-Courier* also liked McLean's ideas on tax fairness and the creation of a tax commissioner. The *New York Tribune* praised McLean's courage to go against the ideas of traditional Republicans who had opposed reforming the legislature for decades.[6]

But the legislature was not as enthusiastic about McLean's reform proposals. On May 28, 1901, the Connecticut House voted against free textbooks by 97 (no) to 63 (aye). Those who opposed the idea argued that it would cultivate a sense of dependence and reliance on government; "Why not furnish clothes and food as well?" one opponent argued. Distributing and housing the textbooks would be costly and time-consuming, opponents said, and re-using books could spread contagious diseases.[7] While the topic of free textbooks was debated at length, McLean's proposal allowing women to vote in city and local elections was killed in committee: "The House decided that it does not want women to have municipal suffrage," the *Courant* succinctly reported on May 30, 1901.[8]

Twenty-first-century critics of uncaring, "laissez-faire" politicians of the Gilded Age should take note that these two seemingly innocuous reform proposals were voted down by a grass-roots representative assembly made up of farmers, mechanics, lawyers, and shopkeepers—a cross-section, albeit male and white, of Connecticut's eligible voters in 1901. These votes illustrate the political world that McLean inhabited: change would come about slowly and painfully.

Early in his term, Governor McLean attended the inaugural festivities of President William McKinley, recently elected to his second term. He traveled to Washington, DC, on March 1, 1901, as a private citizen,

---

5   "The Governor's Message," *New Haven Journal-Courier*, January 10, 1901, 4.

6   "The New Governor's Recommendations Meet with Approval," *New York Tribune*, January 13, 1901, 14.

7   "Municipal Suffrage for Women Rejected," *Hartford Daily Courant*, May 30, 1901, 7.

8   Ibid.

not wanting to ask the legislature to pay for the trip.[9] McLean began his visit sightseeing at George Washington's home, Mount Vernon, and then attended a dinner in his honor hosted by Gifford Pinchot, a Simsbury native, Yale graduate, and head of the US Division of Forestry, who had been appointed to the post by McKinley in 1898. McLean also visited the US Capitol, and spent time on the floor of the House with members of the Connecticut delegation.[10] On March 4, McLean witnessed McKinley's swearing-in ceremony, and sat at the president's reviewing stand during the inaugural parade. That evening he attended the inaugural ball.

Another important ceremonial duty McLean performed in mid-1901 was an official state visit to Buffalo, New York, for the Pan-American Exhibition, a grand display of technological wonder and wizardry which ran from May through November of 1901 and attracted over eight million visitors, or one in ten of every American. It spotlighted new technologies like the X-ray machine and alternating current and featured the electrical illumination of the entire exhibition grounds each night using power generated twenty-five miles away at Niagara Falls.

McLean was part of a delegation of 600 from Connecticut, which participated in a parade on "Connecticut Day," June 18, 1901.[11] McLean was described as a fine horseman, and gracefully doffed his silk hat to the spectators who lined the parade route. The next day McLean was interviewed by reporters as he relaxed in the lobby of the Iroquois Hotel. The forty-three-year-old McLean, wrote the *Buffalo Evening News*, "doesn't look a day over twenty-five." McLean promoted Connecticut's business climate and talked spiritedly with reporters and

---

9   "Personal," *Morning News* (Wilmington, DE), March 2, 1901, 4.

10   "The Governor's Visit," *Hartford Daily Courant*, March 4, 1901, 1.

11   "Governor McLean, Staff and Distinguished Party Arrived This Morning," *Buffalo Evening News*, June 18, 1901, 15.

members of the Connecticut delegation.[12] McLean had personal magnetism to a high degree, one reporter noted. He spent most of the next
two days sight-seeing at the exhibition and ended his trip with a visit
to nearby Niagara Falls.

Meanwhile, McLean's proposal for tax reform and for the creation of a
tax commissioner passed in the state legislature in May 1901. The commissioner's new powers to investigate and fine tax dodgers was picked
up by the national press, making front-page news across the country,
including references to McLean's authorship of the idea.[13] The legislature also passed the so-called tax on moneyed corporations.[14] McLean's
old friend and traveling companion Andrew F. Gates, a Yale-educated
lawyer, was named to the newly-created position of tax commissioner.
During Gates's tenure in the job, the value of assessed taxable property
went from $650 million in 1901 to $720 million in 1905.[15]

After six months as governor, the *Hartford Courant* congratulated
McLean for winning the confidence of those who had doubted him,
and for strengthening the faith of those who already knew and trusted
him. McLean had easily and naturally stepped into the role of governor
and had a winning quality for saying just the right thing. They also
praised the quality of his appointments, which had all won the support
of the legislature. McLean was quiet and unobtrusive, but unmovable
on issues of principle, the *Courant* wrote. His efforts to reform the legislature were viewed "as brave, wise, and sincere." [16]

In early September 1901, President William McKinley was invited
to attend "President's Day" at the Pan-Am Exhibition in Buffalo. The

---

12   Ibid.

13   "Remedy for Tax-Dodging," *Wichita Beacon,* April 19, 1901, 4.

14   "The Work of the Session," *Hartford Courant*, June 15, 1901, 10.

15   State of Connecticut, Report of the Comptroller to the Governor, analysis of "Grand
List" calculations from 1901 to 1905. The Grand List is the aggregate valuation of taxable
property in the state, https://archives.lib.uconn.edu/islandora/search/catch_all_fields_
mt%3A%28comptroller%29, accessed May 2, 2020.

16   "The Work of the Session," *Hartford Daily Courant*, June 15, 1901, 10.

fifty-eight-year-old president was six months into his second term, having won reelection by the highest margin ever at that time. A crowd of about 50,000 turned out to hear McKinley speak at a large outdoor venue called the Esplanade. Tragically, this was McKinley's last speech. Stalking him in the crowd was an obscure anarchist named Leon Czolgosz, an unemployed steelworker who regarded McKinley as the head of a corrupt government. In 1895, Leon Czolgosz first joined a moderate socialist society, and later a more radical group known as the Sila Club, where he became devoted to anarchism and revolution.

At the dawn of the new century, the ideas of Karl Marx (1818–1883) had created deep divisions around the world over income equality and the nature of private property, conflicts rising out of low pay, long hours, and insufferable working conditions for many people. A spirit of anarchism was evident throughout Europe, which witnessed the assassinations of the president of France in 1894, a Spanish statesman in 1897, the empress of Austria in 1898, and the king of Italy in 1900. Labor strikes and political unrest had taken place in the United States during this time, along with the formation of new political parties and groups with varying degrees of radicalism.

It was the third time a US president had been gunned down in just thirty-six years. Two of the killings were politically motivated, and the third killing, of James A. Garfield, had a political dimension (patronage), though the killer (Charles J. Guiteau) was later judged to be insane. These deadly and shocking tragedies seemed to lend credence to the *fin de siècle* anxieties and fears many people felt at the start of the new century.

The day after McKinley died, McLean published a letter in the *Hartford Courant* expressing his sorrow and indignation. McLean wrote that it was time to step up protection for presidents. He then gave further form to his distress by suggesting that a remote island be secured to imprison lawless anarchists like McKinley's assassin.[17] McKinley's murder gave rise to an insidious and growing fear of political anarchism in the nation. The new president, Theodore Roosevelt, wrote to a confidant after the assassination that anarchists should be actively opposed, holding all anarchists and sympathizers responsible for McKinley's murder.[18]

McLean and other moderate reformers saw the very existence of the country hanging in the balance. This was a part of what McLean viewed as the "rot at the core" of society that threatened the American experiment. As much as McLean embraced modernism, he wanted to preserve the best the country had inherited from its puritan forebears, character traits like self-reliance, frugality, honesty, industry, and economy. McLean's centrism is expressed in Yeats's poem "The Second Coming," written in 1919: "Things fall apart; the center cannot hold; mere anarchy is loosed upon the world." McLean lived in the "complicated center," avoiding extremes, and embracing reform and compromise when necessary to make the center hold.[19]

McLean's proposal for reforming the legislature stalled in the summer of 1901. His plan called for one representative for each town, two for those with at least twenty-five thousand, and one additional representative for each twenty thousand over the latter figure. The Connecticut House turned down the measure by a vote of 145 to 61 in June 1901.[20] McLean had no choice but to seek reform by calling for a Constitutional Convention, an option he'd hoped to avoid. In Octo-

---

17 Charles H. Grosvenor, *William McKinley, His Life and Work* (Washington, DC: The Continental Assembly, 1901), 149.

18 Letter from Theodore Roosevelt to Henry Cabot Lodge, Theodore Roosevelt Papers, Library of Congress Manuscript Division, Theodore Roosevelt Digital Library, Dickinson State University. https://www.theodorerooseveltcenter.org/Research/Digital-Library/Record?libID=o179666.

19 Poetry Foundation, n.d., "The Second Coming" by William Butler Yeats, https://www.poetryfoundation.org/poems/43290/the-second-coming.

20 Heath, "Politics and Steady Habits," 134.

ber, a special statewide election was held asking the people if they were in favor of holding a constitutional convention to address the issue of representation in the legislature and other constitutional reforms. The voters approved the calling of a convention by a vote of 47,317 to 26,745, suggesting the public approved of reform.[21]

Before the convention opened at the Connecticut State Capitol on January 2, 1902, however, opponents of reform achieved a major if not familiar victory: the General Assembly ruled that each city or town, regardless of its population, would be allotted one representative to the constitutional convention. This form of representation ensured that the small towns would hold sway. The outcome was *a fait accompli* before the convention began.

For almost five months, delegates wrangled over McLean's proposal to reform the legislature. The depth of opposition to reform is illustrated by the two-day filibuster staged by Joseph L. Bartlett, Democratic representative from Simsbury, McLean's hometown. Bartlett began by offering up his own proposal for representation in the General Assembly—two representatives per town, regardless of size. Bartlett said reapportion would only empower large cities, which were nothing but dens of inequity, filled with corrupt lawyers, politicians, and crooked policemen. For two days, the sixty-six-year-old farmer recounted stories about the virtues of rural Connecticut and the vices of its cities. Bartlett held the floor, speaking sometimes to just one or two people. When all attempts failed to end the filibuster, a bogus telegram was sent to him, reporting that his barn was on fire. Bartlett was unmoved. "Let 'er burn!" he retorted, and continued his filibuster.[22]

Advocates of reform made impassioned pleas for change, citing legal, historical, and political arguments, including "taxation without

---

21   Ibid., 136.

22   John E. Ellsworth, *Simsbury; Being a Brief Historical Sketch of Ancient and Modern Simsbury, 1642–1935* (Simsbury, CT: Simsbury Committee for the Tercentenary, 1935), 149.

representation," but their arguments fell on deaf ears. The "town system" was a revered Connecticut tradition, opponents argued. Besides, adding new assemblymen meant increasing payroll costs. Giving more power to the cities would increase the influence of the lobbyists, "the money power," the "foreign-born," and "undesirable immigrants."[23]

Several of the loudest foes were McLean's political rivals, like Donald T. Warner, the man McLean had recently defeated for the 1900 Republican gubernatorial nomination. McLean's mentor Morgan Bulkeley was another leading opponent of reforming the General Assembly: "For 250 years the state had done very well and there was no need to change things now,"[24] Bulkeley stated in a speech.

In fact, the composition of the state legislature in Connecticut mattered a great deal to Bulkeley. He coveted a seat in the US Senate, and any change to its voting membership could thwart that dream. Along with McLean's initiative to tax moneyed corporations, a widening gulf between the two men began to form. After all, Bulkeley had named McLean's law firm in-house counsel in 1892 and supported him for governor. This was certainly not the kind of treatment he expected in return for all he had done to help McLean's career.

McLean was not in Connecticut when the Constitutional Convention began. Instead, he was in Washington, DC, interviewing for a job with the new president, Theodore Roosevelt. Newspapers reported on January 27, 1902, that Roosevelt would appoint McLean as the next secretary of the navy. (Roosevelt instead named William H. Moody as his secretary of the navy, a man he would later appoint to the US Supreme Court.) Perhaps McLean was looking for a new opportunity, or a way out of the mess back home.

Then in February, McLean ally Orsamus Fyler, a delegate from Torrington, took seriously ill and missed the final two months of the con-

---

23   Ibid., 139

24   "Fessenden Banquet," *Hartford Daily Courant*, November 9, 1901, 9

vention. McLean was so worried about his mentor's health that he took
Fyler and several other friends on a trip to Winter Haven, Florida, beginning on February 27, 1902. McLean said that if Fyler couldn't join
them, he would be as "lonesome as a dis-mated turtledove."[25] Together,
they spent a month in the Florida sunshine, relaxing, tarpon fishing,
and hunting, and then onto Havana, Cuba. The two men shared a
similar penchant for overwork and burnout. McLean wrote to Fyler:
"My liver used to get plugged up and I'd be dizzy for weeks so I know
how you feel. The quickest and best cure in the world for such trouble
is a good time and if I were in your place, I would find a little fun and
have my fill of it."[26] McLean helped Fyler walk a mile a day while in
Florida, a tormenting activity ordered by Fyler's doctor. McLean was
impressed by Fyler's indomitable spirit. In time, Fyler recovered his
health to a large degree.

Ironically, McLean's own health was unraveling about the time of
this Florida trip. The first public indication of his ill-health appeared in
the *Hartford Courant* on April 26, 1902, saying McLean had malaria
and needed six weeks of rest.[27] But by early June, with McLean's condition worsening, it was announced that he had suffered a nervous collapse, and would be taking leave of his office for several months.[28] No
doubt the collapse was triggered, in part, by the failure of his reform
efforts. Opposition from members of his own party had been constant
and vicious. On May 15, the Constitutional Convention ended with
a whimper, resulting in a set of watered-down reforms, none of which
changed representation in the General Assembly.[29] Eventually even
these unsatisfactory reforms were voted down by the public. Reform

25 George P. McLean letter to O.R. Fyler, January 12, 1903, Torrington (CT) Historical Society.

26 George P. McLean letter to O.R. Fyler, n.d., Torrington (CT) Historical Society.

27 "Governor McLean Ailing," *Morning Journal Courier* (New Haven, CT), May 8, 1902, 1.

28 "Governor McLean Not a Candidate," *Hartford Daily Courant*, June 9, 1902, 10.

29 Heath, "Politics and Steady Habits," 146.

of the Connecticut General Assembly was dead and would remain so until 1965.[30]

Diseases of the mind and nervous system were viewed in the early twentieth century as "a curse of our time."[31] After Freud's publication of his landmark work *Studies on Hysteria* in 1895, public awareness and concern dramatically increased over nervous conditions like melancholia, neurasthenia, and other nervous abnormalities.[32] There was a growing awareness in American society at the turn of the century that overwork and unrestrained ambition among the professional classes was taking its toll. "There can be little doubt that disorders of the nervous system are spreading with alarming rapidity," wrote the *Washington Post* in 1907. The writer urged people to engage in practices that improve "mental hygiene," like walking in the woods or engaging in times of silence "so we may hear our own souls speak to us."[33]

During the summer of 1902, newspapers tracked McLean's whereabouts—in June, he was vacationing at Poland Spring, Maine; in July, in Boston with sister Hannah and her three children and then on to the Isle of the Shoals, New Hampshire. While resting at the Isle of Shoals on July 16, 1902, with his sister Hannah, McLean's search for peace and solitude was tragically interrupted.

McLean was staying at the Oceanic resort hotel on Star Island, one of the nine rocky, treeless isles that make up the Shoals, six miles off the New Hampshire coast. McLean organized a sailing excursion for his sister and her three young children on one of the whale boats operated by a local fisherman. Shortly after the sailboat departed, McLean noticed a black cloud gathering in the west, and ordered the captain to return to the dock. The captain said there was no danger, but Mc-

---

30   Ibid., 145.

31   "The Curse of Our Time," *The Washington Post*, November 18, 1907, 14.

32   Stephen A. Diamond, "Who Were the Alienists?" *Psychology Today*, January 26, 2018, https://www.psychologytoday.com/us/blog/evil-deeds/201801/who-were-the-alienists.

33   "The Curse of Our Time," *The Washington Post*, November 18, 1907, 14.

Lean insisted. Waiting on the dock was a party of fourteen wait staff from the hotel, all college age. As they excitedly boarded the boat for a sail, McLean once again warned the captain not to take them out, but to no avail. Within minutes a squall struck, and in full view of the onlookers on the pier, the boat capsized. William Roger Greeley, McLean's nephew who witnessed the tragedy, wrote in 1961: "The pretty waitresses reached out to the strong, young headwaiter and pulled him down with them. All were drowned. Uncle George never spoke of the Shoals again."[34]

Another factor that led to McLean's nervous collapse was his grueling schedule as governor, patronage requests, and the constant demands for speaking engagements. Outside of an executive secretary, Connecticut governors had meager staffs, and the demands upon McLean's time were enormous. His daily activity log as governor often included up to fifty official acts, including bill signings, appointments, proclamations, and even approving the admission of new patients to state hospitals and reformatories. His ceremonial duties were also significant, like dedicating monuments and making speeches at local political gatherings.

For example, on April 4, 1902, a few weeks before his "malaria" disclosure to the press, McLean responded to a request from friend and political ally T.S. Grant to make a speech at a banquet in Enfield, Connecticut. McLean said it was suicidal for him to be out every night, and that he had to cut back on his outside speaking engagements. "The feeling that I must be everywhere is very complimentary, but my friends must realize that I am only human, and not a very tough one at that." McLean agreed that he would accept Grant's invitation, but he would not speak. He ended his letter, "I am tired out right now."[35]

---

34   William Roger Greeley, "A Letter To Hugh Payne Greeley From His Brother" (unpublished manuscript, 1961).

35   George P. McLean to T.S. Grant, April 4, 1902, Connecticut Governor records (RG005) Series 4. Correspondence, 1811–1933, Connecticut State Archives, Hartford, CT.

Despite his protestations, a newspaper reported that McLean not only attended the banquet in Enfield but spoke as well.

Requests for patronage jobs also consumed a significant amount of McLean's time and energy—meeting with job seekers and answering correspondence. For instance, McLean had been pressured by the mayor of Bridgeport about filling the position of Examiner of Barbers to an associate. McLean noted that he had eighty-five applicants for the position, and had already awarded other jobs to Bridgeport residents, and decided to give the job to a "Danbury man." [36]

Temperamentally, McLean was something of a loner, which is seemingly at odds with newspaper accounts describing his charm and personal magnetism. While an introverted politician sounds like an oxymoron, there are many such examples—Abraham Lincoln, Woodrow Wilson, Calvin Coolidge, Richard Nixon, Ronald Reagan, Hillary Clinton, and Barack Obama. Introverts who choose this very public career often learn how to will themselves to communicate in an intentional, calculated manner, almost like an actor portraying a character.

The *Waterbury* (Connecticut) *American* discussed McLean's temperament after his breakdown became public knowledge, in a June 19, 1902, profile. They viewed McLean as naturally high-strung, proud, and sensitive. Additionally, the writer stated, McLean possessed an imaginative, almost poetic streak that gave force, life, and vitality to his speeches. "The very qualities that have made him popular have contributed to his physical breakdown," the article concluded. [37]

McLean's chauffeur, Frank Passini, provided a curious anecdote about McLean's temperament in an unpublished interview after McLean's death. The two men were attending a cattle auction in Rhode Island when McLean was in his sixties. As Passini recalled: "I will never

---

36   George P. McLean to Hugh Stirling, June 26, 1901, Connecticut Governor records (RG005) Series 4. Correspondence, 1811–1933, Connecticut State Archives, Hartford, CT.

37   "Governor McLean Comments on His Withdrawal," *Hartford Daily Courant*, June 19, 1902, 10.

forget one time in Providence, there was a thunderstorm and he [Mc-Lean] was so scared that he didn't want to be alone, so I had to sit with him until the thunderstorm was over."[38]

When McLean's term as governor expired on December 31, 1902, he was just forty-five years old. There was no clear path for his future, but he was still a respected public figure in his state. Consider, for example, this incident at the rival Connecticut State Democratic Convention on September 25, 1902,[39] when they met to choose their candidate to succeed McLean. In his keynote address, the chairman of the state Democratic Party, John J. Walsh, denounced the Republican party for protecting the monopolies and for its corrupt tariff policy. He further cited their undeniable avarice that had led them to drive even their own governor, George P. McLean, out of office. The mention of McLean's name caused a cheer to erupt among these Democrats. As the *New York Tribune* wrote, "[L]ong applause followed the chairman's reference to him and then a delegate jumped up to call for '*three cheers for George P. McLean!*'" This was the first time in Connecticut political history, the *Tribune* writer concluded, that a Republican had ever been hailed at a Democratic state convention.[40] This spontaneous outburst by a member of the Democratic Party was a portent of things to come.

---

38   Frank Passini, "Interview with Frank Passini about Senator McLean" (unpublished manuscript at McLean Care Archives), 8.

39   "Cheers for Republican Governor," *New York Tribune*, September 26, 1902, 3.

40   Ibid.

★ CHAPTER FIVE ★

A TIME TO HEAL

*My breakdown in 1902 took six of the best
years out of my life and left scars that compelled
me to leave many things undone.*
George P. McLean, 1928[1]

On June 9, 1902, the *Hartford Courant* announced that Governor McLean would not run for a second term. He could surely be reelected, the *Courant* wrote, but McLean had decided not to run upon the orders of his doctor.[2] The news was accompanied by the assurance that the governor's ailment is "not organic" but temporary, and that, with rest, he was expected to fully recover.[3] The *Courant* reprinted the empathetic reactions of seven regional newspapers to McLean's decision not to run. For example, *The New York Evening Post* wrote of their surprise over McLean's transformation from a machine politician into a governor with force of character devoted to reform. "Probably his earnest championship of that reform has had much to do with the impairment of his nervous energy." The *Post* also noted that McLean's efforts to reform the unfair system of represen-

---

1   "Senator McLean's Retirement," *Hartford Daily Courant*, April 25, 1928, 8.
2   "Governor McLean Not a Candidate for Governor," *Hartford Daily Courant*, June 9, 1902, 10.
3   Ibid.

tation in the legislature had led to a painful break with many friends and others in his own party. "He is paying a double penalty for political independence."[4]

Sixty-six-year-old Abiram Chamberlain, state comptroller in McLean's administration, succeeded McLean as governor of Connecticut. Chamberlain was described as "upright, diligent, and competent," a former banker and civil engineer who had McLean's unqualified confidence and warm personal liking.[5] McLean's last duties as governor were to accompany Governor-elect Chamberlain to his swearing-in ceremony at the state Capitol.

One newspaper reported that McLean wore a contented smile as he accompanied Chamberlain in a carriage drawn by four gray horses from the governor's residence at the Allyn House to the Capitol.[6] McLean did not attend any of the other inaugural festivities. On January 8, 1903, forty-six-year-old George P. McLean returned to Holly House, his Simsbury home, as an ordinary citizen again, freed from the burdens of office, able to start reordering his life. For the remainder of the decade, McLean largely stayed out of the public eye.

A few weeks after he left office, McLean gave an interview to the *Waterbury American*. He had regained some of the twenty-five pounds lost during his illness; his skin was clear, his eyes bright, and "above all the cheerful responsive manner that made him so magnetic a personality and so good a companion have all come back,"[7] wrote the reporter. McLean refused to discuss his political future, saying only that he was planning a long trip to the South, maybe into Mexico, then to southern California, coming home again for the summer. Repeatedly pressed to discuss public matters, McLean described the competing burdens of

---

4   "Governor McLean," *Hartford Daily Courant*, June 11, 1902, 10.

5   "The Governorship," *Hartford Daily Courant*, November 4, 1902, 10.

6   "Inaugural Parade," *The Morning Journal-Courier* (New Haven, CT), January 8, 1903, 9.

7   "How McLean Appears," *Hartford Daily Courant*, January 17, 1903, 10.

office that he was gladly leaving behind: "The governor of Connecticut ought to have a dual personality: one to perform the public duties of the office and the other to attend the dinners, make speeches and open the fairs."[8]

With Connecticut in the grip of a colder-than-normal winter, McLean went on a golfing holiday in North Carolina and Georgia in January of 1903. It is hard to pinpoint when McLean began playing the sport; the first mention of his golfing came at a campaign appearance in October of 1900 when he was running for governor. Several friends, including McLean's pastor, the Reverend Charles P. Croft, good-naturedly roasted him at a campaign event. "Contrary to what people might think," Croft began, "George McLean is not perfect. After all, he is a left-handed golfer."[9]

One of McLean's favorite golfing destinations was the luxurious Bon Air Hotel in Augusta, Georgia, one of four hotels established and owned by the Vanderbilt family in the early twentieth century. Surrounded by palmetto and magnolia trees, the Bon Air opened in 1889, and it was a favorite resort for wealthy northerners seeking respite from the cold. Presidents Taft and Wilson played the course, and so did Ty Cobb, the baseball great who was an Augusta resident. Over time, the Bon Air became more than a golfing mecca; it was a gathering place for leaders in academia, finance, manufacturing, sports, politics, and motion pictures.

In the summer, McLean often golfed at a resort in Poland Spring, Maine, and in 1905 he joined the Hartford (Connecticut) Country Club, and the honor of his becoming a member was announced in the newspaper, which noted that McLean was a very good player.[10] McLean himself provided a slightly different view of his golf game during

---

8   "He Is Getting Fat and Saying Nothing," *Hartford Daily Courant*, January 17, 1903, 10.

9   "McLean's Neighbors Show Esteem for Him," *Hartford Daily Courant,* September 10, 1900, 5.

10   "Ex-Governor McLean Joins Hartford Golf Club," *Hartford Daily Courant,* April 24, 1905, 2.

an after-dinner speech to the Hartford Business Men's Association annual banquet in March of 1910. McLean said he had just returned from playing golf for three weeks in the South, where he "played better in his dreams than on the links." In fact, when boarding the train for his trip home, a golfing companion bade him goodbye, saying, "Old man, I hope you'll take good care of yourself on your way home, for if anything should happen to you, I'd be the worst golf player on earth."[11]

Golfing was in its infancy in the United States in the early 1900s, reserved for the wealthy, and confined to private clubs around New York City and other large urban areas. With the spread of rail service, wealthy New Englanders increasingly went south during the harsh winters to resort cities in Florida and Georgia. McLean golfed frequently at the village resort in Pinehurst, North Carolina. One regular golfing companion was Charles C. Cook, a wealthy Hartford building contractor and state senator, known for building the Connecticut State Library and Supreme Court Building, a single structure across from the Capitol.

Pinehurst was one of the first golf resorts in the United States, but its association with the game happened almost accidentally. In 1895, a wealthy soda fountain magnate from Massachusetts, James Walker Tufts, purchased six-thousand acres of sandy, clear-cut, unimposing land in Pinehurst. He decided to build a health resort for people suffering from consumption (tuberculosis). Tufts hired landscape architect Frederick Law Olmsted, designer of New York's Central Park, to plan the resort village. In time, to attract more visitors, Tufts added recreational facilities like croquet and tennis courts, riding stables, and skeet shooting.[12] When he saw that many guests were hitting golf balls into an adjacent cow pasture, Tufts thought they were disturbing the milk

---

11   "Business Men Dine and Sing," *Hartford Daily Courant*, March 9, 1910, 13.

12   Audrey Moriarty, *Pinehurst: Golf, History, and the Good Life* (Ann Arbor, MI: Sports Media Group, 2005), 5–114.

production of his dairy herd. To fix that, he decided to build a golf course far away from the cows. Tufts asked Donald Ross, a recent Scottish immigrant, to design the first of four courses at the resort. Ross is considered one of the major forces in the history of American golf course architecture, and Pinehurst was his signature creation.

When McLean and Cook reached Pinehurst by train in February of 1903, a nearby newspaper soon learned of his arrival, and sent a reporter to interview McLean in the dining room of the Hotel Carolina. McLean invited the reporter to lunch with them. "I want to show you that Yankees can be as hospitable as Southern people." McLean inquired about the family of a former Connecticut governor, Joseph Hawley, who was born in North Carolina, and he asked about other people and happenings in the area. McLean was said to be particularly interested in learning about "your native Negro. I love to hear them talk," McLean said. After lunch McLean retired to put on his "golf togs," and he invited the reporter to join them while they played their round.[13]

Near the first tee was a "paddock" where about 100 caddies waited to be assigned to the players that day. Almost all of them were Black, and they ranged in age from five to seventy. McLean was "intensely interested in them," and he asked the caddie master what they did for a living in the off-season. Some worked in the peach orchards or had trades, the head caddie informed him, and a few were ministers. He pointed out one such man nearing seventy with long white hair and chin whiskers. McLean asked to be paired with the old preacher.

On the first hole, the left-handed McLean "managed to stay on the course." On the second hole—a 400-yard par four—McLean's tee shot sliced sharply left into the Carolina pines. In frustration, McLean was "about to make a few remarks appropriate to the occasion" when he turned toward his caddie-preacher and asked:

---

13   "When Governor McLean Took a Vacation in the South," *Hartford Daily Courant*, January 20, 1933, 3.

"Does the discordant language you sometimes hear on the golf course bother you?"

"I caddie for some mighty powerful cussers," the caddie replied.

McLean asked," Do you ever attempt to lead these offenders to a better or purer way?"

"No," the caddie replied, "I always follow the verse in Scripture that says 'no man can serve two masters.' When I caddie, I caddie. When I preach, I preach."

McLean studied the caddie for a moment, and then asked, "Is a golfer ever justified in using words the newspapers represent as dashes when tension and a man's patience reaches its limit?"

The caddie nodded in agreement and said, "Actually after you swatted your last shot into the woods, I said to myself, 'I'll be damned.'"

That response delighted McLean. "You are to caddie for me every day I'm here, Sundays included. You needn't talk to yourself either. Speak up, express your opinions openly, freely, emphatically, with the best profanity you've got—do you understand?"

Yes, the caddie understood and agreed.

At the end of the round, McLean said that he'd enjoyed every moment of the afternoon, tipped the caddie with a bill, praised him for his diplomacy, and told him he would make a great politician.[14]

While McLean spent winters in the South and summers in Simsbury, in the late fall, he habitually went duck hunting at the Princess Anne Club, on Currituck Inlet, North Carolina, which is part of the Outer Banks. Waterfowl hunting was a major form of recreation along the mid-Atlantic Seaboard. The hunting clubs along the seashore attracted the rich and famous—people like President Benjamin Harrison and President Grover Cleveland, Theodore Roosevelt, financier J.P. Morgan, and industrialist George Pullman. Hundreds of hunting clubs operated along the Eastern Seaboard, providing income for local residents

---

14   Ibid.

who offered a full-range of services and accommodations for visiting hunters, including lodging, meals, and guided trips.

For many clients, the sense of "roughing-it" was a big part of the experience. Many came to the clubs to escape urban pressures, getting up before dawn to feel the cold, biting, late fall air, then watching and listening for the ducks to come in through a beautiful sunrise. They enjoyed the companionship of their hunting dogs and camaraderie with their fellow hunters.[15] McLean treasured his hunting trips and the company of close friends, sometimes camping out in the open and sleeping in lean-tos, cooking their meals over an open fire.[16]

Sadly, in time, over-hunting decimated the once abundant supply of wildfowl; sports hunting added to the already substantial bird harvest that resulted from subsistence hunting. One of the early leaders of the hunting conservation movement was President Grover Cleveland, who deplored the practice of killing large numbers of ducks. He wrote several well-publicized articles about hunting, warning that future generations might be deprived of the sport if overhunting went unchecked.[17]

McLean too had long been attuned to the importance of game conservation. In 1888, he helped establish and lead the Connecticut Association of Farmers and Sportsmen for Protection of Game and Fish, which was aimed at publicizing and enforcing game laws that defined the hunting season and placed limits on what could be hunted and how much could be taken.[18] McLean's interest in hunting and fishing played a part in his sensitivity to the need for environmental conservation. As he aged, he would choose conservation over hunting.

---

15 Ibid.

16 William K. Hutchinson, International News Service Staff, "Hobbies of the Great and Near Great: George P. McLean," appearing in *The Herald-Press* (Saint Joseph, MI), August 12, 1925, 4.

17 US Department of the Interior, Parks Service, Ralph E. Eshelman, "Historic Context Study of Waterfowl Hunting Camps and Related Properties Maryland and Virginia," July 21, 2004, 44, http://npshistory.com/publications/asis/hunting-camps-hcs.pdf.

18 "The Protection of Game," *Hartford Daily Courant*, September 8, 1888, 4.

While golfing and hunting were paths to the outside world and important parts of his emotional and physical recovery, McLean also found rest and renewal in the natural beauty surrounding his home, farm, and woodlands—what came to be known as his "estate" in Simsbury. His initial plan upon leaving office was to travel for a full year, but he took weeks and then months off the proposed trip because of the familiar comforts of home.[19] In January of 1903, McLean purchased seventy acres adjoining Holly House, and over the next five years, he acquired another 600 acres. By 1908, he owned 1,600 acres.[20] When he died in 1932, McLean had amassed over 3,000 acres (4.7 square miles), and he made provisions in his will to acquire still more.[21]

"He was a great outdoors person," said great-nephew Roland Greeley in 1996. "We'd love to go down and visit him and walk along the brook."[22] Another relative was "impressed with [McLean's] feelings for nature and living things" and how he enjoyed having visitors, leading tours of the land adjoining his Simsbury home.[23] McLean friend and former US Senator Frederic C. Walcott said that the outdoors had healing virtues for the man.[24]

In 1905, working with the State Fish and Game Commission in nearby Tariffville, he helped create a six-acre holding pen for breeding deer that were released upon maturity to help repopulate the thinning herds in the state.[25] Also around this time, McLean began exper-

---

19   "How McLean Appears," *Hartford Daily Courant*, January 17, 1903, 10.

20   Grant Ellsworth, *The Senator from Simsbury* (West Hartford, CT: Fenwick Productions, 2001), 110–11.

21   Van Alden Ferguson, "George P. McLean Made a Difference, Then and Now," *Hartford Daily Courant*, June 16, 1996, 109.

22   "George McLean Made a Difference, Then and Now," *Hartford Daily Courant*, June 16, 1996, H2.

23   Van Alden Ferguson, "George P. McLean Made a Difference, Then and Now," *Hartford Courant*, June 16, 1996, 109.

24   "Walcott Eulogizes Ex-Senator McLean," *Boston Globe*, June 8, 1932, 4.

25   "Efforts at Propagation Bear Fruit in Connecticut," *Lyon County News and The Emporia* (KS) *Times*, March 17, 1905, 2.

imenting with raising game birds at his estate in Simsbury, including ruffed grouse, quail, bobwhites, and partridges. It was through his experiments in game management that McLean became acquainted with Herbert K. Job, who went on to become the state ornithologist for Connecticut and served on the faculty at the Connecticut Agricultural College from 1908 to 1914. Job's book *Propagation of Wild Birds* (1915) describes his interactions with McLean, which included using bantam hens to incubate quail eggs because wild birds often lose the urge to incubate while in captivity.[26]

During these years after leaving the governor's office, McLean also liked dabbling with modern technology. He bought his first automobile in 1905, and took meandering drives on the primitive Connecticut roads. On August 23, 1905, McLean was spotted driving though Winsted, Connecticut.[27] (Winsted is about sixteen miles west of Simsbury.) McLean owned a 1905 Stevens-Duryea Touring Car, an automobile with twenty horsepower, which retailed for $2,500 (about $73,000 in 2020 dollars). In later years, McLean owned a 1915 Dodge Touring Car and a Rolls-Royce, driven by his chauffeur, Frank Passini, who worked for McLean frm 1910 to 1932. In 1927, McLean told a reporter that he was going to buy a "radio set" for his home as he had been in the habit of rushing out to his garage to listen to prize fights on his car radio.[28]

Then came his honorary degree from Yale in 1904. The tradition of awarding honorary degrees dates to the Middle Ages when universities like Oxford and Cambridge bestowed special academic honors to visiting members of the royal family. In America, Harvard University is believed to have awarded the first honorary degree in 1692 to its incoming president, Increase Mather, an influential puritan minister.

---

26   Herbert K. Job, *Propagation of Wild Birds* (Garden City, NY: Doubleday, 1915), 52.

27   "Winsted," *Hartford Daily Courant*, August 23, 1905, 13.

28   "Farmer McLean," *Watertown News* (Watertown, CT), June 10, 1927, 1.

Yale University has granted honorary degrees since its inception in 1702 to "recognize outstanding achievement," selecting recipients who "have been models of excellence and service to our students, to our graduates, to our community, and to the world." McLean was awarded an honorary master of arts degree from Yale, and invited to address a group of graduates at a dinner following the ceremony. It must have been a welcome development in McLean's life, an encouraging step in his recovery from his nervous breakdown in 1902.

Four to five honorary master's degrees were awarded each year by Yale. Previous recipients of Yale's honorary MA included Benjamin Franklin, Eli Whitney, Gifford Pinchot, and later, Jane Addams, and Orville Wright. McLean accepted his degree at the commencement exercises, and then delivered a short speech to an alumni dinner. Over one thousand students and alumni gathered at University Hall to dine on cold bouillon, lamb chops, fried potatoes, lobster salad, ham and turkey sandwiches, strawberries, assorted cakes, cheeses, and coffee.

Two other speakers at the dinner were Secretary of War William Howard Taft and another honorary degree recipient, Cayetano Arellano, the first chief justice of the Supreme Court of the Philippines under the American Civil Government.[29] Speaking in Spanish, Arellano paid tribute to the United States for its work in the Philippines, especially praising Taft's role as its civil governor from 1901 to early 1904.

McLean opened his speech at the alumni dinner by suggesting that teachers are underappreciated. "Mankind pays best, first, those who destroy—the warrior and the military hero; second, those who cheat them, the preacher and the quack; third, those who entertain them, the dancer, the singer, the actor, and the novel writer; last and least of all, those who tell them the truth, the teachers."[30]

---

29   "Nearly 1,000 Graduates at Yale Dinner," *Bangor Daily News*, June 30, 1904, 2.

30   "Gov. McLean's Speech at Yale Dinner After Being Made an M.A.," *Hartford Daily Courant*, June 30, 1904, 10.

McLean (in top hat) at Yale Bicentennial Parade 1901, Theodore Roosevelt, front row (source: Yale University Library)

McLean then spoke of the duty of each citizen to first learn "self-government," or controlling one's passions and emotions so that one can be guided by reason. This idea of self-management comes from the ancient philosophers and was later echoed by the founding fathers. A civil society depends upon leaders who possess the qualities of self-restraint, goodwill, and moderation, McLean said. Such virtues are fundamental to public-spiritedness and selflessness. Only by curbing one's passions and moderating one's opinions can a people achieve an orderly society.

Later in his speech, McLean warned that the conceit of the privileged has had the effect of turning the minds of those less fortunate toward political radicalism. The man who does hard manual work "is just as much a man as I am," and should be treated with respect, McLean observed. He urged his audience not to flaunt their privileged backgrounds, explaining that their benefits came wholly through the "accident of birth." McLean spoke of the fairness of the "old Maine faculty tax," which was based on an individual's relative skills, abilities, and natural endowments. McLean closed his speech saying that while he was proud to have received this honorary degree, "the man who looks through the grime and dust of hard manual labor…and so gives his life to the doing of something useful is quite as much of a Master as I am."[31]

McLean's restorative routine of duck hunting in the fall, golfing in the winter, and summers in Simsbury, was interrupted by the deaths of his mother, his aunt Sarah Abernethy, and his sister Hannah during 1905–06. These three losses significantly altered McLean's perspective on life, leading him to become rooted in a different reality, and seek new sources of support to move forward. His mother's death in 1906 was an immense loss, since they had lived under the same roof for almost all of McLean's life.

A few days after she died, McLean wrote his close friend O.R. Fyler, summing up his feelings about her death and his own mortality. He told Fyler that he had been at her bedside when she died and was grateful that it happened without pain or struggle. He noted that, at the end, she had called upon the Lord to take her. McLean admired her "absolute faith and belief in an overruling Providence." The scene affected him deeply, calling to mind his own religious convictions. "Doubt and question as we will…we know that neither nations nor men can achieve much without faith." McLean closed the letter, noting that the shadows were lengthening in his own life, quoting Mark 9:23, "Lord I believe, help my unbelief."[32] A month after she died, in December 1906, McLean left Holly House and its association with all his losses for an extended time in the South.

McLean spent the winter of 1906–1907 golfing in Pinehurst with his

---

31 Ibid.

32 George P. McLean letter to O.R. Fyler, November 1, 1906, Torrington (CT) Historical Society.

friends, Charles C. Cook and Dr. Leander P. Jones, his physician from Greenwich, Connecticut. McLean's golf partners were usually professional men, lawyers, doctors, engineers, businessmen, and politicians. Most had families with young children, and it seemed as if an invitation from McLean, a bachelor, provided the excuse they needed to get away from their family responsibilities. After golfing in February and March, McLean spent a week socializing and networking in Washington, DC, till he returned to Simsbury on March 25, 1907.

Maybe these months away had cleared his mind, and helped him manage his grief and come to terms with his other personal and professional challenges. It had been more than five years since he left the governor's office. In any event, two weeks after he returned to Simsbury, on April 10, 1907, George McLean, age forty-nine, married his longtime Simsbury girlfriend, Juliette Goodrich, seven years his junior. The event was a surprise to the public and even some of his extended family, who claimed in later interviews that it was a "spur of the moment" decision.

In an interview in 1971, his niece said that the pair just gathered up a few personal belongings and went to the home of McLean's brother, John McLean, a minister. He performed the wedding ceremony in his living room. Witnesses were summoned and since McLean had no ring, he borrowed one from a guest.[33] Mr. and Mrs. McLean immediately went on a bridal trip to Nova Scotia, the first of many journeys the two took together; travel was one of several of their shared interests.

McLean had known Juliette Goodrich for many years prior to their marriage. There is evidence that he may have met his future wife as early as 1882, the year that McLean began serving in the Connecticut General Assembly, when he was twenty-five and she was eighteen. Juliette's father, Lucius C. Goodrich, also from Simsbury, was a member

---

33   Grant Ellsworth, *The Senator from Simsbury* (West Hartford, CT: Fenwick Productions, 2001), 50.

Juliette (Goodrich) McLean about the time of her marriage to George McLean, 1907 (source: Simsbury Historical Society.)

of the General Assembly with McLean that year, and the two worked together on several legislative committees. McLean and Juliette's father continued their close association at Republican Party functions up until Lucius Goodrich's death in 1893. He owned a substantial farm in Simsbury, only four miles from the McLean farm. A Civil War captain, he was deeply devoted to the Republican Party and active in veterans' groups and veterans' reunions after the war.

Since Juliette Goodrich and McLean had lived in the same town of just 2,000 inhabitants, it is likely that they knew each other and were indeed longtime "sweethearts," as press reports stated upon their marriage in 1907. In addition, newspapers recounted that at McLean's inaugural parade in 1901, Juliette Goodrich was seated in the governor's private box. McLean's mother, Mary, kept a detailed diary where she recorded the numerous visits that Juliette made to Holly House over the years. For example, she recorded eleven visits that Juliette made to the McLean home in 1904, many like the entry on February 3rd: "We had a nice call from Miss Goodrich."[34]

Juliette Goodrich's family was wealthy. Her mother, Martha Abigail Ensign, was part of the family that owned Ensign-Bickford Industries, Inc. of Simsbury. Founded in 1836, Ensign-Bickford invented the safety fuse for mining and military explosives. It was the ubiquitous gunpowder-infused cord that replaced other, very dangerous methods like igniting trails of gunpowder, stuffing kerosene-soaked rags into blast holes, and even filling goose quills filled with black powder. Before the safety fuse was invented, explosions often happened prematurely, leading to the death and dismemberment of countless victims.

Why did McLean wait so long to marry? As McLean's niece, Mary McLean Daniells (daughter of his brother, Charlie), wrote in 1972, "Uncle George's mother and Aunt Sarah [Abernethy] felt that God hadn't created a woman good enough to be his wife." Daniells further stated that McLean broke off a romance, as a young man, with a young lady he deeply loved who was not willing to wait for McLean to earn sufficient money. This was a "sad blow."

McLean's niece further speculated that McLean wanted to see all the old people in his life safely through their lives before marrying.[35] An examination of Mary Payne McLean's diaries show that the twenty-room Holly House was indeed a veritable hotel for family and extended family. For example, McLean's aunt Sarah Abernethy and her retinue of four servants often visited for months at a time. When George McLean married Juliette Goodrich on April 10, 1907, six months had passed since his mother died, and his aunt Sarah had predeceased her, so McLean was now alone and free to look for a companion to share his life.

George and Juliette McLean never had children. In his late sixties,

---

34   Mary Payne McLean, "1904 Diary," unpublished, entry for September 27, 1904.

35   Mary McLean Daniells, "Interview with Mary McLean Daniells, 1972," unpublished, McLean Care Archives, Simsbury, CT, 20.

McLean offered to adopt several of his Greeley great-nephews. One of McLean's great-nephews, Dana McLean Greeley, thought this urge to adopt was not so much motivated out of paternal feelings of love, but more like a desire to put a promising boy through law school and have him follow McLean's footsteps into a political career.[36]

Juliette Goodrich liked to entertain, travel, and attend the theater. In her twenties, she acted in a drama, and after marrying McLean, she and Antoinette Eno Wood, a wealthy Simsbury widow, were patronesses for the performance in Simsbury of Shakespearean actor Ben Greet. Juliette, like her husband, loved dogs. The two raised English Setters and Wirehaired Pointing Griffons, and they entered dogs in shows at the Simsbury Fair. Juliette was also a very avid bridge player. As nephew Hugh Payne Greeley wrote, her love of the game would have interfered with child rearing, but he thought, too, that she "had no maternal instincts."[37]

In the winter of 1908, the newlyweds began a three-month winter tour of the Southwest sponsored by the Atchison, Topeka, and Santa Fe Railroad. They spent over a month in the resort city of Redlands, California, about halfway between Palm Springs and Los Angeles. Redlands was known for its long rows of roses planted along the city thoroughfares, its fragrant lemon and orange groves, and its scenic mountain backdrops. The trip also included stops at the Watrous Valley Ranch in New Mexico; the Grand Canyon, where they stayed at the El Tovar Hotel; and Pasadena, where they spent several weeks at the luxurious Raymond Hotel.

A newspaper account said that the McLeans also made a short visit to Catalina Island, California, but McLean was unimpressed by the tuna fishing there. He complained about the $30 dollar boat and guide

---

36 Van Alden Ferguson, "George P. McLean Made a Difference, Then and Now," *Hartford Daily Courant*, June 16, 1996, 130.

37 William Roger Greeley, "A Letter to Hugh Payne Greeley from His Brother" (unpublished manuscript, 1961).

fee [$800 in 2020 dollars] and failed to catch a single fish.[38] While on Catalina Island, McLean gave a newspaper interview where he mentioned that Taft was his choice for President in 1908. With President Theodore Roosevelt declining to run in 1908, Roosevelt had made it known that he wanted his friend and Secretary of War William Howard Taft to succeed him. In later years, McLean would say that he was a "Taft man from the first."[39]

Throughout his life, McLean was very active in efforts to advance mental health policies and practices, serving on various boards and influencing legislation. His involvement with mental health issues likely began in childhood, growing up in a household with his uncle Lloyd, who had a mental illness. During McLean's lifetime, mental health treatments significantly evolved to conform to the Progressive Era vision of an orderly, almost utopian society. The result was a change from an approach rooted in religious benevolence, education, and assimilation in the mid-1800s to embrace segregation and eugenics by the early 1900s.[40] Progressives applied this same notion of segregation to racial problems as well. McGerr argues in his book *A Fierce Discontent* that many progressives, disgusted by lynchings, race riots, and chronic racial unrest, came to believe that segregation practices and laws would ultimately restore order and stabilize race relations.[41]

From 1898–1914, McLean served on the board of directors of a school for children with intellectual and developmental disabilities. Founded in 1858 by Henry M. Knight (1827–1880) of Lakeville, Con-

---

38   "Governor McLean Returns: Spent Fine Winter in California," *Hartford Daily Courant*, April 2, 1908, 4.

39   "The Coming Convention," *Hartford Daily Courant*, May 4, 1908, 8.

40   Lawrence, B. Goodheart "Rethinking Mental Retardation: Education and Eugenics in Connecticut, 1818–1917," *Journal of the History of Medicine and Allied Sciences* 59, no. 1 (2004): 90–111, accessed August 23, 2021, http://www.jstor.org/stable/24623993.

41   Michael McGerr, *A Fierce Discontent: The Rise and Fall of the Progressive Movement in America, 1870–1920* (New York: Free Press, 2003), 186–87.

necticut, the school initially had a decidedly religious bent, aimed at education and assimilation of children with mental health concerns.[42] Starting out as a religious charity, the school eventually received state aid beginning in 1864. Knight came to realize that at least a third of his students would need perpetual custodial care, but the remainder could be expected to successfully assimilate into society to varying degrees.[43]

When Henry M. Knight died in 1880, his son George H. Knight (1855–1914), a Yale-educated medical doctor, carried on as superintendent of the state-funded school until his death in 1914. George Knight and George McLean were about the same age and were very close friends and professional associates. Knight served as surgeon general during McLean's tenure as governor. They frequently traveled, hunted, and fished together. According to historian Lawrence B. Goodheart, Knight was a model progressive along the lines of Theodore Roosevelt: energetic, politically engaged, and supremely confident that he could solve even the most complex problems arising out of the industrial age. It was said that his ebullience bordered on arrogance.[44]

To George Knight and other progressives, education and assimilation were necessary but not sufficient when treating people with mental health concerns.[45] With the US population rising at an alarming rate, Knight feared the onslaught of a dependent class of persons with mental health concerns requiring permanent custodial care. There was an additional concern among progressives that foreign governments were using the United States as an outlet for persons with mental health concerns. Progressive policy makers feared that this rising number of persons needing care would become a financial burden on society. Moreover, there was an underlying concern that such persons threat-

---

42 Goodheart, 97.

43 Goodheart, 104.

44 Goodheart, 106.

45 Gerald N. Grob, *Mental Illness and American Society, 1875–1940* (Princeton: Princeton University Press, 2019), 166–68.

ened the biological well-being of American society. These concerns led progressives to a variety of interventionist measures, namely marriage regulation, immigration restrictions, and involuntary sterilization.[46] These policies are also seen as an outgrowth of social Darwinism. This is a belief embraced by progressives in the now discredited theory that social relations develop according to the principles of natural selection advanced by Charles Darwin.

McLean's friend George H. Knight led the way to implement these interventionist laws in Connecticut. George Knight believed that his father's emphasis on the benevolent institutionalization of persons with mental health concerns was only a stopgap measure with limited results. While Christian charity requires the humane treatment of persons with a mental health condition, Knight believed that the "terrible increase of this class threatened social disorder," and restrictions on marriage and procreation were justified.[47] According to historian Lawrence B. Goodheart, Connecticut's pioneering marital ban (1895) and sterilization law (1909) were, however, virtually ineffective. The rarely used marital ban was struck down by the courts in 1905, and similarly, the sterilization statute was little used.[48]

McLean was active as an advocate of mental health reform for his entire adult life, playing a pioneering role in establishing a lasting professional association of physicians, psychiatrists, researchers, and other mental health practitioners. In July 1908, McLean was named the first president of the Connecticut Mental Hygiene Society.[49] He remained on the board for the next two decades. The chief purposes of the Mental Hygiene Society were to work for the conservation of mental health; to promote the study of mental disorders; to obtain and disseminate

---

46   Grob, 167.

47   Goodheart, 107.

48   Goodheart, 108.

49   "Mental Hygiene Society," *New York Times,* July 26, 1908, 7.

data concerning them; and to help raise the standards of care and treatment for people with mental disorders.[50]

The Connecticut Mental Hygiene Society was founded by a Yale-educated, Wall Street financier named Clifford Whittingham Beers, who published a widely-read book in 1905 called *A Mind That Found Itself,* an autobiographical account of his hospitalization at an institution and the abuses he suffered. With the nation's rapidly growing population and insufficient government funding especially during economic downturns, these state-owned institutions had grown terribly overcrowded and were often poorly staffed and managed. Beers described the deficiencies in care and the cruel and inhumane treatment people with mental health concerns received, detailing horrific abuse at the hands of his caretakers. At one point during his institutionalization, he was placed in a straitjacket for twenty-one consecutive nights.[51]

The Mental Hygiene Society's first aim was to improve the care and treatment of people in mental hospitals.[52] The society published success stories of improved treatments, such as one person who was restored to good health by "happy and useful labor," or other patients who improved through "fresh air instead of solitary confinement."[53] While improvement of the conditions in mental hospitals was an important aim of the society, it was just one part of a comprehensive plan that included research, and establishing new standards of care and professional excellence.[54]

McLean made speeches on behalf of the society, like his 1914 speech titled "The Conservation of Mental Health: A National Problem,"

---

50 "Mental Hygiene Society to Meet Here," *Birmingham News*, March 26, 1916, 17.

51 Clifford Beers, *A Mind That Found Itself* (New York: Longmans, Green and Co., 1905), xv11.

52 Jonathan Toms, "The Mental Hygiene Movement and the Trapdoor in Measurements of Intellect," *Journal of Intellectual Disabilities Research* (March 2010): 16–27, https://www.ncbi.nlm.nih.gov/pmc/articles/PMC4579550/.

53 "Medical Societies Gather to Discuss Betterments," *Baltimore Sun*, May 26, 1914, 6.

54 Grob, *Mental Illness and American Society*, 150.

which he delivered at the Mental Hygiene Society's first national convention.[55] Mentioning that the nation currently spent $32 million on mental health care, McLean called for "achievements in the domain of the mind" on a par with the government's successful efforts to root out yellow fever.[56] He cited new mental institutions to serve Indigenous Americans in Canton, South Dakota, the Ancon Mental Hospital in the Panama Canal Zone, and the new San Lazaro Mental Hospital in Manilla, Philippines. McLean noted with pride that the only territory under the US flag without a mental hospital was Alaska. McLean also praised the federal government's improved work in mental health screening of immigrants at Ellis Island.

The Connecticut Mental Hygiene Society proved to be a forerunner; by 1911, fourteen other state societies had been formed.[57] McLean's significant role in advocating for the progressive treatment of people with mental health concerns is further evidence of his visionary leadership and openness to reform. The Mental Hygiene Society lives on. It is the antecedent of today's Mental Health America (MHA), the nation's leading community-based nonprofit dedicated to addressing the needs of those living with mental illness and promoting the overall mental health of all.[58]

On August 22, 1908, while he was campaigning for his friend George Lilley's campaign for governor, McLean announced that he was re-entering politics and would run for the US Senate. This meant McLean might challenge his former mentor, Morgan Bulkeley, whose term would end in January 1911. McLean's political detractors quickly denounced his candidacy: "[H]is health is unequal to the effort," said

---

55 "Senator McLean's Report," *The Lancet-clinic* 112, n. 9 (August 29, 1914): 250, https://babel. hathitrust.org/cgi/pt?id=mdp.39015079970235&view=1up&seq=34&skin=2021.

56 Ibid.

57 Ibid.

58 About Mental Health America, Mental Health America, Inc., website, https://www. mhanational.org/about.

one unnamed official in a newspaper article. Another critic doubted McLean's sincerity: "[H]e is too comfortable in his Simsbury home to take up the burdens of public life."[59]

The path for McLean to a seat in the US Senate would not be easy. Did he really want to return to politics? Since leaving the governor's office, McLean had drunk deeply from the cup of the "good life" enabled by his immense wealth: golfing and relaxing at warm, sunny winter resorts in Georgia and North Carolina; enjoying placid summers in Simsbury at his ever-enlarging farm and estate; and duck hunting in the cool, crisp, fall air along the Atlantic Seaboard. His life had taken on a comfortable and relaxing routine, free from after-dinner speech-making, free from the unrelenting criticism that came from leading political change and reform. He was well into a comfortable middle age, and he had recently married. He and his wife had plenty to do—they enjoyed traveling together, raising dogs, and managing their expanding estate in Simsbury, as well as entertaining their extended family and close friends. Why risk another bout with nervous prostration when the last few years had taught him that there was more to life than politics?

What motivated McLean to re-enter politics? McLean loved the partisan clash of political life and was intensely ambitious. After all, he was the eager high school student who arrived in homespuns but upon graduating declared that he wanted to either publish a major newspaper or become president of the United States. What fueled him? What enabled him to try again, knowing the difficulties that might lie ahead, remembering how his dreams of reforming the Connecticut General Assembly had ended so badly, in his own depression and exhaustion?

Perhaps his perseverance was fired by this poem by John Greenleaf Whittier that McLean had read in his youth:

---

59   "Governor McLean Wakes 'Em Up," *Hartford Daily Courant*, August 24, 1908, 8.

Don't Quit

Success is failure turned inside out -
The silver tint of the clouds of doubt,
And you never can tell how close you are -
It may be near when it seems afar;
So, stick to the fight when you're hardest hit -
It's when things seem worst that you mustn't quit[60]

McLean was also a deep thinker who viewed public service philosophically, as America's founders did. American democracy does not automatically sustain itself, McLean knew; it depends upon leaders who conform to moral and ethical principles and strive for moral excellence. Furthermore, if he had ever considered giving up public service for a life of leisure, maybe the Sunday sermons of his youth haunted him on such occasions. It is likely McLean heard the following famous scripture verse from the Congregational pulpit: "For what is a man profited, if he shall gain the whole world, and lose his own soul?"[61]

McLean's supporters were pleased to hear he had re-entered public life. The *New Haven Register* made it clear that only a corrupt vote in the state legislature could derail McLean's election to the US Senate in 1911. A direct vote by the people would certainly result in his election, the *Register* concluded.[62] The headline in the *Hartford Courant* on August 24, 1908, read: "Governor McLean Wakes 'Em Up," stating that McLean was too able and too good a man to remain in the background any longer.[63]

---

60   This poem is in the public domain.

61   Matthew 16:26.

62   "A New Haven Opinion," *New Haven Register*, July 30, 1909, 8.

63   "Governor McLean Wakes 'Em Up," *Hartford Daily Courant*, August 24, 1908, 8.

★ CHAPTER SIX ★

SEEKING THE US SENATE

Yale Bulldogs 17, Princeton Tigers 0.
On the Yale sidelines to watch the defeat of the
Princeton football team were many dignitaries and old
Yale football stars, including former Bulldog footballer
Walter Camp, and ex-Governor George P. McLean.
Hartford Courant, November 15, 1909

L ife was on the upswing for McLean in 1909—his nervous breakdown was behind him, his domestic life settled, and his political
future looked promising for the first time in a decade. McLean,
who enjoyed both football and baseball, witnessed Yale's victory on
November 13, 1909, during a national championship season for the
Bulldogs. Yale and Princeton dominated college football until the
1920s, making the Yale-Princeton game one of the most anticipated
contests in the country.

In 1909, McLean and his wife Juliette observed their second wedding
anniversary and were settling in at Holly House. They had five household servants, a gardener, several herdsmen, and a few farmhands. The
domestic staff included four Irish immigrants: waitress Mary Morgan,
cook Hannah Reardon, kitchen maid Helena Fitzgerald, and laundress

Susie Soden. The lady's maid was French, Cecile Simon.[1] The McLeans traveled with their servants, and appear to have had a close relationship with them; a few would be "remembered" in McLean's will.

McLean had a clear goal: run for the US Senate. That would be determined by a vote of the Connecticut General Assembly on January 11, 1911. The seat was currently held by Morgan Bulkeley, who would be seventy-four years old when his term ended in 1911. Bulkeley was expected to retire, giving McLean a clear path to victory. McLean's plan was to campaign for the Senate seat throughout 1909 and 1910, reintroducing himself to his constituents by making speeches for other candidates, as well as making the rounds at other political events. He still had his legal practice at Sperry & McLean in downtown Hartford.

National political trends provided favorable tailwinds for McLean's Senate run. Republican Theodore Roosevelt, president from 1901 to 1908, had been wildly popular among voters, shaping issues, molding public opinion, and adding progressive, reform-minded voters to the Republican Party. (Roosevelt, who was vice president under McKinley, became president when McKinley was assassinated in 1901.) McLean had actively campaigned in 1904 for Roosevelt's election to the presidency in his own right.

When Roosevelt decided not to run for reelection in 1908, a battle for the soul of the Republican Party commenced. William Howard Taft was Roosevelt's hand-picked successor, and McLean backed Taft without hesitation. However, Connecticut's two US senators, Frank Brandegee and Morgan Bulkeley, were strongly anti-Roosevelt, and they both lined up against Taft for the 1908 presidential nomination. McLean was an astute politician, and knew that hitching his star to Taft could help him win a future US Senate seat. Similarly, McLean

---

1   US Census Bureau (1910), US Household Census, Connecticut, Hartford, Simsbury, District 0237, "George P. McLean," retrieved from Ancestry.com on May 1, 2020.

reckoned that current Senators Brandegee and Bulkeley, by opposing Taft, would be weakened if Taft won.

Matters came to a head when Bulkeley warned McLean that if he dared support Taft he [Bulkeley] "would not let him go to the Senate" in 1911.[2] Bulkeley and other "Old Guard" Republicans wanted nothing to do with Taft. It was high time, they thought, to purge the Republican Party of its progressive tendencies, and nominate a more conservative candidate, namely Bulkeley's friend, Joseph Foraker, a bitter enemy of both Taft and Roosevelt. Foraker had been governor of Ohio and a US senator from that state.

McLean ignored Bulkeley's warning; he campaigned vigorously for Taft throughout Connecticut in the fall of 1908. On October 7, 1908, the *Hartford Courant* wrote that McLean's return to the stump is welcome proof of his recovery of health.[3] McLean's campaigning on behalf of Taft, observed the *Courant*, dispelled any notion that he had given up his interest in politics, or that he was too comfortable in his fine Simsbury home to return to public life.[4]

Embittered by McLean's apparent disloyalty in supporting Taft, Morgan Bulkeley stunned the Connecticut political scene when he announced on March 14, 1909, that he would indeed seek reelection in 1911. *The Meriden Journal* wrote, given Bulkeley's age, (seventy-two), there had been a general understanding that Bulkeley did not desire to succeed himself, but given his immense wealth, Bulkeley's chances for reelection should be in his favor.[5]

Bulkeley had a base of loyal supporters, and a history of ruthless campaigning. McLean could have been rightly concerned that members of the state legislature could be influenced to vote for Bulkeley. In

---

2   "The Senatorship Contest: General Review of the Situation," *Hartford Daily Courant*, September 9, 1910, 8.

3   "Some Good News," *Hartford Daily Courant*, October 7, 1908, 12.

4   "Governor McLean Wakes 'Em Up," *Hartford Daily Courant*, August 24, 1908, 8.

5   "Bulkeley Will Run Again," *The Meriden Daily Journal* (Meriden, CT), March 15, 1909, 6.

November 1909, a muckraking journal called *The Voter* published an exposé charging that highly paid lobbyists were bribing both newspaper reporters and state legislators, sometimes $300 apiece, in exchange for their vote for a US Senate seat.[6] Such an amount could be tempting to any number of Connecticut's part-time legislators who earned just $400 a year for their services. Bulkeley used all kinds of tactics to influence the upcoming election. By mid-1910, for example, several key McLean supporters serving as postmasters in Connecticut cities and towns were fired and replaced by Bulkeley loyalists.[7] Bulkeley was pulling strings and calling in favors in a determined effort to hang on to his senate seat.

Morgan Bulkeley had a history of supporting vote-buying. Quizzed about the practice by a newspaper reporter in 1898, Bulkeley insisted that vote-buying "was in the interests of the party," implying that a voter's acceptance of something in exchange for his ballot was not a serious matter. "It is right for a candidate to secure a man's vote by any means you can use if he is without principle or ignorant," Bulkeley stated.[8]

It was alleged by a crusading political reformer in 1905 that the Bulkeley campaign improperly expended over $150,000 in his successful run for the US Senate that year. Testifying before the Connecticut House Judiciary Committee on March 9, 1905, the Reverend Dr. Newman Smyth alleged that an investigation he led revealed that Bulkeley's lieutenants had likely disbursed money at over one-hundred town caucus sites.[9] Smyth said several officials had been offered bribes ranging from $200 to $300 for their vote. Rev. Smyth concluded his

---

6   Edwin McNeill Dahill Jr., "Connecticut's J. Henry Roraback," PhD diss. (Columbia University, 1971), 12.

7   "General Discussion of Political Ethics," *Hartford Daily Courant*, June 27, 1910, 8.

8   Mark Wahlgren, *Party Games: Getting, Keeping, and Using Power in Gilded Age Politics* (Chapel Hill: University of North Carolina Press, 2004), 96.

9   "Says Senatorship Was Sold," *The Sun* (New York), March 9, 1905, 1.

testimony stating that he had talked to "many men in the game…who have themselves seen the goods handled, that this mass of political corruption has become intolerable."[10]

As McLean braced for an intraparty fight to win the Republican nomination for the 1911 Senate seat, he received some devastating news. His political mentor and best friend Orsamus Fyler died on November 22, 1909, at age sixty-nine. It was a significant personal and professional loss for McLean. The two were exceptionally close for over twenty years, linked by ambition and temperament. McLean idolized the decorated Civil War veteran, who very early saw McLean's potential, took him under his wing, and helped launch and guide his political career. In fact, Fyler was McLean's closest friend. When McLean wrote letters to Fyler, he began with the salutation "My dear good friend and Hero."[11]

McLean would not be adrift without a mentor and close advisor for long. "Boss" Fyler had been grooming a successor for the past twenty years, a fellow Litchfield County Republican activist named J. Henry Roraback. In 1912, Roraback rose to chairman of Connecticut's Republican Central Committee, a post he held until his death in 1932.

Born in 1870, Roraback was from North Canaan, Connecticut, a rural, Democratic stronghold in southwest Connecticut–Litchfield County–about forty miles from New York City. The Depression of 1893 weakened the Democrats there; sensing opportunity, young Henry supplanted the aging Republican leaders of North Canaan and showed remarkable organizing skills in the 1894 election. He helped recruit voters down to the precinct level. In a borrowed horse and buggy, Roraback drove marginal Republicans to the polls,

---

10   "Rev. Dr. Smyth's Bill Against Corruption," *The Journal* (Meriden, CT), March 9, 1905, 3.

11   George P. McLean letter to O.R. Fyler, January 12, 1903, Torrington (CT) Historical Society.

helping Litchfield County, traditionally Democratic, elect a Republican governor in 1894.[12]

The two men were remarkably similar in backgrounds. Like McLean, Roraback grew up poor on a small family farm. He was admitted to the bar via apprenticeship. Roraback and McLean had both done legal work for the railroad industry.[13] Roraback made his fortune by envisioning and constructing some of Connecticut's earliest utilities and power plants. In 1903, Roraback invested in a hydroelectric power plant on the Housatonic River. By 1912, after overseeing the growth and success of his hydroelectric scheme, Roraback sold most of his company stock to focus on politics.[14]

Roraback and McLean first met when McLean ran for governor in 1900. Roraback earned the respect of Fyler during that campaign, who had correctly predicted that "J. Henry would surprise 'em" and deliver the vote for McLean in typically Democratic areas of the state. One biographer says that Roraback considered McLean's gubernatorial election one of the hardest but most satisfying political battles of his career.[15]

Knowing his penchant for exhaustion when campaigning, McLean and his wife spent the winter of 1910 in Augusta, Georgia, at the Bon Air Hotel, resting up for the upcoming senate race. When they returned, McLean went into full campaign mode. He knew the US Senate election in the state legislature on January 11, 1911, was a make-or-break opportunity—maybe his last chance to win a seat in the US Senate. Throughout 1910, he wrote and delivered over two dozen speeches to political, civic, veterans, professional, and church groups.

In February 1910, while McLean was golfing in Georgia, Bulkeley

---

12   "Yankee Boss," *Time* 29, no. 22 (May 31, 1937): 22.

13   Edwin McNeill Dahill Jr., "Connecticut's J. Henry Roraback," PhD diss. (Columbia University, 1971), 61–64.

14   Ibid.

15   Ibid.

Morgan Bulkeley, Governor, Senator, Onetime McLean Mentor
(Source: Connecticut Historical Society)

expressed his deep displeasure with McLean by firing him. Since 1896, the firm of Sperry & McLean had served as in-house counsel for Aetna Life Insurance, thanks to company president Morgan Bulkeley. But on February 9, 1910, the big sign that read "Sperry & McLean" on the fifth floor of the Aetna Building came down, replaced with a new sign that read "Lewis Sperry, Attorney-At-Law."[16] When asked to explain, Senator Bulkeley just chuckled, telling the *Hartford Post* reporter to ask McLean why it had happened. The *Post* concluded that the removal of the McLean sign reflected the bitter political warfare between the two men who had once been so close personally and professionally.[17]

McLean delivered a widely publicized campaign speech in January of 1910 at the eighth annual Connecticut McKinley Banquet. McLean spoke to a gathering of over 200 officials gathered at the Wauregan

---

16   "McLean's Name Down, Sperry's Stands Alone at Aetna Life Office," *Hartford Post,* February 10, 1910, 1.

17   Ibid.

House in Norwich, one of finest hotels in New England.[18] The banquet was also viewed as the opening salvo for his 1911 senatorial campaign. McLean, received a standing ovation when he was introduced, and admitted that he felt a little rusty, it having been eight years since he had been in the political ring.[19]

McLean's speech, entitled "Representative Democracy," spoke to the concerns on the minds of many progressives. "Has our representative democracy fulfilled its promise?" he asked his listeners. What is to be done about rising injustice and a lack of social harmony? McLean believed that the wealthy class had to shoulder much the blame for social unrest. He faulted the laissez-faire attitude of the nation's rich elites whose only interest was "to be let alone so they could get more millions." He was equally critical of "intellectuals," who thought their "hands are too clean to meddle with politics." The nation's wealthy class could no longer ignore the social and economic ills of the nation. In the end, McLean argued, whether one is "strict or loose constructionist, free trade or protectionist…we must remember that all we have won in this world has come to us as a result of compromise."[20]

During his run for governor, McLean had been criticized by an opponent as a "club-man, not a churchman." Perhaps to counter that image for his Senate race, McLean made numerous campaign appearances at Connecticut churches. At the dedication of the Simsbury Methodist Church in June 1909, McLean's wit was on display. The new church was made possible largely by the benevolence of prominent Simsbury resident Ralph Hart Ensign (the brother-in-law of McLean's wife, Juliette). When McLean spoke at the dedication ceremony, he

---

18   "McLean Speech: Interesting Gossip About Missing Statesmen," *Hartford Daily Courant*, January 31, 1910, 8.

19   "McLean Speaks at McKinley Dinner," *Hartford Daily Courant*, January 31, 1910, 8.

20   Ibid.

observed to his audience's delight that "the people had asked for a sign, and got an Ensign."[21]

In the months leading up to the January 11, 1911, election, McLean was faced with a perplexing dilemma: how to handle Theodore Roosevelt, who had declared his public support for McLean over Bulkeley.[22] In the end, McLean decided to put Roosevelt at arm's length. While delighted that the colonel was for McLean, his advisers begged Roosevelt to use his influence quietly.[23] For his part, Roosevelt supported McLean over the dreaded Morgan Bulkeley, but privately said he preferred a man more of the "Joe Alsop type."[24] Alsop was a Republican member of the Connecticut General Assembly, who later became chairman of Roosevelt's breakaway Progressive Party.

McLean and Roosevelt knew each other well, linked through political dealings and shared friendships. Theodore Roosevelt frequently visited his sister Anna Roosevelt Cowles in Farmington, Connecticut, and sometimes went from there to hunt and fish with McLean in Simsbury. McLean's chauffeur, Frank Passini, recalls that McLean and Roosevelt often socialized and campaigned together. Passini said in a 1971 interview: "Colonel Roosevelt was an awfully nice man to know. They don't come that way today."[25] McLean once declared that "Roosevelt is the strongest, grandest personality in the world."[26]

Unlike McLean's previous US Senate election losses in 1904 and 1905, the results of the election in 1911 would be clear and without

---

21 "New Church Dedicated," *Hartford Daily Courant*, June 11, 1909, 12.

22 George Harper, ed., "Scar't of Him," *Harper's Weekly* LIV, no. 2819 (December 31, 1910): 4.

23 Ibid.

24 Letter from Theodore Roosevelt to Anna Roosevelt Cowles and William S. Cowles., January 24, 1911, Theodore Roosevelt Collection, MS Am 1834 (719), Harvard College Library. *See also* Theodore Roosevelt Digital Library at Dickinson State University, https://www.theodorerooseveltcenter.org/Research/Digital-Library/Record?libID=o285240.

25 Frank Passini, "Interview with Frank Passini about Senator McLean" (unpublished manuscript at McLean Care Archives), 7.

26 "Republican Rally in New Britain," *Hartford Daily Courant*, October 30, 1908, 14.

suspense. On January 11, 1911, the Republican members of the state legislature met to choose their candidate.[27] In seventy-five minutes, the vote was complete: McLean received 113 votes to Bulkeley's sixty-three. McLean thus secured the Republican nomination for the US Senate.

On January 17, 1911, the Connecticut General Assembly formally met to elect the state's next US Senator, pitting McLean against the Democratic challenger, Homer S. Cummings. Pundits knew this was little more than a formality, given the large Republican majority. McLean received 177 votes; Cummings received 110 votes, on a strict party-line vote. George P. McLean was now Senator-elect for the state of Connecticut. He would begin his term on March 4, 1911.

The voting ended in the late afternoon, and McLean celebrated with legislators and other well-wishers for several hours. After dining at the Hartford Club, his friends spirited him away to the Parsons Theater to watch a vaudeville show performed by the popular Lew Dockstader. The show, which consisted of a potpourri of soft shoe dancing, comedy routines, brisk songs, and sentimental ballads, included one number where Dockstader sailed high above the audience in a reconstructed Wright Flyer while wisecracking his monologue. Singing the song "An Aeroplane Built for Two," the comedian scanned the audience from his plane (which was supported by invisible wires). When he spied Senator-elect McLean, he cracked, "[T]here's McLean in a box. That was more than his opponents could do."[28]

McLean attended the show with Roraback and several other supporters. Mrs. McLean did not attend, confined to the house with a slight indisposition.[29] A group of McLean's supporters gathered at Hartford headquarters at the Allyn House. One of them contacted the theater by telephone and requested McLean's presence. McLean reluctantly left

---

27 "McLean in Place of Bulkeley," *Norwich Bulletin* (Norwich, CT), January 11, 1911, 1.

28 "Dockstader Makes His Annual Visit," *Hartford Daily Courant,* January 11, 1911, 6.

29 Ibid. 10.

the theater, and joined them at the Allyn House, a reminder that he was no longer a private citizen but once again belonged to the voters.[30]

This rather low-key celebration of his Senate win in 1911 stands in marked contrast to the thousands from Simsbury who turned out for a "jollification" when he was elected governor in 1900. What had changed? McLean had lost many close friends and family members—Fyler; his mother, Mary Payne McLean; his sister, Hannah; and his aunt Sarah. Moreover, in the words of sociologist David Brooks in his 2019 book *The Second Mountain,* McLean was now ascending his "second mountain," experiencing a revised ambition and a newer sense of himself, having been re-fashioned by his extended period in the political wilderness from 1902 to 1911. McLean had also learned that his ambitions came with a cost. As L.M. Montgomery wrote, "We pay a price for everything we get or take in this world; and although ambitions are well worth having, they are not to be cheaply won."[31] McLean had paid an awful price to be governor of Connecticut. What would he have to pay for his seat in the US Senate?

---

30 "Many Congratulate Ex-Governor McLean," *Hartford Daily Courant,* January 11, 1911, 10.

31 L.M. Montgomery, *Anne of Green Gables* (New York: Bantam Books, 1976), 400.

PART TWO

WASHINGTON, D.C.

★ CHAPTER SEVEN ★

ENTER LISTENING

Senator McLean said he was listening and not talking at present, that he had declined all requests for interviews, and would continue to do so for a while.
Hartford Courant, May 6, 1911.

O n Wednesday, January 18, 1911, with the temperature hovering around eight degrees, George P. McLean arrived at the Connecticut State Capitol at eleven o'clock in the morning to formally accept his election to the US Senate. Senator-elect McLean was greeted with hearty applause and a few cheers when he rose to make his speech.[1]

A major theme of his acceptance speech was the "prophetic incident" America had seen in the last election—"the increase in the Socialist vote." The vote in 1910 for Socialist candidates in states like California, Illinois, Wisconsin, New York, and Pennsylvania had doubled since the 1908 election.[2] In Connecticut, the 1910 Socialist candidate for governor had received over five percent of the total.[3]

---

1   "A New Chapter," *Hartford Daily Courant,* January 18, 1911, 8.

2   "Watching the Socialists," *The Sun* (New York), January 15, 1911, 15.

3   "A New Chapter," *Hartford Daily Courant,* January 18, 1911, 8.

In Wisconsin, Victor Berger became the first Socialist elected to Congress in 1910.[4]

McLean portrayed himself as a bulwark against ideological extremes, illustrating the core dilemma of the Progressive Era political leader as articulated by McGerr in *A Fierce Discontent*: the need to reconcile societal regulation with individualism.[5] While McLean believed in many Progressive Era reforms and government interventions, he could not abandon his deeply held beliefs in self-reliance and economic liberty.[6] McLean noted that the political pendulum "seems to be swinging to the side of paternalism," or the increased role of government in solving social and economic problems. But McLean still embraced the notion of limited government espoused by the framers of the Constitution. He warned that liberty was in danger of giving way to "the state as wise father, then as a wet nurse," leading to revolution and "round the circle back to liberty again."[7]

Despite this conflict between liberty and regulation, McLean boldly proclaimed: "I am an ardent Progressive." At the same time, he wanted an "emergency brake to always be in order" when pursuing progressive ideals. Clearly, McLean had demonstrated as governor of Connecticut that he believed in progressive reforms. But as he entered this second stage of his political career, the stakes were growing higher. The Progressive Era was reaching its highwater mark. How far would McLean go in backing future progressive reforms?

At the conclusion of his speech, McLean mentioned that he would be cutting back on public speaking, refraining from "those man-and-time-killing" events like dedicating monuments. He also asked for divine guidance to do the work ahead. In his inaugural speech as gover-

---

4   "Eugene Debs and Victor Berger," Wisconsin Historical Society, https://www.wisconsinhistory.org/Records/Image/IM56204.

5   McGerr, *A Fierce Discontent*, 177.

6   "A New Chapter," *Hartford Daily Courant*, January 18, 1911, 8.

7   Ibid.

Senator McLean, c. 1912
(source: author's collection)

nor eleven years before, he had made no such appeals to Providence; instead, McLean concluded his inaugural address in 1900 by invoking his faith in liberty and the Republican Party. Had the suffering of the past ten years tempered him, made him more open and receptive to spiritual guidance and less reliant on himself?

The following day, the *Hartford Courant* reported that Mr. and Mrs. McLean would escape the New England cold, by "chasing the elusive golf ball about the links at the Bon Air Hotel in Georgia."[8] The McLeans treated many of their staff as family, and most went south with them. Their household staff would be an important part of their new life in Washington, DC, too. Some would stay behind in Simsbury, tending the farm and grounds. In March, rested and tanned, the McLeans arrived in Washington along with their bulldog Peggy, and their many household belongings, including McLean's prized Rolls-Royce, all shipped by train.

Soon after they arrived, however, the *Norwich Bulletin* published a story under the headline "It Cost McLean $14,541 To Be Elected

---

8   "Legislative Notes," *Hartford Daily Courant*, January 18, 1911, 8.

Senator."[9] (That's about $390,000 in 2020 dollars.) Election laws in Connecticut required candidates to file campaign expenditures with the secretary of the state. The expenses were attributed to "automobile hire, newspaper advertisements, printing, and traveling." One newspaper, unfriendly to McLean, displayed the story under the headline "Huge Sum for Toga," implying that McLean used money to influence legislators in exchange for votes.[10]

Later in February, another newspaper published a counter story, stating that the expenses were all legitimate, incurred over a three-year period (not in a single year), and the amount was comparable to what other candidates had spent for US Senate races.[11] It is likely that one of McLean's bitter opponents pushed the bribery narrative to taint McLean's victory and tarnish his reputation. No additional allegations, no charges, and no further investigations ever resulted from the *Norwich Bulletin* story. The allegation also does not square with an account of a visit to McLean's Senate office in 1912 by his nephew, William Roger Greeley. He described watching his uncle open a package he'd received in the mail. Inside was a row of cigars with stacks of $20 bills concealed underneath. McLean carefully re-wrapped it and sent it back.[12]

Arriving in Washington, DC, on March 3, 1911, the McLeans established temporary residence at 1619 Rhode Island Avenue at the home of long-time friend Mrs. Charles (Antoinette Eno) Wood, who had residences in both Washington, DC, and Simsbury. A wealthy widow and socialite, she was active in the women's suffrage movement, and

---

9   "It Cost McLean $14,541 To Be Elected Senator," *Norwich Bulletin* (Norwich, CT), February 4, 1911, 1. The Associated Press story was published in more than 15 other papers across the country, partly because it was a substantial sum and partly because of the rising role of investigative journalism of the era. See also "Election Account of $14,541 Filed by United States Senator-Elect Is Attracting Much Attention – Hartford Prosecutor Takes No Action," *Bridgeport Evening Farmer*, February 4, 1911, 1.

10   "Huge Sum for Toga," *News-Press* (St. Joseph, MO), February 3, 1911, 1.

11   "Public Opinion," *Times-Democrat* (New Orleans, LA), February 23, 1911, 8.

12   William Roger Greeley, "A Letter To Hugh Payne Greeley From His Brother" (unpublished manuscript, 1961), 100.

the aunt of Gifford Pinchot, the former Roosevelt aide who lived next door. Pinchot was a leading progressive and the first chief of the United States Forest Service and a lifelong supporter of Theodore Roosevelt. McLean and Pinchot, both Simsbury natives, were good friends, and held common views, especially on environmental conservation.

The McLeans stayed with Mrs. Wood for most of 1911 until they moved to a townhouse at 1722 Massachusetts Avenue in December. This residence again proved to be only temporary. During the especially frigid January of 1912, Mrs. McLean found the townhouse cold and uncomfortable. She said she didn't mind a cold house, but hated forever fussing with the furnaces and valves like a steamfitter.[13] The McLeans eventually found a more permanent and satisfactory home at 1520 New Hampshire Avenue NW, which is today the Jamaican Embassy.

Only a week after arriving in Washington, DC, McLean cut through government red tape to free an Italian immigrant with Connecticut ties who was detained on Ellis Island. John Pitzinni, a nineteen-year resident of East Hampton, Connecticut, had gone back to visit his family in Italy. On his return trip, officials at Ellis Island refused him re-entry unless he could prove that he would not become a dependent. To help Pitzinni, a contractor-friend from East Hampton, Andrew Ferrigno, went to Ellis Island twice to plead for his release, but to no avail. Ferrigno contacted a local government official in East Hampton who knew McLean, who then contacted the US Secretary of Commerce. Pitzinni's release was soon granted and McLean notified Ferrigno via telegram.[14]

McLean was elected to the sixty-second Congress (congressional sessions encompass a two-year period), which met from 1911 to 1913. These were the dismal last two years of President Taft's term, turbulent

---

13 "While Zero Weather Prevailed, Washington was Unpleasant," *Times Union* (Brooklyn), January 23, 1912, 3.

14 "Appealed to McLean; Red Tape Cut Short," *Hartford Daily Courant*, May 14, 1911, 1.

years marked by increasing polarization within the Republican Party. A powerful group of progressive Republicans, led by Senator Robert La Follette of Wisconsin, were making their mark across the country and gaining seats in Congress. They were in no mood for compromise. It was time to enact major structural reforms that would end the corrupting influence of business in politics, and to legislate lasting social and economic changes to benefit workers and the middle class.

Dissatisfaction with the politically inept President Taft ran deep within the Progressive wing of the Republican Party. Things were so bad that not long after McLean arrived in Washington, rumors began to swirl that Republicans Robert La Follette or Theodore Roosevelt might try to unseat Taft at the 1912 Republican presidential nominating convention.[15]

A landmark vote in the Senate important to progressives occurred in the summer of 1911. As early as 1826, resolutions calling for the direct election of senators had been introduced in the House of Representatives, only to die in the Senate. Progressives believed that direct senatorial elections would curb corruption among state legislatures and give a greater voice to the people. From 1870 to 1906, the Senate had investigated ten cases of alleged bribery or corruption, most having clear evidence of wrongdoing, but all those charges were dismissed.[16]

The corruption issue resurfaced on April 30, 1910, when the *Chicago Tribune* published allegations of a bribery scandal involving the newly elected US Senator from Illinois, William Lorimer, a Republican. The *Tribune's* story was a sensational, first-person account of how Lorimer's election the previous year had been rigged. Charles White, an Illinois state senator, confessed to having sold his vote to Lorimer

---

15   "LaFollette or Roosevelt?" *Star Tribune* (Minneapolis), May 10, 1911, 4.

16   Jay S. Bybee, "Ulysses at the Mast: Democracy, Federalism, and the Sirens' Song of the Seventeenth Amendment" (1997), Scholarly Works, 350, https://scholars.law.unlv.edu/facpub/350539.

for $1,000 and a promise of more to come. The story gained national attention, triggering a US Senate investigation that found no clear trail of corruption. However, the national press picked up the investigation and subsequently alleged that Lorimer had been elected to the Senate with the help of at least seven state legislators whose votes had been bought with $100,000.[17] (Eventually, the full Senate voted to oust Lorimer on July 13, 1912.)[18]

In 1910, a constitutional amendment calling for the direct election of senators had passed the House of Representatives, only to languish in a Senate committee. After the Lorimer case, proponents of the amendment like Wisconsin Senator Robert La Follette pushed hard for its passage in the Senate. He succeeded in getting a vote scheduled on June 12, 1911, for the direct election of senators, just three months after McLean had taken his oath of office.

The vote pitted Old Guard Republicans against Progressive (or "Insurgent") Republicans, and it similarly split the Democrats. Influential Senator Henry Cabot Lodge, a Republican from Massachusetts and a friend and ally of McLean, pledged to vote against the amendment. Connecticut's senior senator, Frank Brandegee, was also a "no" vote. In fact, all Republican senators from New England ultimately voted against the direct election of senators—except George McLean, who voted "Yea" in a 64–24 roll call vote in favor of the direct election of US senators. The proposal would be ratified by the states and become the Seventeenth Amendment.

Historian Sidney M. Milkis views the direct election of senators as a fundamental achievement of the Progressive Era, a clear victory in

---

17   Richard Albert, The Progressive Era of Constitutional Amendment, *Revista de Investigações Constitucionais* 2, no. 3 (2015): 35–59, doi:/10.5380/rinc.v2i3.44528.

18   "Lorimer Ousted by Senate," *Evening Sun* (Baltimore), July 13, 1912, 1.

making government more democratic and more responsible to the popular will.[19] Yale constitutional scholar David N. Schleicher writes that the Seventeenth Amendment resulted in significantly lessening the control of political machines and special interests over state legislatures.[20] Pressure for reform had been building in the country, following a widely circulated article published in *Cosmopolitan* magazine in 1906 entitled *"The Treason of the Senate,"* which offered an unflattering account of US senators as pawns of wealthy industrialists and financiers.[21] The perception was that the Senate was a "millionaire's club."

Why did McLean support the direct election of senators? Wasn't he the poster child of the complacent "millionaire senator," having just been elected by a two-to-one margin in the Connecticut State Legislature? In an interview with the *Hartford Courant* on June 16, 1911, McLean explained his vote. He believed that Americans were losing faith in the US Senate, that senators were not being responsive to the best interests of the nation. The government cannot endure if it loses the confidence and trust of the people, McLean said. The people have demonstrated that they can ably fill the offices of governor and the US president. McLean saw no reason why they could not be trusted to elect US senators.[22]

While these are the reasons he expressed for supporting the direct election of senators, one wonders if there may have been other, unspoken reasons. Perhaps he too was tired of catering to political bosses. Maybe he resented those unsubstantiated press accounts in February criticizing the $14,541 he spent on his campaign for the US Senate,

---

19   Sidney Milkis, *Theodore Roosevelt, the Progressive Party, and the Transformation of American Democracy* (Lawrence: University Press of Kansas, 2009), 42.

20   David N. Schleicher, "The Seventeenth Amendment," National Constitution Center, undated, https://constitutioncenter.org/interactive-constitution/interpretation/amendment-xvii/interps/147, accessed January 5, 2020.

21   "Treason in the Senate," *Washington Post*, June 28, 1906, 4.

22   "McLean's Views on Live Issues," *Hartford Daily Courant*, June 16, 1911, 1.

implying he had bribed state legislators for their support. Perhaps his 1905 Senate loss to Frank Brandegee on the thirty-sixth ballot in the Connecticut legislature had made him cynical about the way state legislatures could be manipulated to elect US senators. And one can see a similarity between McLean's support for the direct election of senators and his reform effort as governor to ensure a more equitable system of representation in the Connecticut legislature. Both reflect his faith in the people and direct democracy. McLean was at heart a reformer who wanted to make democracy more accessible to the people and lessen the influence of the upper classes.

About two weeks after the vote on the direct election of senators, the leading progressive in the Senate, Robert La Follette of Wisconsin, praised McLean for his vote: "Senator McLean is supposed to be a conservative, but, perhaps, he may surprise the Senate Tories. There is an awakening in New England."[23]

Committees are a vital part of the effective operation of the Senate. They enable senators to develop in-depth, specialized knowledge on issues and to draft appropriate legislation. Acting like "little legislatures," the committees screen, monitor, and evaluate information and develop options, ultimately recommending courses of action to the Senate.[24] Senators are assigned to committees through a complex formula based on seniority, input from party leaders, and the expressed interests of the senators.

In 1911, the US Senate was responsible for about twice as many committee assignments compared with those today. McLean was given eight committee assignments in the sixty-second Congress:

---

23 "An Awakening," *Meriden Daily Journal* (Meriden, CT), June 28, 1911, 6.

24 "Senate Committees: Why Committees?" US Senate, Secretary of the Senate, https://www.senate.gov/artandhistory/history/common/briefing/Committees.htm, accessed September 4, 2020.

Forest Reservations and the Protection of Game, Chairman
Canadian Relations
Census
Claims
Education and Labor
Manufactures
Philippines
Territories

Committee work came naturally to McLean, given his reflective and studious nature. "I have an ardent liking for the study of political questions," he once said.[25] When McLean retired from the Senate in 1929, one of his colleagues on the Finance Committee said McLean worked tirelessly behind the scenes; he was always intelligently informed and prepared.[26] McLean's chairmanship of the Forest Reservations and the Protection of Game will be the subject of a later chapter. His other committee work, while varied and important, will be highlighted only briefly, beginning with his work on the Territories Committee and the issue of Arizona statehood.

The Senate debate in 1911 surrounding Arizona statehood illustrates the increasing struggle between the conservative and progressive wings of the Republican party. The proposed Arizona Constitution contained several new provisions espousing "direct democracy"—reforms that gave citizens direct influence on the legislative process and machinery of government. Among the most controversial elements of the proposed Arizona constitution were the initiative, referendum, and recall:

The initiative enabled citizens to bypass their state legislature by placing proposed statutes and constitutional amendments on the ballot.

---

25   "Legislators Hear Senator McLean," *Hartford Daily Courant*, January 19, 1911, 6.

26   "Tribute by Congressman Carter Glass, Banking and Currency Committee," *Hartford Daily Courant*, March 4, 1929, 8.

The referendum is a direct vote of the people on whether to approve or repeal a law enacted by the state legislature.

The recall provisions were especially controversial, particularly the idea that judges could be removed by popular vote. Critics believed that subjecting judges to direct popular control was unwise and a threat to the existence of an independent judiciary.[27]

In a newspaper interview about Arizona statehood on June 16, 1911, McLean expressed his concerns about the proposed Arizona Constitution, saying that, taken together, the initiative, recall, and referendum assume that the average man is wiser than the wisest in the community. "They assume that the man without special training can make as good a watch or as safe a bridge as a skilled mechanic." He was most critical of the recall provision, calling it impeachment without trial and should never be applied to judges.[28]

Replying to a constituent in a letter written on August 15, 1911, McLean provided a more candid assessment of his views on Arizona statehood and its Progressive constitution. He called it a folly, and predicted the radical provisions would have disastrous consequences, leading other states to avoid them.[29] He closed his letter with a comment startling to people today: "Burning darkies alive is bad enough. I hope that we shall never live to see our judges impeached by mobs without hearings."[30]

McLean's word choice is terribly unfortunate; "darkie" is an offensive and disparaging term for a Black person. While Stephen Foster's song "My Old Kentucky Home" (1853) uses the word patronizingly

---

27 "History of Initiative & Referendum in Arizona," Ballotpedia, https://ballotpedia.org/History_of_Initiative_%26_Referendum_in_Arizona, accessed December 1, 2020.

28 "Senator McLean Opposed to Initiative, Referendum, and Recall of Judges," *The Bridgeport Times*, June 17, 1911, 2.

29 Letter from George Payne McLean to Albert H. Walker, August 15, 1911, MssCol, Box 68, New York Public Library Manuscripts and Archives Division.

30 Ibid.

and nostalgically, the term had become increasingly offensive and un-acceptable by the early part of the twentieth century. It reveals Mc-Lean's cultural insulation, his lack of contact with Black people, and it's a sad reminder that racism is embedded in almost every institution in America. McLean, born in 1857, breathed the polluted air of the Jim Crow era, when African Americans were relegated to the status of second-class citizens, segregated, and disenfranchised in many parts of the nation.

In his comment about "burning darkies alive," McLean is actual-ly referring to national, front-page news published just the day be-fore he wrote his letter. On August 13, 1911, in Coatesville, Penn-sylvania, forty miles west of Philadelphia, a Black man named Zack Walker was burned alive for killing Edgar Rice, a white security guard at a steel mill. A mob of 400 people battered down the doors of the hospital where Walker was recovering from a self-inflicted gunshot wound to the head. Still manacled to his hospital bed, the mob carried Walker half a mile to a field and burned him alive while a crowd of 2,000 people watched.[31]

No doubt McLean was appalled by this horrific crime, which he clearly condemned in his letter. McLean inartfully couples the trag-ic mob action in Pennsylvania to his fear over "judges impeached by mobs without hearings." In any event, his comment expresses his long-standing anxiety over mob rule, and his commitment to preventing it. And it reminds us again that it's not always fair to judge our predeces-sors by the standards of the present.

McLean's attitude towards African Americans is shown in a far bet-ter light in a 1913 speech he gave at the fiftieth anniversary of the Kensington (Connecticut) Soldiers' Monument. Erected in 1863, the twenty-foot-tall brownstone obelisk stands on the quiet grounds of the Kensington Congregational Church, in the town of Berlin,

---

31 "Pennsylvania Mob Burns Negro Alive," *The Sun* (New York), August 14, 1911, 1.

Connecticut. More than 1,500 people heard his speech, many of whom were elderly Union war veterans.

McLean spoke eloquently and reverently about the redemptive purpose of the war. The Union soldiers died by the thousands "for a stranger." They died "to square the account we had with the Black man." McLean spoke of the fearful price paid to win the war, but "justice cares nothing for cost." McLean concluded his tribute saying that the sacrifices made by so many were necessary. "The boys in blue died to give the Black man liberty and a chance in the world."[32]

By the summer of 1911, Taft's popularity was in free fall due to a series of political blunders and his tepid leadership style. Worse yet, Taft's former friend and sponsor, Theodore Roosevelt, was now considering a political comeback, challenging Taft for the Republican nomination in 1912. Taft needed his friends and allies more than ever. He coveted McLean's continued loyalty. During their first five months in Washington, the McLeans had been guests of President Taft at the White House on three occasions. And on July 26, 1911, McLean was invited by Vice President James Sherman to watch the Washington Senators play baseball against the Detroit Tigers at the new Griffith Stadium in Washington, DC.

James Sherman was a career politician from upstate New York. A genial man, "Sunny Jim" Sherman earlier in his career was a powerful leader in the House of Representatives, a skilled parliamentarian, and well-liked by his Republican colleagues. (He is often confused with the more famous Senator John Sherman, author of the Sherman Antitrust Act.) James Sherman was chosen by party leaders to be Taft's vice president because of his standing as an Old Guard Republican. In addition, as an Easterner, he provided a balance to Taft, who was an Ohioan with more progressive tendencies. As vice president, Sher-

---

32   Matthew Warshauer, *Connecticut in the American Civil War: Slavery, Sacrifice, and Survival* (Middletown, CT: Wesleyan University Press, 2011), 219–20.

man frequently urged Taft to take a conservative approach on key issues, which alienated Progressive Republicans. For example, in 1910,
Sherman had advised Taft to fire Gifford Pinchot, the Simsbury native
and conservationist whom Roosevelt had appointed to the US Forest
Service. Roosevelt was livid after the firing, seeing Sherman's influence
in the decision.[33]

McLean and Sherman sat in the presidential box along the first-base
line at Griffith Stadium on a sunny Wednesday afternoon, the temperature in the low eighties. Along with 6,000 other fans, they watched
Ty Cobb and the first-place Detroit Tigers face off against the last-place
Washington Senators. But the lowly Washington Senators got the better of the Tigers on July 26, winning 12–5. Cobb scratched out just
one hit, a single. A newspaper account the following day reported that
"McLean enjoyed the game greatly. He likes baseball, as well as hunting
and other sports."[34]

On August 26, 1911, Congress adjourned, ending McLean's first
year as a US Senator. He and Juliette immediately returned to Simsbury. They had made the 350-mile train trip home at least three times
earlier that year. On September 5, 1911, at McLean's invitation, President Taft visited Hartford for a campaign appearance, where he met
leading state officials and attended the state fair. McLean attended a
gala dinner in Hartford with the president, and appeared with him at
several rallies where Taft spoke to large crowds. On October 7, McLean
celebrated his fifty-fourth birthday with a luncheon at Holly House
attended by Juliette and ten friends. He stayed in Simsbury until the
Senate reconvened in December, giving him time to relax and reflect
on his first year in the Senate.

How different he must have felt now compared with those exhaust-

---

33   James S. Sherman, 27th Vice President (1909–1912), US Senate, Secretary of the Senate,
      Washington, DC, https://www.senate.gov/about/officers-staff/vice-president/VP_James_
      Sherman.htm, accessed November 12, 2020.

34   "Senator Sees Ball Game," *Hartford Daily Courant*, July 27, 1911, 1.

ing two years as governor of Connecticut. He was now freed from the demands of a chief executive—the daily decisions, the bedeviling patronage requests, the endless speech-making requests, and the grueling schedule, largely dictated by others. McLean's temperament better fit the Senate, aptly described as a place of sober second thought by former Senator George Hoar in 1897. McLean had seemingly found his niche in the world's greatest deliberative body, his workplace for the next seventeen years.

In March 1912, McLean began his second year in the Senate immersed in committee work, particularly as chairman of the Forest Reservations and the Protection of Game, a low-prestige committee he inherited from Connecticut's senior senator, Frank Brandegee, who had little interest in those matters. McLean had also managed to form a good working relationship with firebrand Progressive Senator Robert La Follette on the Census Committee. The two worked together on a bill authorizing a reapportionment of the country for representatives in Congress on the basis of population shown by the last census.[35]

Despite the heavy demands on his time, McLean exercised daily, frequently walking from the Capitol to his home on New Hampshire Avenue. The two-and-a-half-mile trek took him about an hour, and he would pass the twelve-foot bronze statue of Daniel Webster, only minutes from McLean's house.[36] Webster was one of the Senate's greatest orators, often quoted by McLean in his stump speeches. As Hartford Public High School's "class orator," McLean may have memorized Webster's speeches for declamation exercises. The McLeans' house at 1520 New Hampshire Avenue was in a premier residential area, nicknamed "Millionaires' Row." During the Great Depression, many of the social and political elites who owned these homes were forced to sell.

---

35   Census Committee, "*Sheboygan Press*" (Sheboygan, WI), June 29, 1911, 4.

36   "Senator McLean Busy with Committee Work," *Hartford Daily Courant*, March 18, 1912, 1.

The mansions proved to be well-suited for embassies, and the area was renamed "Embassy Row."

As a member of the Education and Labor committee, McLean participated in a series of well-publicized hearings in March 1912 on a bill that would establish an eight-hour workday. McLean asked many questions, seeking to get all the light on the subject possible.[37] He had invited over a dozen Connecticut manufacturers to testify at the hearings, most of whom opposed the idea. While the bill failed to come up for a vote in the Senate that year, McLean searched for a compromise that would allay the concerns of the Connecticut manufacturers who testified against the bill. In a newspaper interview, McLean disclosed his compromise solution, calling instead for weekly or monthly time limitations, allowing manufacturers some latitude and flexibility in scheduling.[38] While McLean's proposal was not adopted, it does reveal how he carefully listened to his constituents and tried to translate their needs into compromise solutions.

On April 14, 1912, the *RMS Titanic* sank off the coast of Newfoundland, resulting in the deaths of 1,500 people. McLean knew at least one of the passengers who perished, Archibald Butt, an aide to President Taft. McLean and Butt were guests of President Taft at numerous White House gatherings. Theodore Roosevelt had appointed Butt to a position in his administration in 1908, and the well-liked military aide stayed on when Taft assumed the presidency. Butt's health began to deteriorate as a result of worry over the growing feud between his two friends, Taft and Roosevelt. Taft had suggested Butt take a trip to Europe to rest, which resulted in his voyage on the *Titanic*.[39]

A week after the sinking, McLean commented on the tragedy,

37　"The Eight Hour Bill," *Norwich Bulletin* (Norwich, CT), March 14, 1912, 1.

38　"Washington News of Connecticut Interest," *Hartford Daily Courant*, March 14, 1912, 1.

39　"Archibald Willingham Butt, Major, United States Army," Arlington National cemetery website, http://www.arlingtoncemetery.net/awbutt.htm, accessed February 2, 2021.

illustrating his pragmatic approach to solving problems. He proposed that there should be sufficient lifeboats to hold every person aboard a vessel. "When a passenger buys a ticket for a transatlantic voyage, he should find attached a coupon giving the number of the lifeboat in case of emergency."[40]

At the beginning of Taft's term as president in 1908, the Republican Party looked invincible, having won the electoral vote 321 to 162, winning almost every state except the solid South. But midway through Taft's term as president, a serious split in the party emerged. Almost from the start of his presidency, Taft showed that he lacked Roosevelt's zeal for progressive reforms and his astute political instincts. As soon as Taft supported the Payne-Aldrich Tariff, which kept unpopular tariffs high, he began to lose the support of Republican progressives and alienate former President Theodore Roosevelt.[41]

Roosevelt signaled that he might challenge Taft and run for the presidency in 1912 when he made a major speech in Osawatomie, Kansas, on September 1, 1910, now referred to as his "New Nationalism" address. It outlined his progressive vision for the future. Roosevelt's main theme was ending the domination of politics by business interests, which he said controlled both Republicans and Democrats. He called for strict limits on political campaign contributions, registration of lobbyists, presidential primaries, and the direct election of senators. He advocated many social and economic reforms of the Progressive Era, like an eight-hour workday, child labor protection, minimum wages for women, a federal income tax, worker's compensation laws, even a proposal for national medical insurance.[42] Members of the Re-

---

40   "Steamer Ticket to Include Lifeboat," *Hartford Daily Courant*, April 23, 1912, 1.

41   Andrew C. Pavord, "The Gamble for Power: Theodore Roosevelt's Decision to Run for the Presidency in 1912," *Presidential Studies Quarterly* 26, no. 3 (1996): 633–47, accessed March 17, 2021, http://www.jstor.org/stable/27551622.

42   John Murphy, "'Back to the Constitution': Theodore Roosevelt, William Howard Taft and Republican Party Division 1910–1912, *Irish Journal of American Studies* 4 (1995): 109–26, accessed March 17, 2021, http://www.jstor.org/stable/30003333.

publican Party were forced to take sides—align with Roosevelt and the Progressive/Reform wing of the party, or remain loyal to Taft and the conservative wing. This emerging Roosevelt-Taft split proved to be a political tightrope for McLean, and walking it would challenge all of his diplomatic skills.

Taft's worst fears came true on February 21, 1912, when Theodore Roosevelt announced that he would run for president in November 1912. Roosevelt had become deeply disenchanted with Taft's conservatism and his passive leadership style. But the differences between the two men were about far more than the candidate's personalities and ambitions. Historian Sidney Milkis argues in his 2009 book *Theodore Roosevelt and the Progressive Party* that the 1912 presidential election was the climactic battle of the Progressive Era that began at the dawn of the twentieth century. Eventually, four candidates would run for the presidency in 1912, each offering a different set of Progressive-Era solutions to the enormous problems resulting from the rise of industrialization. At the heart of their differences were contrasting views of the role of the executive branch, the courts and the US Constitution, and the appropriate degree of participation of the people in the running of government institutions.[43]

At the contentious Republican National Convention in 1912 at the Chicago Coliseum, fistfights broke out between the Roosevelt and Taft forces. The Roosevelt delegates, feeling cheated over unfavorable or biased convention rulings, eventually walked out. But the embittered Theodore Roosevelt did not quit. Instead, he ran for president as a third-party candidate with the newly-formed Progressive Party.

As the head of this new political party, Roosevelt advocated a series of progressive reforms that would alienate many Republicans, including McLean. As Sidney Milkis writes in his book *Theodore Roosevelt, the Progressive Party, and the Transformation of American Democracy*, Roo-

---

43   Milkis, *Theodore Roosevelt*, xvi–xix.

sevelt reemerged in 1912 from his self-imposed political retirement with a "newfound militant progressivism."[44] Impatient with the pace of reform, frustrated with the courts blocking legislative remedies, and alarmed over persistent social and economic problems, Roosevelt charted a new course for progressives. The stakes were now higher, but the dilemma remained the same—how do government officials reconcile the need for government regulation with American virtues and values like individualism, self-reliance, and economic liberty?[45]

Not only was Roosevelt backing the controversial initiative, referendum, and recall of judges, but he now advocated a judicial referendum, allowing citizens to override certain court rulings by popular vote.[46] Roosevelt also supported women's suffrage, for which he had been lukewarm about in the past[47]; social insurance for the elderly, the unemployed, and the disabled; a version of national health insurance; workers' compensation for work-related injuries; an eight-hour workday; primary elections for state and federal nominations; and an inheritance tax.[48] As the campaign progressed, Roosevelt extended his program of "pure democracy" to even greater heights. In September 1912, he announced at a campaign speech in Phoenix, Arizona, that he would apply the recall initiative to elected officials, including the president of the United States.[49]

Taft sought to reconcile his deep respect for the US Constitution and

---

44   Ibid., 13.

45   McGerr, *A Fierce Discontent*, 177.

46   Logan Stagg Istre, "Theodore Roosevelt and the Case for a Popular Constitution," *American Affairs* IV, no. 3 (Fall 2020): 191–204.

47   Doris Groshen Daniels, "Theodore Roosevelt and Gender Roles," *Presidential Studies Quarterly* 26, no. 3 (Summer 1996): 656–57.

48   Andrew Pavord, "The Gamble for Power: Theodore Roosevelt's Decision to Run for the Presidency in 1912," *Presidential Studies Quarterly* 26, no. 3 (Summer 1996): 633–47.

49   Sidney M. Milkis, "The Transformation of American Democracy: Teddy Roosevelt, the 1912 Election, and the Progressive Party," The Heritage Foundation, June 11, 2012, https://www. heritage.org/political-process/report/the-transformation-american-democracy-teddy-roosevelt-the-1912-election, accessed November 6, 2020.

his restrained view of executive power with the need to make progressive reforms. During his presidency, Taft racked up many progressive reforms, including tariff reform, railroad rate reductions, and the prosecution of antitrust violations (ninety-nine, in all), including Standard Oil Company of New Jersey, the American Tobacco Company, and the American Sugar Refining Company, and tried to break up US Steel, a move Roosevelt opposed, calling it a "good trust." Another progressive reform undertaken by Taft occurred in 1909, when Taft asked Congress to pass a constitutional amendment legalizing a federal income tax, resulting in the Sixteenth Amendment.[50]

As constitutional scholar Jordan Singer writes, Taft believed that executive power was limited by the US Constitution, which clashed with Roosevelt's expansive view of the presidency. Taft abhorred Roosevelt's idea of the public voting to overturn judicial decisions, viewing an independent judiciary as almost sacred.[51] In thought and temperament, Taft was much more like a judge than a politician; he reluctantly ran for the presidency only because his wife and Roosevelt urged him.

Taft and Roosevelt held fundamentally different views of the US Constitution. Taft was a "literalist," or "strict constructionist," interpreting the Constitution based on a narrow definition of the language without regard to modern conditions or societal changes.[52] Roosevelt was a "loose constructionist," and believed in a much more aggressive and expansive use of executive power. Roosevelt thundered at the 1912 Progressive Party convention that "the people themselves must be the ultimate makers of their own Constitution." He called for new ways

---

50   Peri E. Arnold, "William Howard Taft: Domestic Affairs," Miller Center, University of Virginia, website, https://millercenter.org/president/taft/domestic-affairs.

51   Jordan Singer, "Hail to the Chief Justice," Courts Law JOTWELL (June 15, 2018), reviewing Jeffrey Rosen, William Howard Taft (2018), https://courtslaw.jotwell.com/hail-to-the-chief-justice/.

52   Michael J. Korzi, "Our Chief Magistrate and His Powers: A Reconsideration of William Howard Taft's 'Whig' Theory of Presidential Leadership," Presidential Studies Quarterly 33, no. 2 (2003): 305–6, accessed August 25, 2021, http://www.jstor.org/stable/27552486.

where the people could decide fundamental constitutional questions.[53] Taft revered the law and the courts, eventually going on to teach law at Yale University, and then served as chief justice of the US Supreme Court. On the other hand, Roosevelt seems to have had little patience for legal theory. After graduating from Harvard in 1880, Roosevelt began studying law at Columbia. But he soon dropped out to win a seat in the New York State Assembly. He later said that the pleasures of "politicking and writing" soothed his soul more than the law.[54] In this context, McLean, an accomplished lawyer, was much closer in attitude and predilection to Taft than Roosevelt.

Five days after Roosevelt's announcement to run for the presidency, McLean announced that he was squarely for the renomination of President Taft.[55] Later in the campaign, McLean made a sarcastic allusion to Roosevelt's well-publicized claim at the Progressive Party convention, "We stand at Armageddon, and we battle for the Lord!" Using that phrase against him, McLean declared that the Roosevelt supporters were an "army mobilized at Armageddon whose purpose is to destroy. Religion is always a reliable political asset. He is a lucky candidate who gets the Lord on his side first, for the Lord cannot be on both sides."[56]

McLean and Taft had a very close working relationship that had developed over many years. Taft was also a frequent visitor to McLean's estate in Simsbury, where the two fished and hunted. McLean often sought Taft's advice on issues relating to the Philippines, especially relating to McLean's work on the Senate's Philippines committee. They collaborated on the successful passage of a bill in 1912 that led to the

---

53   Michael Les Benedict, "Constitutional Politics in the Gilded Age," *The Journal of the Gilded Age and Progressive Era* 9, no. 1 (2010): 8, accessed August 25, 2021, http://www.jstor.org/stable/27821452.

54   Edmund Morris, *The Rise of Theodore Roosevelt* (New York: Coward, McCann & Geoghegan, 1979), 131.

55   "Connecticut is for Taft," *Hartford Daily Courant,* February 27, 1912, 1.

56   Ibid.

installation of a wireless telegraph system in the Philippines, allowing the country to communicate internationally for the first time.[57]

McLean was the keynote speaker at the Connecticut State Republican convention on September 10, 1912, at Hartford's Foot Guard Armory. McLean reiterated his opposition to Roosevelt's proposals for the initiative, recall, and referendum, arguing that the proposals would destroy representative government, weaken the legislative branch, "and lead us backward to a government based on vagaries, unsound in principle."[58] McLean alleged that Roosevelt had borrowed some of his radical ideas from Eugene Debs, the Socialist Party candidate for president in 1912.[59]

With the Republicans so deeply divided, Democrat Woodrow Wilson won the presidency with just 42 percent of the popular vote (435 electoral votes). The Republicans split their party's vote: Roosevelt got twenty-seven percent of the popular vote (eighty-eight electoral votes) Taft got twenty-three percent (eight electoral votes).[60] Eugene Debs, the socialist party candidate, received a substantial six percent of the vote, double the support he had received in 1908, and made the best showing of a socialist candidate in a presidential election in American history.[61]

Wilson was the first Democrat to win a presidential election since 1892 and one of just two Democratic presidents to serve since the Civil War. Moreover, Congress similarly shifted from Republican to

---

57   Frederick Sammis, "Around the World Wireless," *Popular Mechanics*, September 1912, 331.

58   Ibid.

59   "McLean's Brilliant Speech to Convention," *Bridgeport Times*, September 11, 1912, 4.

60   "The 1912 Presidential Election," 270 To Win, Electoral Ventures LLC, https://www.270towin.com/1912_Election/, accessed December 2, 2020.

61   Milkis, *Theodore Roosevelt*, 236.

Democratic control. The era of Republican dominance in national government, which had lasted since the Civil War, was now over.[62]

The next session of Congress (the sixty-third) met from March 4, 1913, to March 4, 1915. In the Senate, Democrats outnumbered Republicans 51–44.[63] McLean was now a member of the minority party in what appeared to be a promising new era for the Democratic Party because the Republicans were hopelessly split. Without a Republican in the White House, McLean would have to adapt and find new ways to be effective in the Senate. For the next eight years, he would employ persuasion, compromise, and obstruction to achieve his legislative goals, and faithfully represent the interests of Connecticut and the core beliefs of the Republican Party. His legislative skills would be put to the test.

In fact, his greatest legislative achievement would occur during this period dominated by the Democratic Party. This would require years of effort and perseverance, aided in large part not by fellow Republicans, but by working with Democratic President Woodrow Wilson. "New days, new ways," as McLean once said.

---

62 Robert Alexander Kraig, "The 1912 Election and the Rhetorical Foundations of the Liberal State," *Rhetoric and Public Affairs* 3, no. 3 (2000): 363–95, accessed March 17, 2021, http://www.jstor.org/stable/41940243.

63 "Party Division," US Senate, Secretary of the Senate, Washington, DC, https://www.senate.gov/history/partydiv.htm, accessed February 12, 2020.

★ CHAPTER EIGHT ★

SAVING THE BIRDS

> We must use every effort to secure the support of
> the public until the birds of America are saved.
> *George P. McLean, in a letter to Gilbert Pearson,*
> *president of the Audubon Society, March 5, 1913[1]*

Leaving his office at the American Museum of Natural History near Central Park on a sunny spring afternoon in 1886, ornithologist Frank M. Chapman ogled the fashionable ladies strolling along the streets of uptown Manhattan. The twenty-two-year-old naturalist, who would later come up with the idea for the Audubon Christmas Bird Count, was actually conducting research as he walked along Fifth Avenue—how many women wore feathered hats, and what species of bird feathers were adorning those bonnets?

Chapman calculated that over three-fourths of the 700 hats he saw had ornamental feathers on them. He identified over forty species of bird feathers, like the ever-popular egret and heron, but he also spotted the plumage of sparrows, warblers, cardinals, orioles, woodpeckers, flickers, grebes, terns, grouse, quail, jays, bluebirds, waxwings, bun-

1   George P. McLean, letter to T. Gilbert Pearson, March 5, 1913, mssHM 47474, George Bird Grinnell papers, 1879–1951, The Huntington Library, San Marino, CA.

tings, tanagers, grosbeaks, and many others.[2] Estimates vary, but by the late 1800s around 200 million birds were killed annually for making women's and men's hats.[3]

Several key Progressive Era themes are embodied in McLean's efforts in the US Senate to protect migratory birds. Historian Michael Mc-Gerr considers the expansion of federal power to advance the public good as a fundamental characteristic of Progressivism. This expansion of federal power was opposed by many Americans who viewed it as socialistic and dangerous.[4] McLean was clear in his belief that efforts at the state level to protect birds had been unsuccessful, and that only federal protections would be effective.

Senator McLean fits the profile of a "power elite" as advanced by conservation historian Dorceta E. Taylor. Power elites (like Theodore Roosevelt) gave legitimacy to and helped orchestrate the conservation movement in the early 1900s.[5] McLean fits Taylor's definition of a power elite: raised in rural Connecticut with a close connection to nature, as a US senator, McLean sought to reconcile the ravages of industrialization with the rural and wilderness lifestyle of his youth. McLean's nostalgia for his rural boyhood is illustrated by his lament at a Senate hearing over the declining number of woodcock and grouse in Connecticut: "There is not one ruffed grouse today where there were twenty ten years ago."[6]

Taylor's research on the history of the American conservation movement sheds light on the motives behind many Progressive Era conservationists. Many were influenced by the rise of Transcendentalism and

---

2   Frank M. Chapman, "Birds and Bonnets," *Forest and Stream* 26, no. 5 (February 25, 1886): 84.

3   Dorceta E. Taylor, *The Rise of the American Conservation Movement: Power, Privilege, and Environmental Protection* (Durham: Duke University Press, 2016), 196.

4   McGerr, *A Fierce Discontent*, 164.

5   Dorceta E. Taylor, *The Rise of the American Conservation Movement: Power, Privilege, and Environmental Protection* (Durham: Duke University Press, 2016), 168.

6   William T. Hornaday, *Our Vanishing Wildlife: Its Extermination and Preservation* (New York: Scribners, 1913), 94.

Romanticism in the early nineteenth century, believing that there was a spiritual relationship between humans, nature, and God.[7] McLean was an avid reader of nineteenth century Romantic-era poetry, especially during his formative high school years. Such motivation runs deep—nature is important because it reflects universal spiritual truths and must be preserved.

In addition, McLean's motivation for protecting birds grew out of his being one of the era's elite sportsmen, a function of the wealthy leisure class. There was an undercurrent of "class warfare" in conservation reform. Wealthy sportsmen blamed subsistence hunters for ruining recreational hunting. Elite sportsmen, like Roosevelt and McLean, often blamed the decimation of wildlife on unenlightened classes of people who hunted without gentlemanly restraint. Immigrants were also scorned, especially those who killed robins and other songbirds used in cooking native dishes.[8] In addition, many wealthy elites considered birds and other wildlife objects of beauty and study that should be protected by law.

McLean had long been a conscientious sportsman, concerned about overhunting. As early as 1886, he helped organize the Simsbury Game Club, which set bag limits, defined hunting seasons, and re-stocked local hunting grounds. McLean's views about hunting evolved significantly over his lifetime. Interviewed in 1913, he said that he hadn't shot a duck in years.[9] He once loved duck hunting, he said, lying on his back in two inches of sparkling ice water in a floating battery during the coldest days of winter. But now, he had practically quit because the sport wasn't fair anymore, given advances in continuous shotguns.[10] By criticizing continuous shotguns, McLean was voicing disapproval

---

7   Dorceta E. Taylor, *Rise of American Conservation Movement*, 24.

8   Ibid., 211.

9   "The Birdman of the Senate," *Kansas City Times*, September 16, 1913, 12.

10   Ibid.

of the influential firearm manufacturers of his own state, whose new pump shotguns were one of the causes of overhunting.

So great was the slaughter of birds and other wildlife in America that the period between 1870 to around 1900 was called "Age of Extermination" by William T. Hornaday, the director of the New York Zoo and an outspoken naturalist. Perhaps the most infamous example of excessive killing concerns the passenger pigeon.[11] They were once the most abundant bird in North America, numbering around three billion, possibly up to five billion.[12] People ate passenger pigeons in vast amounts, but farmers also exterminated them, believing they were a threat to crops. Passenger pigeon populations went into a death spiral in the early twentieth century; the last known bird, Martha, died ignominiously at the Cincinnati Zoo on September 14, 1914.[13]

While the wholesale killing of birds was real and tragic, it was essentially rational. Market hunting in America originated with the Pilgrims (and indigenous peoples before them), and continued unabated with the westward expansion of the population. Before the advent of commercial refrigeration, freshly killed birds were in high demand as a source of protein for residents in the growing cities, for settlers in the West, and for the rural poor. Chicken was not yet a staple of the American diet; it was considered a luxury meat, not available on a large scale until breakthroughs in poultry science in the 1920s.[14] Similarly, plume hunters were responding to market needs driven by the fads and fashions in the hat trade.

McLean's federal legislative work on behalf of bird protection rep-

---

11 Patrick Duffy, review of "Pilgrims of the Air," by John Wilson Foster, *Dublin Review of Books*, January 1, 2015.

12 Carl McDaniel and John M. Gowdy, "Markets and biodiversity loss: some case studies and policy considerations," *International Journal of Social Economics* 25, no. 10 (January 1998) 1454, 1459.

13 "Martha, The Last Passenger Pigeon," *The Cincinnati Enquirer*, April 4, 1988, 2.

14 Ibid.

resented the culmination of decades of struggles by many individuals and groups opposed to the senseless killing of birds. Women played a crucial role in pioneering bird conservation efforts. Their contributions include forming and giving life to early Audubon societies, advocating bird protection legislation and land conservation, and urging women, through newspaper and magazine articles, to stop the practice of wearing feathers.[15]

Connecticut's Mabel Osgood Wright made significant contributions to ornithology and conservation. Her groundbreaking book titled *Birdcraft* published in 1895 was the most popular bird field guide in the nation until Roger Tory Peterson's *Field Guide to the Birds* was published in 1934.[16] On August 13, 1915, McLean and Mabel Osgood Wright were featured guests at a gathering of Connecticut's seven bird clubs. John Burroughs also attended the meeting, which included talks by both McLean and Wright.[17]

Many prominent women formed and organized the earliest Audubon clubs, like Florence Merriam Bailey, who in 1886 helped create the Smith College Audubon Society, a local chapter of the National Audubon Society. Women are credited with proliferating and giving purpose and energy to local Audubon societies throughout the nation; it is estimated that women comprised eighty percent of the membership of the Audubon clubs in the late nineteenth and early twentieth centuries.[18] Florence Merriam Bailey was also the first female associate member of the American Ornithologists' Union in 1885, which was responsible for developing the "model law" for bird protection adopted by

---

15   Carolyn Merchant, "Women of the Progressive Conservation Movement: 1900–1916," *Environmental Review* 8, no. 1 (1984): 57–85, accessed April 27, 2021, doi:10.2307/3984521.

16   Kathy Van Der Aue, "Mabel Osgood Wright and the History of Birdcraft & the Connecticut Audubon Society," Connecticut Audubon website, https://www.ctaudubon.org/2018/01/mabel-osgood-wright-and-the-history-of-birdcraft-the-connecticut-audubon-society/.

17   "State Meeting of Bird Clubs," *The Journal* (Meriden, CT), August 12, 1915, 9.

18   Jennifer Price, *Flight Maps: Adventures with Nature in Modern America* (New York: Basic Books, 1999), 64.

many states.[19] Despite these decades-long efforts, bird protection laws at the state and local levels did not solve the problem, and over-harvesting continued.[20]

The first successful piece of federal legislation backed by conservation reformers was the passage in 1900 of the Lacey Act, which banned the interstate shipment of birds and mammals taken in violation of state laws. But this law did little to stem the sharp decline in bird populations. Bird preservation legislation lay largely dormant until McLean's election to the Senate in 1911.

Limiting excessive game-hunting was McLean's original focus when he entered the Senate in 1911. Just three months into his first term in the Senate, on May 15, 1911, McLean introduced legislation to protect migratory *game* birds in all states between January 10 and August 15, giving birds protection during their spring migration, the peak time for excessive hunting. Speaking for his bill, McLean told a newspaper reporter that he was as good a sportsman as anybody, but without federal protections, extinction of several species of birds was certain.[21] His legislation failed to get out of committee.

Seeing his legislation stall, on June 28, 1911, McLean took the unusual step of proposing a constitutional amendment to protect migratory birds.[22] In hindsight, it might seem far-fetched to amend the US Constitution to protect migratory birds. There have been over 11,000 proposed constitutional amendments introduced in Congress, though only twenty-seven have been ratified.[23] These unsuccessful amendments

---

19   Minichiello, 33.

20   Kristina Rozan, "Detailed Discussion on the Migratory Bird Treaty Act," Michigan State University College of Law, Animal Legal & Historical Center, 2014, https://www.animallaw.info/article/detailed-discussion-migratory-bird-treaty-act.

21   "McLean Introduces Bill," *Boston Globe*, May 18, 1911, 15.

22   "Ornamenting the Constitution," *Brooklyn Daily Eagle*, July 1, 1911.

23   "Press Kit: Amending America," National Archives, 225th Anniversary of the ratification of the Bill of Rights Exhibit, March 11, 2016–September 4, 2017, https://www.archives.gov/press/press-kits/amending-america.

were not simply frivolous notions, but a way to galvanize public opinion and pave the way for other means of successful reform. McLean may have also thought that a constitutional amendment would be a surefire way to overcome state's rights objections to federal legislation. In fact, to strengthen federal powers, during the Progressive Era four constitutional amendments were passed (Sixteenth-Nineteenth). Progressives believed that the US Constitution needed to be updated to change with the times, reflecting urbanization, industrialization, and the myriad of resulting social and economic problems.

In March 1912, McLean turned his attention to crafting new legislation protecting migratory birds. He staged a series of highly-publicized hearings at his forest preservation committee, taking extensive testimony from game protection groups, leading naturalists, and conservationists. A breakthrough in defining the bill came from Thomas Gilbert Pearson, the president of the National Audubon Society. He urged that McLean expand the scope of McLean's bill beyond just game birds to include songbirds and insect-eating birds as well.[24]

Pearson argued that insectivorous birds provided an indispensable economic role in protecting farm crops from damage by insects. He cited data from economic ornithologists from the US Department of Agriculture's biological survey that insects caused over $800 million in damage to American agriculture.[25] With commercial pesticides still decades away, birds were considered a farmer's best line of defense against crop-eating insects.

At these committee hearings, McLean succeeded in establishing common ground among different interest groups; uniting hunters, state and local game protection groups, conservationists, and gun and ammunition manufacturers to a common cause. In addition to broad-

---

24   Thomas Gilbert Pearson, *Adventures in Bird Protection: An Autobiography* (New York: D. Appleton-Century, 1937), 276.

25   Kurkpatrick Dorsey, *The Dawn of Conservation Diplomacy: U.S.-Canadian Wildlife Protection Treaties in the Progressive Era* (Seattle: University of Washington Press, 1998), 183–84.

ening the legislation to include songbirds, McLean found a new selling point for bird protection: highlighting the role of birds as protectors of American agriculture.[26]

The hearings also led McLean to join forces with Congressman John W. Weeks, a Republican from Massachusetts, who had introduced a similar bird protection bill in the House in May 1909, where it had lay dormant ever since. The two men collaborated to create the Weeks-McLean bill, which made it unlawful to kill or capture both game birds and insect-eating birds, including setting fixed hunting seasons and enforcing penalties for violators.[27]

The bill did have its shortcomings. Initially it provided only $10,000 for implementation, and it did not specify an enforcement mechanism. The bill also used general bird names, not scientific terms. It called for an oversight committee appointed by the Department of Agriculture to address these and other important details. Most importantly to the Audubon Society, supporters of the bill expected a "permanent closed season" for the hunting and capturing of all song and insectivorous birds.[28]

McLean introduced the Weeks-McLean bill in the Senate on January 14, 1913. It was his maiden speech, as he had dutifully followed the custom that new senators wait one year before making their first speech. McLean began by highlighting the economic value of birds to the nation's agriculture industry, but soon focused on the bill's biggest challenge: the exercise of federal authority in matters normally governed by the states.[29]

---

26   Ibid., 187.

27   Act of March 4, 1913, ch. 145, 37 Stat. 828, 847–48 (repealed 1918).

28   George Gladden, "Federal Protection for Migratory Birds," *Outing Magazine* LXII, no. 3, (April 1913): 345–49.

29   George P. McLean (CT), "Migratory Birds," *Congressional Record* 49 (1913), January 14, 1913, 1487, https://www.govinfo.gov/content/pkg/GPO-CRECB-1913-pt2-v49/pdf/GPO-CRECB-1913-pt2-v49-8-1.pdf.

McLean contended that Congress has the implied power to protect and promote the general welfare of the nation. He likened the present ineffectiveness of independent state actions to establishing and regulating post roads one hundred years ago. McLean also invoked the legal doctrine of *ferae naturae,* or the common law understanding that non-domesticated animals are no one's private property but are instead under the dominion of the sovereign power, not individuals or individual states. "Every nation has the power to protect its migratory *ferae naturae,*" McLean stated.

At this point, he was interrupted by Senator James A. Reed, a Missouri Democrat who would become McLean's chief antagonist on migratory bird protection. Reed was a firm advocate of states' rights and opposed all forms of federal usurpation of state power. Reed represented Missouri, a rural state where many poor game and plume hunters vehemently opposed federal interference in setting bag limits or curtailing spring hunting.

Reed asked McLean what clause of the Constitution prevents the killing of game? McLean cited *McCulloch v. Maryland* (1819), one of the first and most important Supreme Court cases on federal power. McLean argued that in this case the Supreme Court held that Congress has implied powers derived from those listed in Article I, Section 8, the "Necessary and Proper" clause, giving Congress the power to establish a national bank. McLean argued that federal power is invoked when the states acting alone cannot accomplish the desired results.[30]

McLean then stated that no one questions the federal government's right to quarantine its borders against plagues and contagious diseases. It is not within the power of a single state to protect the nation as a whole from such threats. Similarly, states acting alone cannot stop the

---

30   McLean was referring to the Supreme Court's 1819 decision in *McCulloch v. Maryland,* which expanded the powers of the national government, including the power "to establish post-offices and post-roads."

Missouri Senator James A. Reed (source: Missouri Valley Special Collections, Kansas City Public Library, Kansas City, Missouri)

wanton destruction of birds, "one of the most beautiful and useful natural blessings of men."[31]

A week later, on January 22, 1913, McLean brought the Weeks-McLean bill before the Senate for a vote. By now, the measure had received much favorable national press coverage and key endorsements from leading conservationists and public figures, including industrialist and bird lover Henry Ford. McLean first introduced two telegrams into the record, one from the nation's leading naturalist-writer John Burroughs, and the other from an everyday farmer from Texas. John Burroughs (1837–1921) was an incredibly popular writer of his time and called "father of the nature essay." A favorite of Theodore Roosevelt, the two men shared a 30-year friendship, including a two-week

---

31   "Protect the Birds," *Boston Evening Transcript*, January 14, 1913, 16.

vacation together at Yellowstone National Park.[32] In his telegram, Burroughs said that public support for the bill was widespread and deep, and no measure before Congress is more far-reaching in its importance. The measure would save one of our most valuable and interesting natural resources. [33]

The other telegram that McLean read was from Thomas Spear, a farmer from Dallas, Texas. Spear said a federal law was desperately needed as local laws were ineffective. Spear described a common practice in Texas where robins were killed in vast numbers when they gathered in flocks during the winter. The birds were hunted for robin pie, a popular regional dish. Using blinding lights, Spear said that robins were killed by the hundreds despite local laws prohibiting it. The rarely-enforced fine for such a practice was a mere $5.[34]

With time running out on the sixty-second Congress (it would end March 4, 1913), McLean requested a unanimous consent agreement to speed the passage of the bird protection bill. Unanimous consent, as a parliamentary device that dispenses with a quorum and roll call vote, is often employed when members feel that it would be useless to oppose a matter. So, on the morning of January 22, 1913, the Senate passed S. 6497 to protect migratory game and insectivorous birds in the United States.

Now the bill would have to pass in the House before it could be signed into law by outgoing President William Howard Taft. The House was unlikely to approve the bill in the short time remaining, but worse yet, McLean knew that Taft would never sign it. As a strict constructionist

---

32   Edmund Morris, *Theodore Rex* (New York: Random House, 2001), 220.

33   George P. McLean (CT), "Protection of Birds," *Congressional Record* 49 (1913), January 22, 1913, p. 1870, https://www.govinfo.gov/content/pkg/GPO-CRECB-1913-pt2-v49/pdf/GPO-CRECB-1913-pt2-v49-16-1.pdf.

34   Ibid.

of the Constitution, Taft had on many occasions pledged to use his veto power to limit the reach of federal power.[35]

So McLean took another tack: on February 27, 1913, he instructed the House to append the Weeks-McLean bird protection bill to a massive agriculture appropriations bill, in effect hiding it from Taft's view. McLean's tactic did not go unchallenged. Senator Nathan Bryan (a Democrat from Florida) objected, but McLean remained firm, saying that there were half a dozen other riders to the agriculture appropriations bill.[36] Senator Asle Gronna, a Progressive Republican from North Dakota, supported McLean's amendment, as did the Senate's presiding officer, Jacob Gallinger, a Republican from New Hampshire.[37]

The appropriations bill containing the Weeks-McLean rider passed the House, and with little fanfare it was sent to the White House for Taft's signature. It arrived late in the day on Taft's final day in office, March 4, 1913. After nearly two years of political maneuvering, McLean and the bill's supporters now fretted that Taft would veto it. But Taft, worn out and eager to leave the White House, signed the agriculture appropriations bill without reading it. In later years, Taft insisted that he would have never signed the bill had he known that it contained the rider for federal migratory bird protection, telling a friend, "I would have given it my veto."[38]

Shortly after the passage of Weeks-McLean, a California newspaper published a personal portrait of McLean, calling him the "bird man of the Senate." The writer praised McLean for his persistence and toughness in getting Weeks-McLean passed. At the appropriate time,

---

35   Kurkpatrick Dorsey, *The Dawn of Conservation Diplomacy: U.S.-Canadian Wildlife Protection Treaties in the Progressive Era* (Seattle: University of Washington Press, 1998), 187.

36   Sen. Nathan Philemon Bryan (FL), "Agriculture Appropriation Bill," *Congressional Record* 49, February 27, 1913, 4149.

37   Sen. Asle Jorgenson Gronna (ND), "Agriculture Appropriation Bill," *Congressional Record* 49, February 27, 1913, 4149.

38   Dorsey, *The Dawn of Conservation Diplomacy*, 188.

when the "persimmons were ripe," McLean "shook the tree" to get his bill passed. McLean was in no way a tender-hearted man, the writer observed. "No man who has been in Connecticut politics for thirty years can be of a timorous nature."[39] A former prosecutor, McLean had gained a reputation for "unjointing" the guilty party as "neatly as any legal butcher in the business." The writer recalled McLean's efforts to reform the Connecticut Legislature as governor, saying McLean went after the "rotten borough" system "with a mop."

Despite passage of Weeks-McLean, serious questions remained. Would it withstand a constitutional challenge in the Supreme Court? How could the new law be implemented and enforced? In addition, McLean would now have to work with a Democratic president, Woodrow Wilson. New approaches to deal with changing circumstances were needed or measures to protect migratory birds would be rendered ineffective.

On the day that Weeks-McLean passed, McLean intimated that he knew what needed to be done: only an international treaty protecting birds would have lasting impact.[40]

As early as 1906, the idea of solving international conservation problems via treaties was proposed by Secretary of State Elihu Root to resolve boundary water disputes for fisheries. Root thought the idea might apply to protecting birds, and advocated for it as a US senator for New York in January 1913, but with Taft on his way out, the idea went nowhere.[41]

McLean now believed that international treaties to protect migratory birds had a better chance of withstanding a Supreme Court challenge than legislation did. Root and other treaty proponents pointed out

---

39   "Senator McLean Quits Duck Hunting," *The Sacramento Bee,* October 31, 1913, 6.

40   Charles A. Lofgren, "Missouri v. Holland in Historical Perspective," *The Supreme Court Review* 1975 (1975): 81, accessed March 22, 2021, http://www.jstor.org/stable/3108809.

41   Dorsey, *The Dawn of Conservation Diplomacy,* 188.

that the Supremacy Clause of the Constitution establishes that treaties made under the authority of the Constitution constitute the "supreme Law of the Land," and thus take priority over any conflicting state laws.[42] In addition, treaties would be more effective in protecting birds since migrating birds have no respect for state or national boundaries. Birds were in equal danger when they migrated outside the country.

With President Wilson in office for less than a month, McLean introduced a Senate resolution on April 7, 1913, "asking the President to enter into treaty discussions with the Governments of other countries for the mutual protection and preservation of birds." Two days later, McLean met with President Wilson and a team of conservation officials to solicit Wilson's support for the treaty effort. After agreeing to support the concept of a treaty, Wilson told Secretary of State William Jennings Bryan that he wanted to begin negotiations, and asked Bryan to explore timing and potential treaty partners.[43] Bryan conferred with experts in the agriculture department; it was soon agreed that the United States would initiate treaty discussions with the governments of Canada, Germany, France, Denmark, the Netherlands, Russia, Japan, Argentina, Venezuela, and several Central American nations.[44] With Wilson's expressed support and the cooperation of Bryan's Department of State, McLean's Senate resolution asking the president to pursue international treaties to protect migratory birds passed on July 7, 1913.[45]

McLean's efforts to save the birds did not end with the success of his treaty resolution. A more immediate opportunity to curtail the trade in plumes used for women's and men's hats emerged shortly after the Senate approved his treaty pact. In January 1913, Audubon Society official Henry Oldys first voiced the idea that the nation should prohibit

---

42   Charles A. Lofgren, "Missouri v. Holland in Historical Perspective," *The Supreme Court Review* 1975 (1975): 81, accessed March 22, 2021, http://www.jstor.org/stable/3108809.

43   Ibid.

44   Dorsey, *The Dawn of Conservation Diplomacy*, 195.

45   "Resolution for Treaty Passed," *Montpelier* (VT) *Morning Journal*, July 11, 1913, 3.

the importation of feathers by modifying the nation's tariff code.[46] Every year, US milliners imported a large amount of exotic bird feathers from nations like New Guinea, Venezuela, Nicaragua, and Costa Rica. Oldys' idea of a ban on feather imports was aggressively publicized by the Audubon Society and gained the interest and support of the public.

McLean led the fight in the Senate to amend the tariff bill in a prominent speech on August 16, 1913. In the speech, McLean meticulously documented the history of the plumage trade and identified the nations where birds were being hunted to near extinction. McLean highlighted the popular species prized by the feather trade and pilloried the greed of the milliners. For example, he described a coat composed of hundreds of hummingbird hides that recently sold for $10,000 in Cuba. While his speech was largely factual, evidence-based, and lawyerly, he also spoke of the aesthetic value of birds and the "intense pleasure many people find in the companionship and study of birds." McLean revealed that his motives for protecting birds went beyond the interest of an elite sportsman. He stated that he wanted to "save the birds for their beauty alone." He confessed on the floor of the Senate that people may view it as a weakness, but a world without birds would not interest him.[47]

McLean's speech was interrupted numerous times by his nemesis, Senator James A. Reed of Missouri, who provided his unvarnished opinions on the plumage trade. Referring to the egret, a bird nearing extinction and prized by milliners for its beautiful white feathers, Reed sarcastically asked, why is there sympathy for "a long-legged, long-beaked, long-necked bird that lives in swamps and eats tadpoles?" Let

---

46 Dorsey, *The Dawn of Conservation Diplomacy*, 193.

47 George P. McLean, Speech Reprint, *The Plumage And The Tariff Extermination Of Useful Birds For Their Plumage, A Grave Economic Blunder Speech Of Hon. George P. Mclean In The Senate Of The United States*, August 16, 1913 (Washington, DC: US Government Printing Office), 11.

humanity utilize birds for the only purpose God intended, namely, to adorn the "bonnets of our beautiful ladies," Reed intoned.[48]

It's interesting to note that while Reed and McLean disagreed strongly on bird protection, away from the Senate, they socialized together. Beginning in 1913, McLean's wife, Juliette, and Reed's wife, Lura, were partners at a weekly bridge club.[49] This kind of civility in politics today seems as antiquated as the feathery hats so in vogue in the early 1900s. A 2016 study concluded that incivility among government leaders inhibits action on important issues and inspires distrust of public institutions and those who serve in them.[50] While McLean was generally civil and courteous in his Senate floor communications, he could be tough and impatient at times. In his maiden Senate speech, McLean noted that the spirit of courtesy so evident in the Senate can be taken too far. McLean thought that chivalry and individual conceit among Senators often resulted in needless delays and inaction.[51]

McLean succeeded in getting the plumage ban added to the Underwood tariff bill, which passed and was signed into law by President Wilson on October 3, 1913. McLean had cultivated an important ally in Woodrow Wilson for the protection of birds. Historian Michael McGerr the places conservation movement among the top Progressive Era reforms, a striking example of using federal power to achieve a social good at the expense of individualism and personal freedom.[52] Woodrow Wilson and George P. McLean would clash often in the years ahead; for now, at least, they had a shared vision for environmental conservation.

---

48   Ibid.

49   "Bridge Party at Rock Creek," *Washington Times,* August 19, 1913, 8.

50   Angela Andrews, "Civility: Does It Matter?" *Newsletter of the National Conference of State Legislatures* 24, no. 23 (June 2016), https://www.ncsl.org/research/about-state-legislatures/civility-does-it-matter.aspx, accessed February 7, 2021.

51   "Senator McLean Chides Colleagues for Inaction," *Coffeyville Daily Journal,* January 14, 1913, 1.

52   McGerr, *A Fierce Discontent,* 165.

Wilson was highly attuned to conservation, and he would one day be among The Wilderness Society's thirteen presidents inducted into its Hall of Fame. In his first inaugural address, Wilson voiced his support for environmental conservation measures, praising the nation's economic and material achievements, but warning of the consequences of unchecked growth. He deplored the squandering of the nation's natural resources, calling for the conservation of the beauty and bounty of nature.[53]

President Wilson may have been further sensitized to the need for protecting birds by his wife and daughters. In early 1913, while vacationing, First Lady Ellen Wilson wrote her husband a letter urging him to support McLean's proposed plumage ban in the pending tariff bill. The president complied, saying he would do what he could "about the birds," and he remained true to his word.[54]

President Wilson's daughter, Margaret, had a passionate interest in birds. From 1913 to 1915, the Wilson family vacationed at a home they leased in Cornish, New Hampshire, known as Harlakenden House. There, his daughter, Margaret, volunteered at the nearby Meriden Bird Club, one of the nation's first sanctuaries for wild birds. During the summer of 1913, the club's manager commissioned a New England poet to write a play to increase public awareness and support for bird conservation. Wilson's daughters, Margaret and Ellen, were given prominent parts in the play.[55]

The Wilson-McLean bird preservation alliance advanced another step forward when Wilson issued a presidential proclamation implementing the Weeks-McLean law on October 13, 1913. This proclama-

---

53 Woodrow Wilson, First Inaugural Address, Tuesday, March 4, 1913, retrieved from Miller Center website February 3, 2021, https://millercenter.org/the-presidency/presidential-speeches/march-4-1913-first-inaugural-address.

54 Gregory Dehler, *The Most Defiant Devil: William T. Hornaday* (Charlottesville: University of Virginia Press, 2013), 154.

55 "Sanctuary for Birds—A Remarkable Pageant's 100th Anniversary," September 12, 2013 by Barbara Orbach Natanson, Prints and Photographs Division at the Library of Congress.

tion banned the killing of all insectivorous birds and songbirds (except by naturalists for scientific purposes), following expert advice provided by the Department of Agriculture. It also defined opening and closing dates of bird hunting seasons for the states to follow. The proclamation further declared that when state and federal regulations differed, the federal rules would supersede the state laws. A five-year ban on hunting several vulnerable bird species was imposed, including whooping cranes, wood ducks, and swans.[56]

Wilson's proclamation provided seven federal field agents to supervise 172 local game wardens placed on the rolls of the US Agriculture Department with a nominal salary.[57] The Weeks-McLean law was now a reality, not just a concept, with a provision for enforcement, however inadequate. It also set up a constitutional showdown about the power of the federal government in areas historically ruled by state governments.

Everything seemed to be going McLean's way. President Wilson had supported McLean's bird protection efforts in several important ways:

First, the new tariff bill passed with the plumage ban intact.

Second, McLean's Senate resolution asking the president to pursue international treaties to protect migratory birds passed on July 7, 1913.

Third, Wilson issued his presidential proclamation implementing the Weeks-McLean bill, which included enforcement resources and a clear ban on hunting song birds and insectivorous birds.

Meanwhile, opponents of Weeks-McLean in the Senate sought to cripple the bill by defunding or repealing it. Congressman Frank W. Mondell, a Republican from Montana, introduced a bill on August 19, 1913, to repeal the Weeks-McLean law. The Montana senator called

---

56   "How National Game Law Effects State," *Hartford Daily Courant,* October 9, 1913, 3.

57   Clement E. Vose, "State Against Nation: The Case of Missouri vs. Holland," *Prologue: The Journal of the National Archives,* Spring 1984, 238, https://babel.hathitrust.org/cgi/pt?id=mdp.39015020435403&view=1up&seq=253&q1=%22game%20wardens%22, accessed on May 22, 2020.

the law a "revolutionary extension of Federal authority and a Russianizing of the Republic."[58] On April 9, 1914, Senator Joseph T. Robinson, a Democrat from Arkansas, submitted an amendment to the agriculture appropriations bill to eliminate funding for enforcement of the Weeks-McLean rider. Other senators called for funding increases. On April 15, 1914, Senator Henry Ashurst, the first US senator elected from the new state of Arizona, proposed that the enforcement appropriation be raised to $100,000.

On May 12, 1914, McLean and Missouri Senator James A. Reed had another spirited floor debate over these proposed defunding amendments. Calling McLean a "most loveable and intelligent gentleman," Reed said the Connecticut senator was only fooling himself and the country since Weeks-McLean would most certainly be stricken down as unconstitutional.

McLean replied that he was trying to save the birds so that they'd be enjoyed in the future by the humblest families in the country. Reed opposed the law, McLean countered, so that millionaire sportsmen in Missouri could hunt without restraint.[59] McLean had clearly lost patience with Reed. Exasperated, he conjectured that in Reed's view, "the only good bird is a dead bird. I cannot understand the Senator's antipathy toward anything that wears wings."

The first test of the constitutionality of the Weeks-McLean law occurred on January 13, 1914. Opponents of the law persuaded hunter Harvey C. Shauver of Jonesport, Arkansas, to plead guilty to shooting two coots "out of season," as defined by the new federal regulations, arguing that the birds had been shot "in-season," according to Arkansas

---

58   Frank Mondell (WY), "Enforcement Funds for Birds," *Congressional Record-House* 49 (1913),March 3, 1913, 4799, https://www.govinfo.gov/content/pkg/GPO-CRECB-1913-pt5-v49/pdf/GPO-CRECB-1913-pt5-v49-5-2.pdf.

59   George P. McLean (CT), "Weeks-McLean Migratory Bird Law," *Congressional Record* 51 (1914), May 12, 1914, p. 8449, https://www.govinfo.gov/content/pkg/GPO-CRECB-1914-pt9-v51/pdf/GPO-CRECB-1914-pt9-v51-3-1.pdf.

state law. Shauver was reluctant to file the case in federal court until his legal fees were picked up by a local duck club.

The case was tried before federal judge Jacob Trieber, who found the Weeks-McLean law unconstitutional. The decision was immediately appealed to the US Supreme Court.[60] The case, *United States v. Shauver*, galvanized both sides of the debate; it looked like the long-anticipated legal showdown was finally at hand. Fearing defeat, in early September of 1915, McLean considered re-introducing his constitutional amendment protecting migratory birds as a fallback if the Supreme Court ruled against the Weeks-McLean law.

To raise public awareness of his bird protection initiatives, McLean undertook a highly-publicized trip in November 1915 to a Louisiana bird sanctuary, 300,000 acres of marsh land set aside by the McIlhenny family, producers of the famous Tabasco sauce. The sanctuary tour was the brainchild of Herbert K. Job, a Connecticut ornithologist and McLean friend who chronicled the trip for a leading sporting magazine. McLean insisted upon and provided first-class train travel for all from New York to New Orleans, sumptuous meals in the dining car, and drawing rooms for Herbert Job and their other traveling companion, Audubon President Thomas Gilbert Pearson. Job's article, entitled "Ducks and a Senator," portrayed Senator McLean as a "live wire" and one of the "true lovers of wildlife today."[61]

After arriving in New Orleans and meeting with the local press, the party embarked for the Avery Island Bird Sanctuary, where they were met by their host Edward McIlhenny.[62] They talked with local game wardens at the sanctuary, who praised the Weeks-McLean bill, especially the provision ending spring hunting. Job included photos

---

60   Clement E. Vose, "State Against Nation: The Case of Missouri vs. Holland," *Prologue: The Journal of the National Archives,* Spring 1984, 160–61.

61   Herbert. K. Job, "Ducks and the Senator," *Outing Magazine* 69, October 1916, 161.

62   Ibid. Today the sanctuary is called Bird City, and it is a small part of the Avery Island Jungle Gardens.

Senator McLean and Party,
Marsh Island, Louisiana,
November 1915.
(source: Watkinson Library,
Trinity College, Hartford,
Connecticut)

of thousands of ducks swarming around the sanctuary, with McLean noting with a twinkle in his eye that he counted "fifty thousand billion" of them. The trip lasted for a week and produced over 3,000 feet of documentary film, which was later edited and shown at many of the nation's Audubon Bird clubs. Press coverage of the trip was extensive, and provided favorable publicity for the Weeks-McLean bird law and the need for additional enforcement resources.[63]

With the outbreak of war in Europe on July 28, 1914, treaty negotiations for migratory bird protection stalled. While Mexico had been the State Department's first candidate for a treaty, a coup d'état in that country in February of 1913 stopped the talks before they even got started. So the State Department turned to Canada as their first treaty partner, but as a dominion of the British Empire, negotiations were conducted with both the British government and Canadian provincial officials. With Britain at war with Germany beginning in 1914, little progress was made on the bird protection treaty.

In October of 1915, *United States v. Shauver* was argued before the US Supreme Court. Fearing defeat, conservationists pressed the State

---

63   "Senator McLean Shoots Birds Only with Camera," *Hartford Daily Courant*, December 19, 1915, 20.

Department to step up progress on treaty negotiations with Great Britain. The ever-zealous naturalist William T. Hornaday took matters into his own hands by going to the British embassy in Ottawa, Canada, on February 12, 1916, to "demand satisfaction" and get a response from Canadian officials about the treaty.[64] Hornaday's visit proved fruitful as the treaty was subsequently rescued from inactivity and bureaucratic neglect due to the war in Europe. Treaty negotiations were soon reignited, with officials from the United States, Canada, and Great Britain meeting frequently to resolve the many thorny scientific and legal difficulties posed by the treaty.

Finally, on August 16, 1916, the treaty between the United States and Great Britain for the protection of migratory birds in the United States and Canada was agreed to by negotiators. The Senate gave its consent to the treaty two weeks later by a show of hands.[65] Before the vote, however, Missouri Senator James Reed demanded that the Senate go into executive session to discuss it. Eyewitnesses to the executive session say that Reed immediately launched into a blistering "rough-house" speech denouncing the treaty, calling for delay or its outright defeat.

Reed's nearly three-and-a-half-year campaign against McLean's work to protect birds, accompanied by his florid, silver-tongued denunciations of the bills on the Senate floor, had exhausted even his own supporters. An unnamed "Southern Senator" cut Reed's speech short. "We have to protect these birds," he told Reed, "and we are going to do it *now*, so *sit down, Jim!*"[66] The battle was over—the irrepressible Reed had been silenced, at least for now.

Wilson signed the treaty in late October 1916 and then sent it to officials in Great Britain for their ratification. Because communications were slow and the Great War was still raging in Europe, King George V

64   Dorsey, *The Dawn of Conservation*, 208.

65   Ibid., 213.

66   Ibid., 213.

of Great Britain eventually signed the treaty on December 8, 1916. Despite this apparent victory, without enforcement, the treaty alone would do little to stop the wanton killing of birds. Enforcement was a bedeviling problem for Progressive Era reformers.[67] One progressive leader wrote in 1909: "we must not stop with the mere enactment of a law. We must also provide for a means of enforcement."[68]

An additional piece of federal "enabling legislation" that would add teeth to the treaty was needed. The Wilson administration realized this, but instead of putting Senator McLean in charge of the new bill, Wilson wanted a fellow Democrat to get credit. As a result, Wilson selected Democratic Senator Marcus Smith from Arizona to lead the bill through the Senate, and Democratic Congressman Henry Flood of Virginia to do the same in the House.[69]

How did McLean react to this slight? While the choice of Senator Smith over McLean greatly displeased Audubon President T. Gilbert Pearson, McLean, however, understood Wilson's dilemma and told Pearson: "Our opposition in the past has come from Democratic sources, and as my sole object has been to secure able and effective legislation, I am always willing to submerge myself in the interest of the cause."[70] McLean's willingness to take the backseat for the greater good is a testament to his character. One is reminded of the political adage: "There is no limit to the amount of good you can do if you don't care who gets the credit."

Officials in Wilson's Department of Agriculture drafted the enforcement legislation, which included an annual appropriation of $275,000

---

67 Champe S. Andrews, "The Importance of the Enforcement of Law," *The Annals of the American Academy of Political and Social Science* 34, no. 1 (1909): 85–89, accessed March 22, 2021, https://doi.org/10.2307/1011347.

68 Ibid.

69 Dorsey, *The Dawn of Conservation*, 217.

70 McLean to Pearson, December 13, 1916, Box 78, Folder "District of Columbia, I-O," Audubon records; E.W. Nelson Papers, Smithsonian Institution Archives, Washington, DC.

to pay for wardens (nearly $7 million in today's dollars), and six months in prison and/or a fine of $500 to violators (about $10,000 in 2021 dollars).[71] At the same time, the Audubon Society mounted a massive letter-writing and newspaper publicity campaign utilizing a New York City-based public relations firm, Thomas R. Schipp and Company.[72] As a total effort, conservation historian Kurkpatrick Dorsey views the strategy and tactics used to pass the Migratory Bird Treaty Act a pioneering example for future environmental legislation.[73]

Despite McLean's selflessness to let someone else lead the way, he spent more time than any other senator fighting for the bill.[74] For example, after America's entry into the Great War on April 6, 1917, even many conservationists figured that the new treaty enforcement bill would be put on hold. Missouri Senator James Reed expressed this sentiment, telling the Senate on June 27, 1917, that the Senate should focus solely on war measures, and that the shooting of birds out of season hardly seemed like a preparedness issue.[75]

McLean responded to Reed by directly linking bird protection efforts to the war effort, a key plank in the lobbying campaign undertaken by the Audubon Society. McLean called the bird protection bill a food-conservation measure and had statistical evidence to prove it.[76] McLean cited the Audubon Society's estimate that agricultural losses due to insect damage amounted to $800 million annually. "Real preparedness comes first from the soil. Birds are worth millions to our farmers," McLean stated.[77] McLean also read aloud a letter in support of the bill written by Wilson's Secretary of State Robert Lansing.

---

71 Dorsey, *The Dawn of Conservation*, 217.

72 Ibid.

73 Ibid., 236–37.

74 Ibid., 217.

75 James Reed (MO), "Bird Protection Measures," *Congressional Record* 55, June 27, 1917, 4399.

76 George P. McLean (CT), "Bird Protection Measures," *Congressional Record* 55, June 27, 1917, 4400.

77 "How Can We Be Prepared for Conflict," *South Alabamian* (Jackson, AL), March 2, 1917, 5.

Despite Reed's objections, the Migratory Bird Treaty Act passed the Senate on July 30, 1917, by a show of hands; only Reed and three other Senators opposed it.[78] The bill now required passage in the House, where it stalled. Wilson's hand-picked leader, Congressman Henry Flood of Virginia, viewed it as non-essential to the war effort and shelved it. The bill sat dormant in Flood's committee for eight months. On April 30, 1918, McLean complained angrily in a letter to President Wilson about Flood's foot dragging.[79] Wilson subsequently told Secretary of State Lansing that he sympathized with McLean and told Lansing to intervene. A few days later, Congressman Flood received a sharp letter from the State Department.[80] On June 7, 1918, the House passed the treaty enabling act for the protection of migratory birds.[81]

The Migratory Bird Treaty Act had taken McLean and others nearly seven years of negotiating, alliance building, public relations, and tactical skill to overcome resistance from hunters, laissez faire government officials, federal and state judges, and vehement states' rights advocates. All that remained was for President Wilson to sign the bill into law.

At the Migratory Bird Treaty Act bill signing ceremony on July 3, 1918, in the Treaty Room at the White House, President Wilson signed the law using his trademark nibbed, wooden-shafted pen. After signing the bill on the "Treaty Table," a magnificent Victorian desk originally used as a cabinet meeting table by Ulysses S. Grant, Wilson looked up through his round and rimless pince-nez glasses, extended his hand, and presented the signatory pen to Senator George Payne McLean.[82]

Oh, how I wish I had that pen today.

---

78 Dorsey, *The Dawn of Conservation*, 226.

79 Ibid., 227–28.

80 Ibid., 228.

81 "House Passes Treaty Enabling Act," *New York Herald*, June 8, 1918, 10.

82 "Migratory Bird Treaty is Signed," *Edmonton Journal* (Canada), July 27, 1918, 9.

★ CHAPTER NINE ★

WORKING WITH WILSON

President Wilson's "New Freedom"?
Why the Democrats have freed more men from
their jobs than Abraham Lincoln freed slaves by
his Emancipation Proclamation.
George P. McLean, October 23, 1914[1]

President Wilson and Senator McLean may have worked profitably together on migratory bird protection measures, but in no way did this shared accomplishment usher in an era of good feelings between the rival politicians. Eight of McLean's eighteen years in the Senate were spent with the Wilson administration, longer than his time with any other president. While their relationship was at times cordial and cooperative, more often it was contentious and combative.

McLean and other Republican leaders viewed Wilson's 1912 presidential victory as something of a fluke, and were quite confident of unseating him in 1916. As a result, Congressional Republicans were in no mood to help Wilson win reelection by supporting his first-term legislative agenda. Though Wilson had dominated the electoral college vote in 1912, he had received three million fewer popular votes

---

1   "McLean's Keynote Address," *Hartford Daily Courant*, October 24, 1914, 16.

than the combined totals of his three opponents (Taft, Roosevelt, and third-party candidate Eugene Debs).

Republican Party unity was critical, McLean believed, if Republicans expected to recapture the White House in 1916. Within weeks of Wilson's win in 1912, McLean publicly called for party unity, beginning with a new name: the "Progressive Republican Party." It was time to welcome back Roosevelt's "Bull Moosers," and go "two-thirds of the way" with our "progressive friends" on issues important to them, McLean said in a newspaper interview shortly after the 1912 election.[2]

In early 1913, President Wilson began work on his "New Freedom" progressive reform agenda. Conducting himself much like a British prime minister, he appeared before Congress to unveil it. Political cartoonists came to characterize Wilson as a stern schoolmaster, replete with mortarboard and spectacles, ridiculing him for his frequent speeches to Congress, and for keeping Congress in session continuously for almost a year and a half—from April 1913 to October 1914—the longest session to date. There would be no winter break in Georgia for the McLeans in 1913.

Wilson's first legislative priority was to lower tariffs and to institute a national income tax to make up for the lost tariff revenue. McLean, who vehemently opposed tariff reform, became a leading spokesman against the Underwood tariff bill, named after the bill's sponsor, Oscar Underwood, a Democrat from Kentucky.

McLean's opposition to tariff reductions was a clear departure from progressivism. Wilson and other progressives had long argued that tariffs made goods cost more, hurting the working class, and unfairly enriched wealthy business owners.[3] Why was McLean such a staunch advocate of protective tariffs? Essentially, he believed that tariff

---

2 "Senator McLean's Plan," *Rutland Daily Herald,* November 25, 1912, 4. Roosevelt's followers were referred to as "Bull Moosers."

3 Milkis, *Theodore Roosevelt,* 12.

reductions would "throw thousands of workmen in Connecticut out of employment."[4] Connecticut, from its earliest days, had been a hotbed of manufacturing ingenuity and innovation unrivaled by any other state. It boasted of such industrial firsts as the cotton gin, the revolver, the typewriter, the sewing machine, the ice-making machine, the tape measure, the can opener, the pay telephone, even the collapsible toothpaste tube.[5]

William A. Countryman, a Hartford native and statistician with the Census Bureau in Washington, proudly reflected upon the ingenuity and inventiveness of his home state in an article appearing in *Connecticut Magazine* in 1902.[6] So many items of his everyday life were made in Connecticut, he wrote. The Yale key he uses to unlock his Washington, DC boardinghouse, his pocket watch and pocket knife—all made in Connecticut. The pen and typewriter he uses at work, the paper and envelopes, the letterbox for mailing—all made in Connecticut. And the shop windows he views on his walk home are filled with items made in his home state: axes, hammers, augers, hardware, hats, and shoes. The automobile rushing by, it too was made in Connecticut. Even the trousers he puts away at night go onto a hanger of the best kind—made in Connecticut.[7]

---

4   "Republicans Against a Filibuster," *Norwich Bulletin,* May 13, 1913, 1.

5   "Connecticut's Historical Facts," Connecticut's official state website, https://portal.ct.gov/About/Connecticut-Historical-Facts, accessed December 15, 2020.

6   The author of these remarks, William A. Countryman, worked for the Census Bureau in Washington from 1900 to 1922, when he was required to retire at age seventy due to the government's mandatory retirement policy. Not wanting to leave his job, the Hartford-native approached McLean for help, requesting a two-year extension. McLean wrote then-Commerce Secretary Herbert Hoover, asking that an exception be made, citing Countryman's excellent work record. "I wish it were possible to comply with his request," Hoover wrote McLean on June 21, 1922, but an exception could not be granted. See Correspondence from Herbert Hoover to George P. McLean, June 22, 1922, Box 543: Senate – McLean, George P., 1921–1928, Herbert Hoover Papers—Secretary of Commerce Files, Herbert Hoover Presidential Library-Museum, West Branch, Iowa.

7   William A. Countryman, "Connecticut's position in the Manufacturing World," *Connecticut Magazine,* vol. 7 (1902), 323.

McLean's state was also the nation's arsenal. Much of the infrastructure supporting Connecticut's manufacturing sector originated with the making of arms and ammunition for the American Revolutionary War. Connecticut was home to many legendary gun makers—Samuel Colt, John Marlin, Christian Sharps, Richard Gatling, Oliver Winchester, and Daniel Wesson. During the Civil War, Connecticut arms makers supplied 43 percent of all rifle muskets, breech loading rifles, carbines, and revolvers bought by the War Department, along with staggering quantities of ammunition for arms and artillery.[8] After World War I, McLean stated with equal parts hyperbole and pride that Paris would have surrendered to Germany in 1914 "but for munitions made in Connecticut."[9]

The success of Connecticut's munitions industry attracted other types of manufacturing to the state. In 1900, 185,000 or 20 percent of Connecticut's total population was employed in manufacturing in over 9,000 establishments, up from 50,000 employed in 3,700 establishments in 1850, or 14 percent of the total population employed in manufacturing.[10] McLean understood the special value and importance of manufacturing jobs—their high "multiplier effect." For every one manufacturing job, many more jobs are created in other industries to support it.[11]

The idea of cultivating and protecting manufacturing jobs in America originated with Alexander Hamilton. Rather than import manufactured goods from other nations, Hamilton posited, Americans should

---

8   Dean E. Nelson, "Civil War: Connecticut Arms the Union," *Connecticut Explored*, Spring 2011.

9   "Claims Connecticut Saved Surrender of Paris," *Hartford Courant*, July 13, 1922, 14.

10   *U.S. Census of Manufacturing, 1900*, Table 1 Connecticut Comparative Summary, 1850 to 1900, 75, https://www2.census.gov/library/publications/decennial/1900/volume-8/volume-8-p2.pdf, accessed January 3, 2021.

11   Josh Bivens, "Updated employment multipliers for the U.S. economy," Economic Policy Institute, January 23, 2019, https://www.epi.org/publication/updated-employment-multipliers-for-the-u-s-economy/, accessed January 6, 2021.

make their own finished goods, creating jobs and ending their status as a colony dependent upon other nations for vital goods.[12] Manufacturing was doubly important because the nation's tax revenue was based primarily on duties placed upon imported goods—tariffs. This concept too originated from Hamilton. To wipe out the enormous war debts resulting from the Revolutionary War, Hamilton had to come up with the least unpopular way to raise taxes. Tariffs were his answer. Taxes on imported finished goods would not only raise desperately needed revenues, they would also give fledgling American manufacturers a chance to compete.[13] Hence the "protective tariff" was born.

McLean fought unsuccessfully to stop Wilson's Underwood tariff reductions in an impassioned Senate speech on April 9, 1913. Wilson's bill "would help Old England and hurt New England," McLean argued. Tariff reductions would throw Americans out of work and result in lower wages for workers.[14] McLean introduced petitions, letters, and reports into the Senate record representing over 132,000 Connecticut citizens opposed to tariff revisions. One such protest came from H. Backus & Company, which claimed to be the largest fireworks manufacturer in the United States. The owner said he paid his workers $1.50 per day while competitors in China paid just six cents per day. He could not compete without the tariff adjustments.[15] Tariff rates, McLean summarized, equalized the cost of production with other nations, raised wages in America, and created jobs.

McLean's efforts to stop the bill failed, but his protests became a rallying point against Wilson and a source of unity for the Republican Party. Since a national income tax was included in the Underwood tariff bill, McLean's vote against the tariff reductions was also a vote

---

12   Willard S. Randall, *Alexander Hamilton: A Life* (New York: HarperCollins, 2003), 403–5.

13   Randall, *Alexander Hamilton: A Life*, 404.

14   "McLean Comments on New Tariff Bill," *Hartford Daily Courant*, April 10, 1913, 1.

15   "Over 132,000 Wage-Earners Represented by McLean," *Norwich Bulletin*, May 26, 1913, 1.

against the income tax. But it's important to note that, in July 1912, McLean had told a newspaper reporter in July 1912 that he had supported a national income tax "for some time."[16] In December 1913, McLean again stated that he "believes in the principle of the income tax," stressing that he was eager to work with then Treasury Secretary James McAdoo on making it intelligible and fair.[17]

A second major legislative victory for the Wilson administration was passage of the Federal Reserve Act, which was signed into law by President Wilson on December 23, 1913. The need for an effective central banking system had long been recognized in Congress; the issue urgently resurfaced after the Panic of 1907. Periodic financial panics were distressingly common in the United States, but by the twentieth century the consequences of such disruptions were amplified by the increasingly interconnected and industrialized nature of the economy. Wilson's proposal for a new national banking system was based upon recommendations from the "Aldrich Plan" produced by the National Monetary Commission, which had been formed in response to the Panic of 1907.

Rhode Island Republican Senator Nelson Aldrich, a pillar of the Eastern establishment, led a team of experts to study European national banks and craft a central banking system suitable for the US economy. The Aldrich Plan called for one central institution with the power to issue currency, supported by a group of regional branch banks throughout the country. The most contentious issue concerned control of the central bank, with the Aldrich Plan calling for private control and Progressives like William Jennings Bryan favoring government control.[18] The Wilson administration drafted a central banking bill

---

16 "Senator McLean In Favor of Income Tax," *Hartford Daily Courant*, July 27, 1912, 1.

17 "The Protest of Mr. McLean," *Hartford Daily Courant*, December 10, 1913, 8.

18 Roger T. Johnson, "Historical Beginnings of The Federal Reserve," Public and Community Affairs Department, Federal Reserve Bank of Boston, revised, February 2010, 18, https://www.bostonfed.org/-/media/Documents/education/pubs/begin.pdf, accessed October 29, 2020.

that occupied a middle ground between these divergent views. After months of negotiations, a compromise plan emerged: private banks would control the twelve regional Federal Reserve Banks, but a central board governed by presidential appointees would retain controlling interest in the system.[19]

Most of the negotiations leading to the Federal Reserve Act occurred in the Senate Banking and Currency Committee, of which McLean was a member. McLean was "at variance" with the committee, and made an hour-long speech on the Senate floor on December 9, 1913, explaining his position. McLean favored a central bank controlled by the government, but he opposed the proposed system of regional banks, fearing they would be subject to political horse-trading and controlled by "selfish banking interests."[20]

In his Senate speech, McLean first took a swipe at Wilson's recently passed Underwood tariff, contending that tariff rate reductions had put the economy in a precarious position, so now was an "inopportune time to create a new banking and currency system." McLean liked the idea of a central bank, viewing it as a check against bad banking practices and a means to better regulate the swings in economic activity. He called the proposed Federal Reserve the "supreme court of finance," and backed it in principle.[21]

McLean embraced the idea of a central bank but foresaw the potential for political horse-trading and corruption if the system of regional reserve banks were allowed. The decision on locating regional reserve banks was wrought with local and sectional jealousies, he believed. All sorts of political deals would be possible. McLean was prescient in foreseeing horse trading in the establishment of the regional Federal Re-

---

19   Ibid.

20   "McLean's Pleas for a Central Bank," *Hartford Daily Courant*, December 10, 1913, 1.

21   George P. McLean (CT), "Federal Reserve," *Congressional Record* 51 (1913), December 9, 1913, 545, https://www.govinfo.gov/content/pkg/GPO-CRECB-1914-pt1-v51/pdf/GPO-CRECB-1914-pt1-v51-8-1.pdf, accessed January 3, 2021.

serve banks. Recent studies have suggested that political considerations weighed heavily in their selection. To pass the Federal Reserve Act, Wilson needed to persuade reluctant Southern Democrats who balked at the idea of federal dominance over the sovereign rights of states. How did Wilson win their support?

Richmond, the site of one of the regional banks, was located in the state represented by influential Democrat Congressman Carter Glass.[22] Similar deals were made in Texas and Colorado.

Missouri Senator James A. Reed, initially hostile to the idea of a central bank, was a late convert who "broke the deadlock in the Senate Banking Committee, allowing the Federal Reserve Act to pass."[23] Reed, who opposed the migratory bird act for similar states' rights reasons, got something in exchange for the change in his vote: Missouri is the only state with two of the regional Federal Reserve Banks—one in St. Louis, and one in Kansas City.[24]

The political deals made with southern Congressmen to pass the Federal Reserve Act were a sign of things to come. While during his first term President Wilson compiled an impressive domestic legislative record unrivaled at the time, historian Patricia O'Toole concludes that many of these legislative victories were purchased through an "immoral bargain."[25] The expansion of federal power advocated by Wilson was anathema to many Southerners in Congress. In some cases, their loyalty and cooperation on such issues as the Federal Reserve system, women's suffrage, anti-trust laws, and child labor came at a price, namely

---

22   Robert Craig West, *Banking Reform and the Federal Reserve* (Ithaca: Cornell University Press, 1977), 107.

23   Ibid.

24   James Neal Primm, *A Foregone Conclusion: The Founding of the Federal Reserve Bank of St. Louis* (St Louis: Federal Reserve Bank, 1989), https://www.stlouisfed.org/a-foregone-conclusion/chapter-three#thirtynine, accessed August 5, 2020.

25   Patricia O'Toole, *The Moralist: Woodrow Wilson and the World He Made* (New York: Simon & Schuster, 2018), xvi.

Wilson's push to institutionalize segregation of the federal government, including the civil service and many federal departments.[26]

In 1914, President Wilson unveiled two new antitrust bills aimed at strengthening previous legislation and adding more enforcement power to stem monopolistic business practices. Proponents of the new legislation argued that large corporations controlled whole portions of the economy through predatory pricing, exclusive dealings, and anti-competitive mergers that stifled competition. Wilson's two anti-trust measures were the Clayton Act, named after the bill's sponsor, and the Federal Trade Commission Act. Together, these statutes gave the federal government new tools to deal with price discrimination and anti-competitive mergers.

Though the Clayton Act easily passed the Senate, McLean opposed it for both political and philosophical reasons. Still smarting over the tariff rate reductions, McLean argued that the new antitrust measures were untimely and would further erode business confidence and create more unemployment. McLean warned the public that Wilson's continued tinkering with the economy would have grave consequences. In addition to these political jabs, McLean believed that the Clayton Act was not needed. "The men who framed the Sherman Antitrust Act in 1890 turned out a good piece of work," McLean said. It already prohibited "everything that in reason and good conscience is monopolistic." It was the job of the Supreme Court to apply and enforce the Sherman Act, so new antitrust legislation was largely unnecessary.[27]

The McLeans were quite active in the Washington social scene during Wilson's first term, especially after they moved to their permanent home on New Hampshire Avenue in March of 1913. Several times a month, McLean's wife, Juliette, hosted teas, receptions, dinners, and

26   Ibid.
27   "Wilson's Reforms," *Hartford Daily Courant*, January 24, 1914, 8.

bridge parties, and she patronized artistic events, often with Wilson administration officials, including First Lady Ellen Wilson on at least one occasion. On February 19, 1917, they had dinner with Franklin D. Roosevelt, who was then Assistant Secretary of the Navy, and his wife, Eleanor.[28] The McLeans met the Roosevelts at the home of Senator Willard Saulsbury Jr., a Democrat from Delaware, who assembled a group of senators and their wives to meet with Chinese Ambassador Wellington Koo and his wife. Koo was a Columbia University graduate who would serve as president of the Republic of China in 1926. (Tragically, Mrs. Koo would die in 1918 from the Spanish flu.)

The McLeans were close friends with Wilson's vice president, Thomas R. Marshall, and his wife, Lois. The two couples frequently attended diplomatic and political receptions together and hosted each other for dinner. It's interesting to note that Marshall was listed among *Time* magazine's "worst vice presidents of all time" in 2008. A former governor of Indiana, he was chosen vice president by convention delegates, not by Wilson, and he never gained the president's trust or confidence. The neglected vice president was actually a good-natured and gregarious dinner companion. His memorable witticisms include an inscription he wrote in a book he gave to the stoic and businesslike Woodrow Wilson: "From your only vice."[29]

Another high-profile Democrat that McLean grew to know was a Wilson cabinet member, William Jennings Bryan, the three-time presidential nominee who never won the office. Wilson appointed Bryan as his secretary of state in 1913, and McLean worked with Bryan to pass the migratory bird treaty law. In fact, McLean once arranged to host Bryan at his home in Simsbury, though circumstances intervened.

---

28 "Society," *The Washington Herald*, February 20, 1917, 8.

29 "America's Worst Vice Presidents," *Time*, August 21, 2008, https://time.com/4314491/americas-worst-vice-presidents/, accessed December 18, 2020. Others have argued that the quip properly belongs to Frank McKinney Hubbard, a Hoosier humorist, http://www.billhogan.com/1988/01/post-mortem-the-willard-hotel/.

It seems that Bryan worked the lucrative lecture circuit to supplement his meager government salary. Bryan was especially active in the "Chautauqua" lecture series, a highly popular adult-education program in the late nineteenth and early twentieth centuries. The goal of "Chautauqua" was to deliver educational, spiritual, and cultural stimulation to rural and small-town America. Bryan made over 3,000 Chautauqua lectures in his lifetime, including a stop in Simsbury, McLean's hometown. McLean was the leading underwriter of the Simsbury Chautauqua and was set to host and introduce Bryan at his lecture there on Sunday, August 2, 1914. However, Germany's declaration of war on Russia on August 1, 1914, forced Bryan to cancel the engagement. As a result, Bryan was unable to earn his $250 Chautauqua lecture fee (around $6,500 in 2020 dollars). McLean told a newspaper reporter the following day that the "Europeans had deprived Secretary Bryan of his pin money."[30]

The outbreak of war in Europe in the summer of 1914 had major repercussions for McLean and the nation in both the near term and long term. McLean went immediately to work assisting Connecticut residents stranded across the Atlantic, fielding a deluge of inquiries from the press and anxious family members. The rescue efforts were led by McLean's Executive Secretary W . H. "Bill" Sault, who worked with the State Department and US Embassy officials, seeking the whereabouts of dozens of missing persons.[31] McLean's office also arranged money transfers from the Treasury Department to those who needed it.

Examples of citizens they helped include Hartford resident Emma G. Allen, who was on a guided tour of Moscow, Warsaw, Vienna, and Nuremberg from July 25 to August 7, just when the war began; another was Hartford's Carl Morba, a teacher at Hartford Public High

---

30 "The Secretary of State Lost Pin Money Yesterday," *Kansas City Star*, August 3, 1914, 6.

31 "More Names Go to State Department: Senator McLean Looking After Missing Connecticut People," *Hartford Daily Courant*, August 12, 1914, 2.

School, who had been visiting relatives in Thuringia, Germany, since July 27. Miss Allen reported to the *Courant* on August 21 that she was safe and on her way to England. On August 25, McLean got word from a US official in Berlin that Morba was safe and well, his passage home assured.[32] *The Hartford Courant* newspaper joined the effort, which continued well into September.[33]

Up until the outbreak of war in 1914, foreign policy issues had generally played a secondary role in American politics. It's true that Wilson made reluctant military excursions into Mexico and other parts of Latin America to quell political instability and protect American interests, but the new administration sought to stay neutral and avoid entry into international conflicts. The biggest challenge came on May 7, 1915, when a German U-boat torpedoed the British-owned steamship *Lusitania*, killing 1,195 people, including 123 Americans. This incident has been likened to events like the bombing of Pearl Harbor on December 7, 1941, or the attack on the World Trade Center on September 11, 2001, greatly shocking and outraging the American public. While many called for reprisals against Germany, President Wilson took a cautious approach, demanding an apology, compensation, and a pledge from Germany to discontinue submarine warfare.[34]

McLean's response to the *Lusitania* sinking was also restrained. Several weeks after the *Lusitania* sinking, McLean traveled to Hartford to visit his friend, the newly-elected governor, Marcus Holcomb, at the Connecticut State Capitol. At the end of their visit, Holcomb asked McLean to make an impromptu speech to the legislature. During his fifteen-minute address, McLean recalled first coming to the chamber in

32   "Tourists Returning from Trouble Zone," *Hartford Daily Courant*, August 21, 1914, 18.

33   "American Tourists Well Out of Europe," *Hartford Daily Courant*, September 18, 1914, 2.

34   John W. Chambers, *The Eagle and the Dove: The American Peace Movement and United States Foreign Policy, 1900–1922* (Albany: Syracuse University Press, 1991), 59.

1883, in his mid-twenties. He said he thought he knew it all, then—how wrong he was, he now realized.[35]

McLean spoke about his struggles as governor. He felt he had been criticized unfairly, often by unjust, dishonest men. Patience and forbearance were needed to survive in the realm of politics, he had learned. McLean turned to the war in Europe, saying these were trying and strange times, stressing the importance of people now staying cool and avoiding rash responses.[36] McLean concluded his remarks by expressing gratitude for what the people of Connecticut had done for him. The current governor, his good friend Marcus Holcomb, is the best the state has had since 1901, McLean quipped. McLean encouraged the new governor to consult with the people often to learn what they want. That type of communication will lessen the need to veto bills. He had never used the veto as governor, he added with pride.

Meanwhile, Theodore Roosevelt, no longer a Republican but the head of his breakaway Progressive Party, was not so cool-headed about the *Lusitania* sinking. He wanted an immediate military reprisal and a declaration of war against Germany. In June of 1915, Roosevelt wrote to an acquaintance, criticizing Wilson's handling of the incident, likening it to Lincoln ignoring the firing on Fort Sumter, the flash point of the American Civil War.[37] Roosevelt came to despise Wilson, privately calling him a "very adroit and able (but not forceful) hypocrite,"[38] and planned another run for the presidency in 1916. Would he run as a "Bull Moose" Progressive or return, hat in hand, to the Republican Party?

---

35   "The Legislature Adjourns . . .[McLean] In the House," *Meriden* (CT) *Daily Journal,* May 18, 1915, 1.

36   Ibid.

37   Theodore Roosevelt to Oscar King Davis, June 23, 1915, GLC08003, Gilder Lehrman Collection, https://www.gilderlehrman.org/sites/default/files/inline-pdfs/t-08003.pdf, accessed March 1, 2021.

38   Lewis L. Gould, *Grand Old Party: A History of the Republicans* (New York: Oxford University Press, 2015), 207.

In the months leading up to the 1916 US presidential election, several newspapers suggested that McLean run for the presidency. In January 1915, *The Bridgeport Post* wrote that he would make an admirable president. The editorial praised McLean's keen grasp of the great issues and balanced views. "He can honestly be classed as conservatively progressive. He would move forward, but do it slowly."[39] That same month, Connecticut's other US senator, Frank Brandegee, told the *Hartford Courant* that he was enthusiastic over McLean's prospects for the 1916 Republican presidential nomination.[40]

The McLean for President idea got exposure in other parts of the country, too. In an opinion piece entitled "Senator McLean for President" on August 15, 1915, in Kansas City's *Topeka Daily Capital,* Arthur Capper, the governor of Kansas, praised McLean for his shrewd sense, honesty, independence, and courage. Acknowledging McLean's immense wealth, Kapper said there are no strings on McLean. He acts with independence, and is not attached to corporate interests. Viewing McLean as essentially conservative, the Kansas governor applauded McLean's remarkably progressive record since he entered the Senate. McLean was nothing like former Connecticut Senator Morgan Bulkeley, whom Capper called an "extreme tool of big business."[41]

The Topeka Capital opinion piece boosting McLean was reprinted in other newspapers in the country, including the *Waterbury Republican,* which added a local perspective. They commented that since McLean acted with humility and little flourish, people in New England had taken him for granted and needed an expression from outside the state to help them appreciate the man. In Vermont, *The Burlington Free Press* wrote that McLean would be the kind of compromise candidate that

---

39   "Fine But No Chance," *Hartford Courant*, January 4, 1915, 8.

40   "Boom: McLean for President," *Hartford Courant*, January 1, 1915, 19.

41   "Senator McLean for President," *Record-Journal* (Meriden, CT), August 16, 1915, 6.

could strongly reunite both wings of the party.[42] A friend sent McLean a clipping of the flattering editorial. McLean replied that such calls for his running for president were "a little nonsense."[43]

McLean likely had no interest in the presidency. He knew firsthand the differences between executive and legislative leadership; the Senate was a better fit for him intellectually and temperamentally. About this time, rumors appeared that McLean would not run for a second Senate term in 1916. A series of national press reports claimed that ex-President William Howard Taft, now a Yale Law School professor living in New Haven, would replace McLean in the Senate in 1916.[44]

Rumors aside, McLean ran for reelection to the Senate in 1916. He had the solid backing of Connecticut's Republican Party Chairman J. Henry Roraback, the "political general," who helped McLean win the governor's race in 1901 and his first Senate race in 1911. This time Connecticut would choose its senator by direct election of the voters, not a vote of the Connecticut State Legislature as it did in years past. To secure reelection to the Senate in 1916, McLean needed to unite the Taft wing (the conservatives) and the Roosevelt wing (the progressives) in the Republican Party.

McLean's opponent for the 1916 US Senate race was Democrat Homer S. Cummings, thirteen years younger than McLean, who was now fifty-nine. A Yale Law School graduate active in Democratic committee politics, Cummings lost to McLean in the 1911 Senate race by a party-line vote in the Connecticut legislature. Cummings, still young, would go on to a colorful career in national politics and leave his mark on the nation's history.

Later in life, Cummings would attain his highest office as attorney general in Franklin D. Roosevelt's administration. As the nation's at-

---

42   "The Republican Situation," *The Burlington* (VT) *Free Press,* August 20, 1915, 4

43   "Senator McLean and a Little Nonsense," *Hartford Courant,* January 12, 1915, 6.

44   "Taft May Run for Senate," *New York Tribune,* August 19, 1916, 5.

torney general, he would announce the capture of Bruno Hauptmann in the kidnapping and murder of the Lindbergh baby.[45] He would also be credited with conceptualizing and building the Alcatraz prison, and he would be instrumental in Roosevelt's disastrous attempt to pack the Supreme Court. And during the 1924 Democratic presidential convention, Cummings would try unsuccessfully to mediate a dispute between the Ku Klux Klan and anti-Klan factions in the writing of the party platform. After a raucous debate, the proposed plank condemning the Ku Klux Klan would be defeated by a narrow margin.[46]

The climax of the race between McLean and Cummings was a debate before an audience of 4,000 people at the Waterbury Auditorium on November 1, 1916. Hundreds had been turned away from the eagerly awaited event. Cummings began by launching attacks against McLean for opposing Wilson's domestic reforms, and criticized the "impatient and bloodthirsty" Republican politicians who wanted Wilson to take the nation to war in Europe. McLean's resistance to tariff reform, Cummings alleged, was motivated out of concern for special interests, not helping American workers, as McLean claimed.[47]

McLean countered by condemning the Wilson administration's utter failure to provide for the impregnable defense of our borders and to ensure national peace and prosperity. He especially blamed Democrats for their opposition to military preparedness, then documented how far behind the American Navy and other service branches were compared

---

45 Ken Armstrong, "The Suspect, the Prosecutor, and the Unlikely Bond They Forged," *Smithsonian Magazine*, January 2017, https://www.smithsonianmag.com/history/charming-story-homer-cummings-harold-israel-180961429/, accessed February 2, 2021.

46 Matthew Wills, "A Really Contested Convention: The 1924 Democratic 'Klanbake,'" *JSTOR Daily*, May 11, 2016, https://daily.jstor.org/contested-convention/, retrieved March 2, 2021.

47 "Joint Debate at Waterbury," *Hartford Daily Courant*, November 1, 1916, 10.

with leading nations of the world. McLean then detailed Wilson's "yard-wide incompetence and assumed infallibility" in foreign policy.[48]

McLean defended his votes against Wilson's domestic legislation, saying that most of Wilson's reforms had originated in the Republican party, including the income tax and central bank, both of which he supported in concept. McLean said the Federal Reserve Act was better than the old system, but the act benefited immensely from the "300 amendments" he and other Republicans had crafted. Cummings interrupted McLean: "Didn't Democrats make some of those amendments?" McLean scoffed: "I have no time to chase mice through dark cellars."[49]

About the tariff bill, McLean said he was only looking out for the interests of the working man, and predicted a drop in jobs as a result of the tariff rate decreases. Cummings charged that McLean ducked voting on Wilson's child labor reform bill when it passed the Senate. McLean said Cummings was deceiving the voters with that claim. McLean said he took particular pains to ensure that the child labor vote would pass by a very large majority before making the "pairing" arrangement with Senator Henry Myers of Montana. (Such "vote pairing" practices were common in the Senate, given transportation challenges of the time.) McLean said his absence from voting was due to a family illness, an excuse Cummings later ridiculed.[50]

McLean won reelection by just 8,000 votes, garnering fifty percent of the total to Cummings' forty-six percent. (Third-party candidates made up the other four percent, namely 2.5 percent for Socialist Martin Plunkett).[51] McLean matched Cummings in Connecticut's two largest urban counties, Hartford and New Haven; McLean's winning

---

48   Ibid, 19.

49   Ibid.

50   Ibid.

51   "1916 CT US Senate Race," OurCampaigns, https://www.ourcampaigns.com/RaceDetail. html?RaceID=267949, accessed March 1, 2021.

margins came mostly from Connecticut's smaller, more rural counties. But McLean also performed well in the city of Bridgeport in Fairfield County. J. Henry Roraback, State Chairman of the Republican State Committee, played an important role in helping McLean win Bridgeport.[52] Roraback later stated that McLean's vote tally in Bridgeport was the key to his 1916 Senate win.[53]

Days after the election, Cummings charged that "something was wrong" with the unusually high vote for McLean in Bridgeport.[54] US Attorney Thomas J. Spellacy, a future political foe of McLean, led the investigation, which included opening and inspecting several voting machines used in the election. Nothing was substantiated to prove Cummings' theory about voting irregularities in Bridgeport.[55]

It is likely that McLean's stance on the protective tariff appealed to many of Bridgeport's manufacturers and workers.[56] The war in Europe had created a boom in arms and ordinance production in Bridgeport, helping companies like the Union Metallic Cartridge Company (cartridge ammunition for small arms), Lake Torpedo (submarines), the American British Manufacturing Company (rapid-fire guns), the Bridgeport Projectile Company (artillery shells), American Fabrics Company (army blankets), Sikorsky (aircrafts), and Remington Arms (rifles, pistols).[57]

The 1916 presidential election was close in Connecticut and nationally. Connecticut voted for Republican Charles Evans Hughes over President Wilson, fifty percent to forty-six percent, matching McLean's

---

52   "Connecticut During the 1930s," Yale-New Haven Teachers Institute, https://teachersinstitute. yale.edu/curriculum/units/1981/cthistory/81.ch.09/2, accessed February 12, 2021.

53   Roraback to McLean, October 2, 1922, Connecticut Governor records (RG005) Series 4. Correspondence, 1811–1933; Incoming Letters, 1811–1933, Connecticut State Library.

54   "Bridgeport Voting Machines Opened," *Hartford Daily Courant*, November 16, 1916, 17.

55   Ibid.

56   "War Brings Business," *Hartford Courant*, November 29, 1914, 36.

57   "Bridgeport Working: Voices From the 20th Century," Bridgeport Library website, retrieved December 4, 2020, https://www.bridgeporthistory.org/News.aspx.

1916 McLean for Senate campaign pin (source: from the collection of Dr. Kenneth Florey)

margin over Cummings.[58] Wilson's opponent was not the firebrand Republican Theodore Roosevelt, who had stepped aside in favor of the more moderate Republican, Charles Evans Hughes, a former progressive governor of New York, who had brought considerably less political baggage to the contest than Roosevelt.

Hughes almost united the conservative and progressive Republican wings that had been so fractured in 1912. In fact, Hughes went to bed on election night believing that he had won the presidency after the *New York Times* announced that he was the winner, although returns from California were incomplete. Calling Hughes early the next morning, a reporter was told, "The President is asleep." The reporter responded, "When he wakes up, tell him he isn't the president."[59] Hughes had lost California by just 4,000 votes, tipping the election to

---

58   "1916 Presidential General Election Results – Connecticut," Dave Leip's Atlas of U.S. Elections, https://uselectionatlas.org/RESULTS/state. php?year=1916&fips=9&f=1&off=0&elect=0, accessed November 11, 2020.

59   Bruce J. Evensen, *Journalism and the American Experience* (New York: Routledge, 2018), 172.

Wilson. Republicans were first shocked, then angered by the results.[60] Bitterness set in after the election, as many disappointed Republicans deepened their animosity toward Wilson.

On January 31, 1917, just two months after the election, Germany declared its intention to restart unrestricted submarine warfare in the Atlantic. In response, President Wilson severed diplomatic relations with Germany, but left open the possibility of further negotiations. However, throughout February and March of 1917, German submarines targeted and sunk several US ships, killing many Americans. Then, in March of 1917, the American government intercepted several telegrams between the German and Mexican governments showing that Germany had approached Mexico about forming a military alliance. After years of avoiding war in Europe, circumstances had finally forced Wilson's hand. The so-called "Zimmermann Telegrams" were the last straw. Along with Germany's policy of renewing unrestricted submarine warfare, the threatening diplomatic communiqués convinced the Wilson administration that it had to enter the war in Europe.[61]

Events in Washington during the first week of April 1917 are among the most dramatic ever chronicled. On April 2, 1917, for only the fourth time in US history, the president appeared before Congress and called for a declaration of war. With war casualties in Europe exceeding one million each year since 1914, the seriousness of the moment was surely not lost on members of Congress. Wilson arrived ten minutes early at the Capitol for his 8:30 p.m. speech in a limousine surrounded by Secret Service agents, a motorcycle escort, and two mounted cav-

---

60   James A. Henretta, "Charles Evans Hughes and the Strange Death of Liberal America," *Law and History Review* 24, no. 1 (2006): 115–71, accessed March 24, 2021, http://www.jstor.org/stable/27641353.

61   Puong Fei Yeh, "The Role of the Zimmermann Telegram in Spurring America's Entry into the First World War," *American Intelligence Journal* 32, no. 1 (2015): 61–64, accessed March 24, 2021, http://www.jstor.org/stable/26202105.

alry regiments with "sabers glittering in the arc lights."[62] Hundreds of police, both uniformed and plain clothes, blanketed the area. The Capitol dome, shrouded in a misty rain, was illuminated by powerful electric floodlights.[63]

Inside, members of the House were already seated, and minutes before the president entered the House chamber, the Senators, en masse, strode to their seats, each of them carrying a small, silk American flag mounted on a handheld staff. The flags, made in Manchester, Connecticut, by Cheney Brothers (who owned the silk mills there), had been presented to each senator by George McLean. When the President entered amid deafening cheers, members of both sides of the chamber stood and applauded; a few senators waved their miniature American flags.[64]

Two days later, the Senate voted to declare war on Germany 82–6 (eight senators did not vote). McLean voted "aye." The House voted 373–50 for the declaration. Those congressional majorities favoring war belied the significant opposition to American military action. This anti-war movement, though small, was made up of pacifists, religious groups, socialists, internationalists, intellectuals, women's suffrage groups, peace activists, some immigrants and labor unions, and prominent industrialists like Henry Ford and Andrew Carnegie.

The strength of the anti-war dissent and protests eventually led the Wilson administration to push for controversial legislation which restricted free speech and protests during wartime.[65] The Espionage Act passed 77–6 in the Senate on May 14, 1917, and the Sedition Act

---

62 "Congress Cheers U.S. Call to Arms," *Evening Star* (Washington, DC), April 3, 1917, 12.

63 Ibid.

64 "Congress Cheers U.S. Call to Arms," *Evening Star* (Washington, DC), April 3, 1917, 12

65 "Sedition Act of 1918," Encyclopedia.com, https://www.encyclopedia.com/politics/legal-and-political-magazines/sedition-act-1918, accessed March 20, 2021.

passed 48–26 on May 4, 1918;[66] McLean voted in favor of both, but he never spoke publicly about the issue in the newspapers or on the floor of the Senate. More than two thousand Americans would be arrested for sedition, including Socialist Party leader Eugene Debs after making an anti-war speech. Debs was subsequently convicted and sentenced to ten years in prison.[67]

Congress also voted for a military draft, and by war's end, nearly five million Americans would serve in the military. Wartime industrial production needs increased dramatically, boosting employment, and leaving openings in the workforce filled largely by women. In short order, women took on a variety of jobs traditionally held by men. To supporters of women's suffrage, these developments proved beyond a doubt that women deserved the right to vote.

With pressure mounting for women's suffrage, on February 10, 1919, Congress voted on the Nineteenth Amendment, establishing that citizens of the United States shall not be denied the right to vote by any State on account of sex. After passing the House, the Senate voted on the amendment. If it passed the Senate by two-thirds majority, it would then be subject to ratification by three-fourths of the states. While the resolution passed 55–29, it failed to meet the necessary two-thirds majority—by just one vote. George P. McLean had voted "no."[68]

Why was McLean among the "last men standing" against granting women the right to vote? He was not insulated from or ignorant

---

66 TO PASS H.R. 291, May 14, 1917, GovTrack.us, https://www.govtrack.us/congress/votes/65-1/s50; TO AGREE TO H.R. 8753, May 4, 1918, GovTrack.us, https://www.govtrack.us/congress/votes/65-2/s247, accessed March 12, 2021.

67 Eddith A. Dashiell, "Espionage and Sedition Acts of 1917–1918," https://immigrationtounitedstates.org/482-espionage-and-sedition-acts-of-1917-1918.html, accessed May 22, 2020.

68 "Woman Suffrage Fails in Senate; One Vote Lacking," *Hartford Courant*, February 11, 1919, 16.

about the issues surrounding women's suffrage. He knew many people who supported the cause. For example, his two sisters were both suffragists. Hannah McLean (Greeley) helped found the Lexington Equal Suffrage Association in Massachusetts on November 6, 1900, serving as vice president and corresponding secretary.[69]

McLean's wife, Juliette, however, was an anti-suffragist. In fact, many of the most ardent opponents of extending the vote to women were women. On December 13, 1915, in Washington, DC, Juliette hosted a reception for delegates to the convention of the National Association Opposed to Woman Suffrage (NAOWS). Earlier, in 1910, Juliette was active in the Connecticut Association Opposed to Woman Suffrage.[70] Corrine McConnaughy, a scholar at Princeton University concludes that female leaders of the US anti-suffrage campaign were generally women of wealth and privilege.[71] Anti-suffrage groups opposed giving women the right to vote because they believed that many women did not want to vote, and that their husbands adequately represented their political views. They warned that women's suffrage would create competition, not cooperation, between the sexes, blurring the roles of men and women, ultimately destroying families. And since political matters sometimes included decisions of war, they believed women should naturally be excluded from voting.

While McLean embraced many aspects of modernity, such as industrialization, urbanization, owning and driving automobiles, spending increased leisure time on travel and golf, there were other ways in which he remained rooted in traditional nineteenth-century values.

69   Emily A. Murphy, "Something Must Be Done: Bold Women of Lexington," white paper #3 for Lexington Historical Society exhibit, https://www.lexingtonhistory.org/uploads/6/5/2/1/6521332/3wp_voteswomen.pdf, accessed March 12, 2020.

70   Carole Nichols, *Votes and More for Women: Suffrage and After in Connecticut* (New York: Haworth Press, 1983), 15.

71   "American Women Who Were Anti-Suffragettes," National Public Radio History Dept., October 22, 2015, https://www.npr.org/sections/npr-history-dept/2015/10/22/450221328/american-women-who-were-anti-suffragettes, accessed March 14, 2020.

He adhered to the notion that men and women inhabited "separate spheres." Women occupied the private sphere, he believed, which included family life and the home. Men operated in the public sphere, in politics and matters of business and wealth creation. The line sometimes blurred—women could and did lead many civic causes like the Red Cross and church and philanthropic organizations. But generally their domain was the home and family.

This idea of separate spheres seems to have hardened as a result of industrialization during the nineteenth century. When most people spent life on the farm, men and women often worked side-by-side, but industrialization made gender roles more rigid. To adapt to the social and economic upheaval brought about by industrialization, these demarcated roles brought stability and comfort in a time of change and upheaval to those who held these views.[72]

Juliette and George McLean, like many wealthy and upper-class people, were content with their respective roles, and they viewed any change in roles as disruptive and threatening.[73] As historian Vanessa Beasley writes, although some states had granted women the vote in national elections long before 1920, "most American women did not want the vote, and most American men liked it that way."[74]

McLean was never an outspoken opponent of women's suffrage. He once stated that the right to vote was a "solemn obligation to be wisely and faithfully performed," a sober responsibility that most women did not desire.[75] On another occasion, he stated that voting rights were a matter best left to the states. Like many other states in America, Con-

---

72 Barbara Easton, "Industrialization and Femininity: A Case Study of Nineteenth Century New England," *Social Problems* 23, no. 4 (1976): 389–401, accessed March 24, 2021, https://doi.org/10.2307/799850.

73 Joe C. Miller, "Never A Fight of Woman Against Man: What Textbooks Don't Say about Women's Suffrage," *The History Teacher* 48, no. 3 (May 2015): 437–82.

74 Vanessa B. Beasley, "Engendering Democratic Change: How Three U.S. Presidents Discussed Female Suffrage," *Rhetoric and Public Affairs* 5, no. 1 (Spring 2002): 84.

75 "McLean's Wise Words," *Hartford Daily Courant*, June 15, 1919, 10.

necticut was split on the issue of women's suffrage, and it was one of the last states to ratify the Nineteenth Amendment, on September 14, 1920. (The amendment had taken effect when it was ratified by the required three-fourths of the states—36 of the 48 states—on August 18, 1920.)

McLean had several public encounters with the proponents of women's suffrage. Some suffragists thought they had a chance of turning McLean to their side, since he had been open and courteous while other senators who voted "no" were dogmatic and disrespectful in their opposition. On May 1, 1918, a group of fifty Connecticut suffragists visited their two US Senators at their offices in Washington, DC. The visit, organized by the Connecticut Woman Suffrage Association, and preceded by much national press coverage, was aimed at persuading both Brandegee and McLean to support the Nineteenth Amendment the next time it came up for a vote in the Senate. Brandegee, whom McLean said in his eulogy loved the word "no," told the group of women that he fully intended to vote against the measure and that it was useless to waste their time on him. He also acerbically noted that their heckling of him did more harm than good. For his part, McLean did not give them any encouragement, but said he was watching with interest suffrage experiments in states like New York, which had adopted women's suffrage in 1917.[76]

McLean had an even more personal experience with a suffragist on January 8, 1919, when Connecticut native Josephine Bennett and other suffragists ignited a "Watch Fire" in front of the White House. Bennett addressed a large crowd as she burned a speech that President Wilson had recently delivered honoring Christopher Columbus. Dropping pages of Wilson's speech into a bonfire, Bennett asked her listeners: How could Wilson praise Columbus for discovering a land

---

76   "'Suffs' Get No Encouragement on Washington Trip," *Hartford Daily Courant,* May 2, 1918, 10.

of freedom when twenty million of her citizens are still denied the right to vote? How could Wilson fight for the freedom of Europeans but ignore it in America?[77]

The police arrested Bennett and took her in a patrol wagon to jail. Convicted of illegally starting a fire in front of the White House, Bennett was sentenced to pay a five-dollar fine or spend five days in jail. She chose jail, and immediately began a five-day hunger strike. On the second morning of her stay, Senator McLean arrived to visit her. "I suppose you will say I'm entirely to blame for this," he remarked with a slight smile. She promptly agreed with him, saying his vote would likely make the difference in passing the amendment. She then called his attention to the filthy, unsanitary conditions of her cell, the open sewage, the way rats had run over her bed in the night, and a prostitute who occupied the neighboring cell.

"You must leave this place at once," McLean replied, offering to pay her fine. "You owe too much to your family and to your friends, to endanger your life in this place." Bennett invited him to stay in the jail for a night so that he would "realize the intensity of our demand which enables us to endure such hardships." McLean was "very distressed on leaving," she later said, "and appeared much shocked by the conditions at the jail."[78]

Another controversial issue that engulfed Wilson's second term was passage of the Eighteenth Amendment, prohibiting the manufacture and sale of alcoholic beverages. Prohibition was decades in the making, and its ultimate passage and enforcement took years of political maneuvering before it was ratified by the requisite number of states on January 16, 1919. The prohibition of alcohol was a quintessential

77 Mark Jones and Nancy O. Albert, "Women's Suffrage: Setting the Watch Fires of Liberty," *Connecticut Explored*, Fall 2005, https://www.ctexplored.org/womens-suffrage-setting-the-watch-fires-of-liberty/, accessed December 4, 2020.

78 "Rats Ran Across Her Bed In Jail, Says Mrs. Bennett," *Hartford Daily Courant*, January 16, 1919, 8.

Josephine Bennett, Suffragist
(source: Connecticut State Library)

Progressive Era accomplishment. It is a clear example of reformers successfully imposing their middle-class Victorian values upon others who needed moral improvement.[79] McLean, however, was not a supporter of this reform effort.

McLean voted against the Eighteenth Amendment and the subsequent acts to enforce it throughout his Senate career. "It is a seventeenth century throwback," McLean stated, "impossible of enforcement and unsound in principle."[80] His stance on the doomed reform measure is further evidence of his independence of thought and his capacity to avoid partisan, lockstep voting to suit party leaders. Many of his conservative Republican peers realized prohibition was popular with voters, and that was enough to justify their support. But although Prohibition was aimed at improving morality, its subsequent failure

---

79   McGerr, *A Fierce Discontent*, 81–88.

80   "Senator McLean on Prohibition," *Hartford Daily Courant*, June 8, 1931, 10.

and unpopularity sowed increased dissatisfaction with the reform impulse itself that had been active for so many decades in government.[81]

The defining issue of Wilson's second term, perhaps of his whole life, was the fight to create the League of Nations, the first global, intergovernmental organization to maintain world peace. Technically, the League was part of the Treaty of Versailles that ended World War I, negotiated by Wilson and other world leaders in Paris from January through June 1919. Since it was a treaty, the US Constitution provides that the Senate must concur with the president, providing advice and consent through a two-thirds majority vote.

President Wilson hand-delivered the 264-page treaty to the Senate on July 10, 1919, and then addressed the chamber. For the next two months, the Senate's Foreign Relations Committee, headed by Henry Cabot Lodge, a Republican from Massachusetts, held hearings and ultimately modified the treaty by including fourteen "reservations" relating to the proposed treaty's influence over US decision-making and autonomy.

The primary objection to the treaty concerned "Article 10," which required member nations to work together—even supply troops—to keep the peace. Senator Lodge and other "Reservationists" believed that the decision to go to war was derived solely from the US Constitution, which grants Congress the power to declare war.[82] As a compromise, the Reservationists demanded that Article 10 be changed to read, "The United States assumes no obligation to preserve the territorial integrity or political independence of any other country unless Congress shall so provide."[83]

---

81   S.J. Mennell, "Prohibition: A Sociological View," *Journal of American Studies* 3, no. 2 (1969): 173–75, accessed March 24, 2021, http://www.jstor.org/stable/27552891.

82   Article I, Section 8, Clause 11, US Constitution.

83   William G. Ross, "Constitutional Issues Involving the Controversy Over American Membership in the League of Nations, 1918–1920," *The American Journal of Legal History* 53, no. 1 (2013): 29–30, accessed February 27, 2021, http://www.jstor.org/stable/23416464.

McLean numbered among the "Reservationists." Wilson viewed him as one of a handful of swing voters, and he invited McLean to the Oval Office for a private one-hour meeting on July 23, 1919. Waiting outside the White House, a group of reporters interviewed McLean after their 2:15 p.m. meeting concluded. McLean said he told the president that "we want to save all of [the Treaty] that can be saved," and urged Wilson to broker a compromise on Article 10, the provision that compelled League member nations to take collective military action.[84]

The president responded that he would not attempt any such compromise. While the major European nations might be willing to modify Article 10, the president explained, some of the smaller League nations would undoubtedly oppose any changes guaranteeing collective military security. Wilson said that if the United States urged changes to Article 10, that might be interpreted that the United States was only half-hearted in its engagement in the peace pact. McLean suggested that the president take up the matter with the Senate Foreign Relations Committee. Wilson said he would do no such thing.[85]

McLean's nephew, William Roger Greeley, recalled discussing the League with his uncle that summer (1919). Greeley, a strong supporter of the League, was disappointed in his uncle's opposition, and along with his brother Hugh, both in their thirties, tried to persuade McLean to vote for Wilson's version of the treaty. He and his brother had fortified themselves with arguments favoring the League, but after an evening's discussion with their uncle George, the pair retreated, completely overwhelmed by his counter arguments.[86]

McLean made a last-ditch effort on behalf of the treaty (with the "Lodge Reservations") on the Senate floor on March 2, 1920. Quot-

---

84 "McLean Suggests League Changes to President Wilson," *Hartford Daily Courant*, July 24, 1919, 1.

85 "Wilson Won't Allow Change in Peace Pact," *Green Bay Press-Gazette*, July 24, 1919, 2.

86 William Roger Greeley, "A Letter to Hugh Payne Greeley from His Brother" (unpublished manuscript, 1961).

ing Edmund Burke (1729–1797), the great Anglo-Irish statesman and philosopher, McLean said all governments are founded on compromise, and such an approach ought to be welcomed at this historic moment. While it was a constitutional necessity to keep the war-making power in the US Congress, the Senate should not abandon the League, which he called an "experiment for the promotion of international peace." While calling for compromise, McLean did not shy away from blaming Wilson for the months of fruitless debate on the treaty. An "adjusted agreement" could have been achieved months ago, blocked only by the "uncompromising spirit of a single individual."[87]

The Lodge Reservations were authored by Senator Henry Cabot Lodge, the Republican leader in the Senate. The two men had a close working relationship. McLean's nephew, Hugh Payne Greeley, wrote that he remembered Uncle George saying that Lodge "was the only gentleman in the Senate and the only one of his confreres with table manners."[88] Lodge and Wilson, however, both stubborn men, loathed each other, which eventually turned into freezing hatred. In fact, it was hard to imagine reconciling the three blocs that emerged.

The "Reservationists" numbered around twenty-five senators, including Lodge and McLean.

Another voting bloc of around forty-five Senators, the "Internationalists," mostly loyal Democrats, backed Wilson's version of the League.

That left a third group, the so-called "Irreconcilables," approximately fourteen bitter treaty opponents from both parties. One of the most outspoken of the Irreconcilables was Senator James A. Reed, the

---

87   George P. McLean (CT), *Congressional Record* 59 (1920), March 2, 1920, 3734, https://www.govinfo.gov/content/pkg/GPO-CRECB-1920-pt4-v59/pdf/GPO-CRECB-1920-pt4-v59-10-1.pdf, accessed March 4, 2020.

88   Hugh Payne Greeley, "Reminiscences" (unpublished, ~1970), author's collection.

Missouri Democrat who was McLean's opponent on the bird treaty. Wilson hated Reed with a passion second only to Lodge.[89]

Unwilling to compromise on the treaty, Wilson decided to embark on a grueling public speaking tour during the fall of 1919 to win the support of the American people. The exhausting trip led to a massive stroke on October 2, 1919, that nearly killed Wilson. When the League of Nations treaty (with the Lodge Reservations) came up for a vote on November 19, 1919, the Senate passed the treaty 55–39, with McLean voting in the affirmative. But that meant it still fell short of the votes needed for the required two-thirds majority.

Undeterred, Wilson called for another vote in early 1920. On March 19, 1920, the Senate rejected the League of Nations for the second and final time, falling seven votes short of the needed two-thirds majority. McLean voted "Yea," for the treaty (with the Lodge reservations). As the *New York Times* reported on March 20, "the treaty was now dead."

Some historians like to play a parlor game listing the worst years in history.[90] On many of those lists is the year 1919. The year leading up to the presidential election of 1920 delivered a toxic mixture of world war, a pandemic, race riots, violent labor strikes, and rising unemployment. It is believed that one-third of the world's population became infected with the Spanish flu virus in 1919; about 50 million died worldwide with 675,000 flu deaths in the United States.[91] After the war ended in November 1918, many of the nation's five million war-weary veterans could not find jobs. Fears of the spread of communism after the Russian Revolution led Wilson's Attorney General Mitchell Palmer to undertake a series of law-enforcement raids directed

---

89 Michael Cronan, *James A. Reed: Legendary Lawyer; Marplot in the United States Senate* (Bloomington, IN: iUniverse Books, 2018), 91, 1413.

90 Staff of *The Atlantic*, "What Was the Worst Year in History?" *The Atlantic*, December 2013, https://www.theatlantic.com/magazine/archive/2013/12/what-was-the-worst-year-in-history/354687/, accessed March 1, 2021.

91 Laura Spinney, *Pale Rider: The Spanish Flu of 1918 and How It Changed the World* (New York: PublicAffairs, 2018), 2.

at leftist radicals and anarchists in 1919 and 1920. Even the national pastime, baseball, was tainted when players on the Chicago White Sox threw the World Series—the 1919 Black Sox scandal.

As the decade closed, Americans seemed unmoored from traditional values, institutions, organizations, and cultural norms. Progressivism and its perpetual search for reform and perfection seemed irrelevant and outdated. Weary of war, disease, strikes, and economic hardship, the nation looked for new political leadership, deeply disenchanted with Woodrow Wilson. Who would lead the country out of arguably the "worst ever" year of 1919? And in what direction?

★ CHAPTER TEN ★

THE GOOD SHIP *NORMALCY*

I am profoundly conscious of the great honor
you have conferred upon me. My platform,
in the future, as in the past, will be:
"Connecticut first and a fair deal for all."
*George P. McLean, accepting the nomination for
a third term in the US Senate, September 13, 1922[1]*

Nearly every US president since Benjamin Harrison has attended the annual Gridiron Club dinner, sponsored by the oldest journalism fraternity in the nation's capital. The white-tie affair is a gathering of news reporters and Washington's political elite, featuring skits lampooning current events, quips and self-deprecating humor by representatives of each political party, culminating in an off-the-record speech by the president of the United States.

The Gridiron Club was founded in 1885 when a group of newspaper reporters gathered over dinner to discuss restrictions to the press gallery proposed by some hostile congressmen. They met to talk the matter over, but instead of serious deliberations, the journalists descended into wit and revelry. A participant suggested that they repeat the affair and invite congressmen and other politicians, and engage in some

---

1   "McLean's Wires Acceptance," *Hartford Daily Courant*, September 14, 1922, 1.

good-natured "roasting on the griddle," hence the club name "Gridiron."[2] The tradition lives on. At the 2015 Gridiron dinner, then President Obama made headlines when he poked fun at the people accusing him of "not loving" America. Obama quipped: "Of course I love America. If I didn't, I wouldn't have moved from Kenya."[3]

On December 9, 1921, the Gridiron Club dinner was held at the grand ballroom of Washington's new Willard Hotel, an exquisite setting with its buttercup yellow, pale blue, and soft green hues, large beveled wall mirrors, six crystal chandeliers suspended from a high-arched ceiling, parquet floor, and a beautifully hand-painted mural. George P. McLean attended the dinner along with 350 other invited guests, including his friend, the newly-installed Vice-President Calvin Coolidge; President Warren G. Harding and his cabinet; the recently-appointed Chief Justice of the United States, William Howard Taft; select members of Congress; foreign embassy dignitaries; and a large contingent of Washington newspaper correspondents.

Harding had been president for about ten months, the GOP having retaken the White House after an eight-year hiatus. December 9, 1921, was a good time to be a Republican, and the evening's festivities reflected their celebratory mood. Hip flasks may have been in evidence that evening as the nation's new Prohibition law barred the hotel from serving alcohol. A new word had entered the American lexicon—the "hipster"—perhaps coined by a writer from the *New York Tribune* in describing the surreptitious use of hip flasks in New York hotel dining rooms at the start of Prohibition.[4]

Dinner organizers had set up a Marconi wireless device manned by

---

2   "Gridiron Dinner Roasts Capitol's Sacred Cows," *Star Tribune* (Minneapolis, MN), April 1946, 15.

3   Robert Lehrman, "Seriously, the Gridiron Club dinner matters," *The Hill*, March 6, 2016, https://thehill.com/blogs/pundits-blog/media/271900-seriously-the-gridiron-club-dinner-matters, accessed January 3, 2021.

4   "Word History: The Original Hipsters," *Merriam-Webster Unabridged Dictionary*, https://www.merriam-webster.com/words-at-play/the-original-hipsters, accessed March 1, 2021.

an "operator" wearing black, Bakelite headphones, who periodically received messages from the "good ship *Normalcy.*" (Harding had campaigned on the theme that his administration would bring about a "Return to Normalcy.") The festivities were periodically interrupted by Morse-code beeps and clicks emanating from the Marconi device, followed by the reading aloud of a message. One such communication: "This just in from Milwaukee: no sand bars reported in the vicinity. No bars of any kind are in view."[5]

Another joke that evening involved Charles Evans Hughes, the party's unsuccessful candidate for president in 1916, but recently named US Secretary of State by Harding. Someone from the dining area approached the front table holding an oversized key with a large tag attached, bearing the inscription: "Key to the Back Door of the League of Nations." The bearer of the key attempted to give it to Secretary of State Hughes, who waved him off, exclaiming, "all my pockets are sewn shut."

William Howard Taft, whom Harding had appointed in June to Taft's dream job of Chief Justice of the Supreme Court of the United States, was sung to his feet when the "Gridiron Singers" performed the 1919 Jerome Kern hit song, "Look for the Silver Lining," in barbershop quartet style. A prank occurred later in the evening during the club's new member induction ceremony for reporter Robert McGinter of the *Pittsburgh Gazette.* Suddenly the room lights went off, and a spotlight followed three hooded, white-robed figures galloping on hobby horses, mimicking Ku Klux Klan riders. The pair abducted McGinter and rode out of the ballroom to much applause and laughter.[6]

During a break in the evening's festivities, a hospital orderly entered the ballroom, wheeling a sickly man in a plaid bathrobe, his forehead

---

5 "Gridironers Hold Officials Over Fire at Annual Dinner," *Evening Star* (Washington, DC), December 11, 1921, 2.

6 "World Leaders Guests of Gridiron Club," *Washington Herald,* December 11, 1921, 16.

heavily bandaged, his arm in a sling, and one leg rigidly cast and elevated. "I am a sick American businessman," he moaned, "run over by a motor truck of the International Deflation Company." Asked if there was a cure for him, he replied, "Yes, tell the politicians to leave me alone. I am willing to take a prescription from Dr. Warren G. Harding, but I am through with quacks."[7]

At the conclusion of the evening, a final message beeped and clicked from the Marconi machine. The operator transcribed and read it aloud: "Captain Harding on the bridge of the good ship *Normalcy*. Pilot Hughes at the wheel. Head winds dying down. Skies clear. Now pointing straight for port. Prosperity light abeam. Eight bells and the larboard watch. All's well."[8]

Warren G. Harding and running mate Calvin Coolidge won the presidency on November 2, 1920, by the greatest popular vote margin to that time. Ranking dead-last in today's presidential greatness polls, Harding received over sixty percent of the popular vote in 1920 (16 million votes), twenty-six percentage points higher than his Democratic opponent, James Cox, and his running mate, Franklin D. Roosevelt (9 million votes).[9] This twenty-six-point victory margin is the largest in American presidential history. At his death from a heart attack twenty-seven months later, Harding still enjoyed tremendous popularity.[10] His presidency has been eclipsed by personal and political scandals that were largely unknown to the public at the time.

---

7   "Gridironers Hold Officials Over Fire at Annual Dinner," *Evening Star* (Washington, DC), December 11, 1921, 2.

8   Ibid.

9   United States Presidential Election of 1920, Encyclopedia Britannica, https://www.britannica.com/event/United-States-presidential-election-of-1920, accessed March 12, 2021.

10   James D. Robenalt, "If we weren't so obsessed with Warren G. Harding's sex life, we'd realize he was a pretty good president," *Washington Post*, August 13, 2015, https://www.washingtonpost.com/posteverything/wp/2015/08/13/if-we-werent-so-obsessed-with-warren-g-hardings-sex-life-wed-realize-he-was-a-pretty-good-president/.

Harding was elected on a wave of anti-Wilson sentiment and widespread social and economic discontent. During 1920–1921, the nation was mired in a painful economic depression, with the unemployment rate peaking at 11.7 percent in 1921. Industrial production declined sharply: from May 1920 to July 1921, automobile production was down 60 percent and total industrial production fell 30 percent.[11] Many businesses failed, including a haberdashery in Kansas City, Missouri, called "Truman and Jacobson." Opened in 1919 by a returning Army infantry captain, Harry S. Truman, the men's clothing store went bankrupt in 1921.

McLean and Harding had a close professional and personal relationship. They served in the Senate together from 1915 to 1921, toiling together on two Senate committees, Territories and the Philippines. When Harding came to Connecticut for political meetings and appearances, he often visited McLean's estate in Simsbury.[12] Before settling into the White House in February 1921, Mrs. Harding spent a few days with Juliette McLean.[13]

But Harding was much closer to Connecticut's other US Senator, Frank Brandegee, bulwark of the Republican Old Guard, who played a leading role in promoting Harding's dark-horse candidacy at the 1920 Republican National Convention in Chicago.[14] Brandegee was up for a tough reelection bid to the Senate in 1920, under siege for his opposition to Prohibition, the Federal Reserve System, child labor laws, the direct election of senators, and for opposing women's suffrage. His reelection strategy was to hitch his coattails to the 1920 Republican

11   "Diagnosing depression: What is the difference between a recession and a depression?" *The Economist*, December 30, 2008, https://www.economist.com/finance-and-economics/2008/12/30/diagnosing-depression, accessed November 5, 2020.

12   Frances Hallahan and Eleanor Lathrop, "Wilderness in Suburbia: The Management Dilemma," *Yale School of Forestry and Environmental Studies*, 1981, 3.

13   "Mrs. Harding to Go to Washington," *Daily News* (New York), February 5, 1921, 2.

14   Herbert Janick, "Senator Frank B. Brandegee and the Election of 1920," *The Historian* 35, no. 3 (1973): 434–51, http://www.jstor.org/stable/24443018, accessed March 24, 2021.

presidential nominee, whoever it might be, as he sensed the national mood turning against the Democratic party.

Brandegee was one of Harding's chief supporters at the deadlocked Republican nominating convention in Chicago. (McLean was not a delegate). Harding biographer Robert K. Murray disputes the myth that a Senate cabal in a "smoke-filled room" manipulated the convention toward Harding. Murray portrays Harding as a charismatic, likable figure who skillfully united the various factions of the Republican party that had been so hopelessly split since Theodore Roosevelt formed the Progressive "Bull Moose" party in 1912.[15] Brandegee later became a regular at Harding's frequent White House poker games.[16] While McLean did not comment publicly on Harding's candidacy before the convention, he quickly extended his heartiest congratulations after he received the nomination.[17] Along with other party leaders, McLean attended a victory dinner honoring Harding in Columbus, Ohio on July 22, 1920.

In some rankings, Warren G. Harding has been called America's "worst president,"[18] but scholarly reappraisals now recognize him for many achievements that have often been overlooked. These accomplishments include:

Economic plan to restart the post-war economy;

Negotiating global disarmament treaties;

Earmarking over $150 million ($2.2 billion in 2020 dollars) for roads and highways;

---

15 Robert K. Murray, *The Politics of Normalcy* (New York: Norton & Co., 1973), 6–14.

16 Karl Schriftgiesser, *This Was Normalcy* (New York: Oriole Editions, 1948), 81.

17 "Harding Told of United Support," *Salt Lake Tribune*, June 25, 1920, 1.

18 A 1996 poll of academics by noted historian Arthur Schlesinger, Jr., views Warren Harding as the nation's worst president. See Arthur M. Schlesinger, Jr., "Rating the Presidents: Washington to Clinton," *Political Science Quarterly* 112, no. 2 (Summer, 1997): 179–90, Stable URL: http://www.jstor.org/stable/2657937, accessed March 1, 2021.

Regulating and investing in infrastructure for radio broadcasting and aviation;

Advocating federal anti-lynching legislation;

Rebuilding the nation's merchant marine fleet; and

Promoting the Sheppard-Towner Act, which provided $1 million annually in federal aid for prenatal and newborn care, leading to a decrease in infant mortality. It was the first federally funded social welfare program.[19,20]

Harding also created the Bureau of Budget (now called the Office of Management and Budget) and the Government Accounting Office. Before Harding's presidency, the US government had no systematic budgeting process. Each government department would approach Congress separately, asking for approval. After the federal budget ballooned during World War I, a more business-like approach was needed. For the first time, the president was required to submit an annual budget for the entire federal government.

Harding also went to great lengths to ease political tensions arising from the arrests under the Sedition Act during the Wilson era. Harding pardoned twenty-five nonviolent political protesters imprisoned during the Wilson administration, including Socialist Party US presidential candidate Eugene Debs, who was serving ten years in prison for sedition. "I want him to eat his Christmas dinner with his wife," Harding said upon Debs' release on December 23, 1921. Debs later told a bank of reporters waiting outside the White House that Harding was a "kind gentleman" who "possesses humane impulses."[21]

---

19 Gary M. Pecquet and Clifford F. Thies, "Reputation Overrides Record: How Warren G. Harding Mistakenly Became the 'Worst' President of the United States," *The Independent Review* 21, no. 1 (2016): 29–45, accessed March 24, 2021, http://www.jstor.org/stable/43999675.

20 See Robert K. Murray, *The Harding Era* (Minneapolis: University of Minnesota Press, 1969).

21 Charles L. Mee, Jr., *The Ohio Gang: The World of Warren G. Harding* (New York: M. Evans and Co., 1981), 193.

Between 1901 and 1929, more than 1,200 African Americans were lynched in America. Forty-one percent of these lynchings occurred in two states: Georgia (250) and Mississippi (245).[22] The passage of federal anti-lynching legislation became one of the National Association for the Advancement of Colored People's central goals. A landmark NAACP report, *Thirty Years of Lynching in the United States, 1889–1919*, created national awareness and urgency for congressional action. Just one month into his term, on April 12, 1921, President Warren G. Harding sent a civil rights legislative message to Congress, calling for an end to the "stain of barbaric lynching" in America, and urged passage of the Dyer Anti-Lynching bill introduced by Missouri Congressman Leonidas C. Dyer in 1918. This was followed by Harding's speech in October 1921 to a segregated audience in Birmingham, Alabama, where the new president called for an end to Jim Crow laws and the disenfranchisement of African Americans. "We cannot go on, as we have for more than half a century, with one section of our population…set off from real contribution to solving national issues, because of a division on race lines," he said.[23]

Dyer's bill sought to try lynching cases in federal court and charge lynch mobs with capital murder. The bill also imposed jail time and fines of up to $5,000 on state and local law enforcement officials who refused to make reasonable efforts to prevent a lynching or protect a prisoner in their custody. In addition, the bill established guidelines for fair courtroom proceedings by excluding lynch mob participants and supporters from juries. Finally, a fine of up to $10,000 would be paid to the victim's immediate family.[24]

---

22   Carter et al., *Historical Statistics of the United States: Government and International Relations*, vol. 5, 252–55.

23   Alan S. Felzenberg, *The Leaders We Deserved* (New York: Basic Books, 2008), 303.

24   *Congressional Record*, House, 65th Cong., 2nd sess., May 7, 1918), 6177.

On January 2, 1922, the Hartford branch of the NAACP hosted a rally at the historic Center House Church in support of the Dyer bill. A letter from Senator McLean was read aloud, pledging his support for the bill without amendments.[25] Two years earlier, McLean had signaled his support for anti-lynching legislation when he introduced a petition in the Senate on October 19, 1919, calling for a national investigation on mob violence and the lynchings of African Americans.[26] An op-ed in the *Cincinnati Enquirer* subsequently criticized McLean for supporting the Dyer Anti-Lynching bill, cynically charging that McLean was "under obligation to Negro voters" in his state.[27]

The Dyer Anti-Lynching bill was passed by the House of Representatives on January 26, 1922. With Harding having already promised to sign the bill, pressure now mounted on the Senate to similarly pass it. Although the Senate Judiciary Committee eventually moved the bill to the Senate floor for a vote, its passage was blocked by a filibuster in the Senate by Southern Democrats in December 1922 and twice more thereafter.[28] The defeat of the Dyer Anti-Lynching bill illustrates the power of the Old Confederacy in the United States Senate during much of the twentieth century. Bills aimed at advancing the rights of African Americans sometimes passed in the House of Representatives only to die in the Senate. Representing straight-line Democratic Party voters, southern senators faced token opposition, resulting in lengthy tenures in office. Because of the seniority system, many key Senate committees were controlled by southern senators, enabling them to

---

25   "Comments on Lynching," *Hartford Courant*, January 3, 1922, 19.

26   "Asks Probe of Negro Lynchings," *Hartford Courant*, October 17, 1919, 12.

27   "Dyer Anti-Lynching Bill," *Cincinnati Enquirer*, November 22, 1919, 5.

28   Robert L. Zangrando, *The NACCP Crusade Against Lynching, 1909–1950* (Philadelphia, PA: Temple University Press, 1980), 66.

obstruct substantive civil rights advances for decades, often aided and abetted by like-minded northern senators.[29]

President Harding's number one priority upon taking office in March 1921 was ending the economic depression that had gripped the nation since around January 1920.[30] War debts were an eye-popping $25 billion in 1919, and unemployment was on the rise, peaking at 11.7 percent in 1921. After years of very high tax rates to fund the war, there was a consensus in Congress that taxes needed to fall, but how?

McLean was a member of the Senate Finance Committee, the epicenter of a protracted debate on how to design a new postwar taxation system. At one end of the spectrum, favoring individualism and economic liberty, were conservative Republicans like Senator Reed Smoot, a prominent Mormon from Utah, who wanted to replace the income tax with a national sales tax. Strongly opposing that approach were progressives like Senator Robert LaFollette of Wisconsin, who not only wanted to preserve Wilson's graduated income tax but keep the rates high on wealthy taxpayers. When the federal income tax was first enacted in 1913, the top rate was just 7 percent; but by the end of World War I, rates had been greatly increased at all income levels, with the top rate reaching 77 percent. LaFollette viewed high tax rates on the wealthy as a permanent feature of the income tax, not just a temporary war measure.

During the campaign, Harding promised that if elected he would consult the "best minds" available to guide his administration. For Treasury Secretary, he chose Andrew Mellon, a businessman, banker, art collector, and a philanthropist. Part of Mellon's fortune came from starting up or investing in companies like ALCOA, Carborundum,

---

29   Keith M. Finley, "Southern opposition to civil rights in the United States Senate: a tactical and ideological analysis, 1938–1965," 2003, LSU Doctoral Dissertations, 5–7.

30   Elmus R. Wicker, "A Reconsideration of Federal Reserve Policy during the 1920–1921 Depression," *Journal of Economic History* 26, no. 2 (1966): 223–38.

214

Koppers, and Gulf Oil.[31] Mellon is regarded as one of Harding's best appointments, often described as the second greatest treasury secretary of all time, behind only Alexander Hamilton.[32] Mellon sought to roll back federal income tax rates to stimulate consumer spending and encourage capital investment in businesses. While Mellon's "scientific taxation" plan called for lowering the overall tax rates, he was still committed to the principles of progressive income taxation.[33] Proponents of the national sales tax were not. The goals of Mellon's tax reforms were to reform but preserve the progressive income tax system established under Wilson; and stimulate business activity and capital investment by reducing tax rates.[34]

After months of Congressional debate, McLean came out in favor of a compromise tax bill (later called the Revenue Act of 1921) and on October 7, 1921, spoke in the Senate on its behalf. The proposed tax rate reductions, McLean began, would return the nation's six million employed to profitable employment. Ending the wartime excess profit tax would free up cash for companies to invest in new plants and equipment. The proposed bill would end the first-ever "excess profits tax" on corporations enacted in 1917, with tax rates of up to 60 percent on the profits of businesses in excess of prewar earnings. McLean argued that high excess-profits taxes were retarding a return to normal business

31   David Cannadine, *Mellon: An American Life* (New York: Knopf, 2006), 184.

32   Joseph J. Thorndike, "Was Andrew Mellon Really the Supply Sider That Conservatives Like to Believe?" Tax Analysts, Inc., March 24, 2003, http://www.taxhistory.org/thp/readings.nsf/ArtWeb/1D6628F544D4A43C85256EE0004D414D. See also Lawrence W. Reed, "Andrew Mellon: The Best Treasury Secretary in US History," Foundation for Economic Education, May 26, 2016, https://www.valuewalk.com/2016/05/andrew-mellon-history/.

33   Susan M. Murnane, "Selling Scientific Taxation: The Treasury Department's Campaign for Tax Reform in the 1920s," *Law & Social Inquiry* 29, no. 4 (2004): 819–56, http://www.jstor.org/stable/4092770, accessed August 28, 2021.

34   Ibid.

conditions and that in the interests of labor they should be reduced as fast as is possible to stimulate new investment and employment.[35]

McLean voted for the Revenue Act of 1921, which passed in a close vote in the Senate (42–39, with 15 not voting).[36] The bill repealed the wartime excess profits tax; in addition, the marginal rate on individuals fell from 73 to 58 percent by 1922. Mellon had hoped for a more significant tax reduction. Progressive Senator Robert La Follette voted against the bill. A month earlier, he called for Mellon to resign. Calling Mellon a "menace," La Follette criticized him for brazenly protecting the wealthy from a fair level of taxation.[37]

As passed, the 1921 Revenue Act pleased almost no one. Critics complained that it was a patchwork quilt of politically-driven compromises. Secretary of the Treasury Mellon insisted that deeper tax reductions were needed to spur economic expansion and restore prosperity. Senator Reed Smoot's proposed national retail sales tax still had considerable support in the Senate. For example, Senator George Moses (R-New Hampshire), viewed the national sales tax as a way to "strike down the vicious principle of graduated taxation which is but a modern legislative adaptation of the Communistic doctrine of Karl Marx."[38] Meanwhile, a strong coalition of Democrats and progressive Republicans remained committed to permanently high tax rates on the wealthy along with high corporate tax rates. The Revenue Act of 1921 was only the opening salvo for Secretary of the Treasury Andrew Mellon. Undaunted, he would bide his time for now, fully intending to return to Congress with more legislation on tax reform.

---

35   George P. McLean (CT), "Tax Reform," *Congressional Record* 61 (1921), October 7, 1921, 6091–93.

36   67th Congress, Senate, Vote 197 on HR8245, November 23, 1921, https://voteview.com/rollcall/RS0670197.

37   "LaFollette Asks Mellon to Resign," *The Daily Tribune* (Wisconsin Rapids, WI), November 5, 1921, 1.

38   Sidney Ratner, *Taxation and Democracy in America* (New York: Wiley, 1967), 410.

During Harding's time in office, the economy rebounded. American GDP per capita rose from $5,401 in 1920 to $6,016 in 1923, an impressive 11.7 percent increase. During the same time, the national debt fell from $24.3 billion in 1920 to $22.3 billion. [39] Unemployment by 1923 had returned to a level consistent with full employment (2.4 percent). The nation's finances stabilized, and Harding made a consistent push to reduce government employment from wartime highs. The economy had been rejuvenated despite the challenging circumstances.[40] And the Progressive Era achievement of a graduated income tax had been preserved, stopping a serious effort to replace it with a national sales tax.

At the start of the 67th Congress (1921–1923), the Senate abolished 41 of its 75 committees, weeding out some and consolidating many others.[41] McLean's new committee assignments went from eight to four and had a clear focus on economic matters: chairman of Banking and Currency, and a member of three others: Finance, Interstate Commerce, and Territories and Insular Possessions. McLean's tenure on the Interstate Commerce committee was marked by legislative and regulatory challenges stemming from heretofore unknown technologies like radio, telephone, and aviation.

McLean was chairman of the Banking and Currency Committee, which helped create the Federal Reserve System in 1913. The infant "Fed" was a work in progress, requiring much attention and amending. McLean was one of the Senate's leading experts on the Federal Reserve System, and did much to influence its development during the first fifteen years of its existence. While much of McLean's

---

39 John A. Moore, "The Original Supply Siders: Warren Harding and Calvin Coolidge," *The Independent Review* 18, no. 4 (2014): 604, http://www.jstor.org/stable/24563172.

40 Ibid.

41 David T. Canon, "Committee Hierarchy and Assignments in the U.S. Senate, 1789–1946," Delivered at the Norman Thomas Conference on Senate Exceptionalism, Vanderbilt University, October 21–23, 1999, 11, http://web.mit.edu/cstewart/www/papers/vanderbilt.pdf.

Banking and Currency Committee work was detailed and highly technical, the committee gained front-page headlines following the sudden death of Theodore Roosevelt on January 6, 1919. A letter-writing campaign to the Senate Banking Committee led McLean to introduce a bill in November 1919 authorizing the coinage of a Roosevelt two-cent piece. Not surprisingly, Republicans favored it but Democrats did not. The only US president's likeness on a coin at that time was Abraham Lincoln, thanks to the strong advocacy of the coin by Roosevelt himself in 1909.[42]

For months, the proposed coin generated spirited Congressional and public debate. On May 3, 1920, the Senate passed McLean's bill, authorizing the Roosevelt coin over the objections of Democrats. The bill was then sent to the House, where its fate was decided on practicalities. The streetcar industry vigorously opposed it, since their conductors used a standard dispenser on their belts that had slots only for the coins then in use. Bankers also complained that they would have to re-tool their coin storage containers because of the new coin. McLean then contacted leading manufacturers of coin carriers and cash registers, hoping to broker a solution.[43] His efforts came to naught. Admirers of Theodore Roosevelt would have to wait twenty-one years for a proper tribute, when on October 31, 1941, the public got their first glimpse of his likeness on the Mount Rushmore National Memorial.

At the end of World War I, public opinion swung solidly toward neutrality and isolationism. Having rebuffed Wilson's proposed League of Nations, Republicans sought responsible alternatives. Early in his presidency, Harding gathered the world's largest naval powers in Washington for a conference to discuss naval disarmament. Many Americans believed the arms buildup early in the century by the Europe-

---

42 "Model of Coin," *Evening Star* (Washington, DC), November 20, 1919, 22.

43 George P. McLean (CT), "Roosevelt Two-Cent Coin," *Congressional Record* 59 (1920), May 3, 1920, 6451, https://www.govinfo.gov/content/pkg/GPO-CRECB-1920-pt6-v59/pdf/GPO-CRECB-1920-pt6-v59-22-1.pdf.

an powers was a cause of World War I. Reducing military armaments around the world, so they thought, would prevent another war. In addition, the Harding administration sought to limit the growing military power of Japan, viewing them as a threat to American interests in the Pacific.[44]

The Washington Naval Conference is hailed as the first disarmament conference in history and generated real hope that another world war could be averted. Public reaction to news of the disarmament conference was extremely positive. *The Times-Tribune* called the conference inspiring news that offered great promise for the future. "The President is truly responding to the desire of all nations. He has given to this country the high distinction of leading a noble work for civilization."[45]

Between 1921 and 1922, under the able leadership of Secretary of State Charles Evans Hughes, the world's largest naval powers met in Washington and established limits on the number and tonnage of warships of each nation. When the conference opened, McLean praised President Harding's leadership and vision, saying that the time has come when reason must be substituted for force if the world is to be rescued from perpetual wars.[46]

While McLean voiced support for Harding's disarmament conference, he also believed in the deterrent effects of US military power. He advocated for maintaining adequate navy and air services, as well as staffing the army with enough commissioned officers to handle an expanded army at any time. McLean thought it a great folly to underfund a proper national defense. A strong navy and air force were needed to

---

44   Timothy P. Maga, "Prelude to War? The United States, Japan, and the Yap Crisis, 1918–22," *Diplomatic History* 9, no. 3 (1985): 215–31, http://www.jstor.org/stable/24911662, accessed March 24, 2021.

45   "The President Acts," *The Times-Tribune* (PA), July 12, 1921, 6.

46   "McLean Speaks, Endorses Harding," *Hartford Daily Courant*, November 21, 1921, 10.

219

keep the country from becoming embroiled in another catastrophe like the recently ended Great War.[47]

In May 1921, McLean led an effort in the Senate to modernize the nation's naval fleet by sponsoring an amendment for the construction of a new fleet of submarines. During World War I, the Navy viewed submarines largely as a novelty, of minor importance compared to the battleship. US naval planners were beginning to see an expanding role for submarines, given the terrible successes of German submarine warfare during World War I.[48]

In a speech on the Senate floor on May 26, 1921, McLean decried the economic and strategic folly of building battleships at a cost of $25 million each over submarines at a cost of $2 million, especially when all the other naval powers of the world were constructing submarines at an alarming rate. McLean urged senators to support the construction of submarines and aircraft, armaments that will "bring us the most for our money." He cited national and international experts who insist that the submarine will give us the greatest degree of protection for the amount of money invested.[49] Only three subs were under construction in the United States, McLean noted, while Japan had thirty-six and Great Britain fifty-two. McLean proposed that the United States build at least six submarines.

In the aftermath of World War I, US policymakers saw Japan as a rising military threat. Heavily militarized and seeking to expand its influence and territory in Asia, Japan had the potential to disrupt US trade in Asia and threaten US colonial possessions in the region. McLean viewed submarines as a vital deterrent to Japanese military activity in the Pacific. A fleet of modern US submarines "would cause Japan

---

47 "Farmer McLean," *Watertown* (CT) *News*, June 10, 1927, 4.

48 Karl Lautenschlager, "The Submarine in Naval Warfare, 1901–2001," International Security 11, no. 3 (1986): 113–14, accessed August 29, 2021, https://doi.org/10.2307/2538886.

49 "Submarines and the Navy," *The Bridgeport Telegram*, May 27, 1921, 13.

to hesitate, and hesitate again," McLean argued.[50] McLean's submarine amendment was hotly debated. Battleships were viewed as more important, while other senators criticized armament spending of any kind during peacetime. McLean reminded his colleagues of how President Lincoln had put faith in the innovative ironclad warships built for the Union Navy during the American Civil War. "It seems to me," McLean concluded, "there is something in the submarine," and it's a grave mistake "that we have only three under construction at this time."

McLean's support for submarine construction had some political benefits back home. His remarks were featured in the *Bridgeport Telegram*, home of the Lake Torpedo Boat Company, the principal builder of submarines for the US Navy. The company was founded in 1912 by Connecticut's Simon Lake. Even after persistent lobbying of his Senate colleagues, McLean's submarine amendment was not adopted. With disarmament ruling the day, the demand for submarines dwindled; the Lake Torpedo Boat Company in Bridgeport, Connecticut, closed its doors in 1924, resulting in the loss of 2,000 jobs.[51]

McLean faced an uphill battle for his reelection bid to the Senate slated for November 7, 1922. With the nation still feeling the effects of an economic depression, voters took out their frustration on their elected representatives. Eight incumbent Senators had been defeated in 1920, seven in the 1918 elections, including Senator John W. Weeks, the Massachusetts Republican who had joined with McLean to create the Weeks-McLean migratory bird law in 1913. With his reelection in doubt, McLean scrambled for support.

The soldier's bonus bill was crafted in the Senate Finance committee, one of McLean's four committee assignments. After the war ended in 1918, many in Congress felt that a bonus should be awarded to the nation's veterans, many of whom were unemployed. Then there was

---

50   Ibid., 18.

51   "Ex–Submarine Yard is Razed," *The Bridgeport Post,* November 26, 1969, 44.

also the "lost pay" argument—compensating servicemen for the difference they lost between pay in the military versus their civilian jobs. (According to the Bureau of Labor Statistics, the average household earned $125 per month in 1918; a private in the US Army received $30 a month.[52])

McLean was certainly aware of the voting power veterans had: sixty-three thousand residents of Connecticut had served in World War I, including 694 who died.[53] McLean supported the bonus bill for patriotic, practical, and political reasons. In a June 10, 1922, letter to a constituent, McLean praised the bonus because it helped the many veterans who were out of work; it restored lost pay; and he also feared that denying it might turn the "American Legion posts into hotbeds of sedition."[54]

Veterans and workers in Connecticut's arms and munitions industries were key voting blocs for McLean. Connecticut's munitions industries had churned out much-needed war supplies and material during the war. In addition, many civilians served in the Connecticut Home Guard, a force of over 10,000 men tasked with standing guard over the state's railroads, factories, ports, and bridges. Connecticut's proximity to the Atlantic Ocean caused many to fear a potential German invasion of the Nutmeg State.

On May 13, 1918, the Connecticut Home Guard staged a mock attack, including five battalions mounting an "invasion" of the state

---

52 Logan Nye, "This is how much troops were paid in every major American war," December 4, 2018, Inside Hook (website), https://www.insidehook.com/daily_brief/news-opinion/how-much-were-u-s-troops-paid-during-every-american-war.

53 "November 11: Connecticut's Last World War I Casualty," November 11, 2018, Office of the Connecticut State Historian, https://todayincthistory.com/2018/11/11/november-11-connecticuts-last-world-war-i-casualty/.

54 George P. McLean letter to Mr. Francis T. Maxwell, June 10, 1922, Francis Maxwell Autograph Collection, 1910–1936, MS 51622, Connecticut Historical Society.

Capitol in front of an audience of thousands.[55] That attack probably reminded people of a fictional serialization in the national magazine *McClure's* in 1915, a chilling, fictional account of a German military assault of Connecticut later released in a widely-circulated book called *The Conquest of America*. The frightening narrative described 150,000 German troops easily overrunning Connecticut's coastal cities, then capturing the state's vast arms and munitions factories. After taking Hartford in the fictional narrative, the German high command made hostages of former governor Morgan Bulkeley and *Hartford Courant* editor Charles Hopkins Clark.[56]

Throughout 1921, Harding made it clear to Congress that he strongly opposed the bonus bill, calling it a wasteful gratuity that would imperil the country's financial stability.[57] On June 2, 1922, the *New York Times* criticized McLean's support of the soldier's bonus bill, calling it a selfish catering to the soldier vote just in time for his reelection bid to the Senate. After both houses of Congress passed it in mid-September 1922, Harding vetoed the bonus bill, just six weeks before the election. The following day, the House voted to override Harding's veto 258–54, but the vote to override in the Senate fell short by four votes.[58]

On October 19, 1922, just two weeks before McLean's bid for reelection, he received the coveted endorsement of the Connecticut Veterans of Foreign Wars.[59] At a meeting of the Republican Club of

---

55   Jonathan Gonzalez, "Home Guard Patrols Helped in Connecticut During WWI," Southern Connecticut State University Journalism blog, November 2018, http://www.scsujournalism. org/home-guard-patrols-helped-out-in-connecticut-during-wwi/, accessed June 12, 2020.

56   Walter W. Woodward (Connecticut State Historian), "The German Invasion of Connecticut," *Connecticut Explored*, Spring 2017.

57   Niall A. Palmer, "The Veterans' Bonus and the Evolving Presidency of Warren G. Harding," *Presidential Studies Quarterly* 38, no. 1 (2008): 50–51, accessed March 24, 2021, http://www. jstor.org/stable/27552303.

58   Ibid., 57.

59   "Veterans for McLean; Call Him Friend; Call Spellacy Unfair," *Hartford Daily Courant*, October 19, 1922, 1.

Hartford, a group of ex-servicemen formed the "McLean Club," a group of ex-servicemen, veterans of the World War and other of the country's wars, some of whom were disabled and members of both political parties. The club's president Captain Anson McCook spoke of the many things McLean had done for veterans, calling McLean "the ex-serviceman's best friend."[60]

McLean had significant work to do to mend fences with women, having voted against women's suffrage four times between 1914 and 1919 in the Senate. One way McLean sought to win women voters was his civil service reform bill in December of 1919.[61] McLean's bill, although never enacted, would have allowed women equal access to any federal civil service position, except those where physical strength might play a role.[62] McLean's bill received the enthusiastic endorsement of the Women's Trade Union League, a leading organization representing thousands of women who had filled many government jobs during wartime. Speaking for his bill in the Senate, McLean said it was time to ensure equal access and compensation for women in employment. While his bill was aimed at civil service jobs, he said he hoped the principles of equal access and pay would spread to "any occupation whatsoever."[63]

In January of 1922, the president of Connecticut's Woman's Christian Temperance Union (CWCTU) announced that their "big task" was the defeat of Senator George P. McLean in November, since he had voted against Prohibition (the Eighteenth Amendment).[64] While many "Old Guard" Republicans supported Prohibition, McLean

---

60   Ibid.

61   "Senator McLean Champions Women in Civil Service," *The Labor Journal* (Everett, WA), December 12, 1919, 2.

62   Ibid.

63   "Senator McLean Champions Women in Civil Service," *The Worker's Chronicle* (Pittsburg, KS), December 12, 1919, 1.

64   "McLean Sought End of Profit in Bootlegging," *Hartford Daily Courant*, December 10, 1933, 30.

eschewed his party's conventional wisdom on the issue and went his own way. One wonders if there may have been some political calculation behind McLean's opposition to Prohibition. Knowing that his Democratic opponent for the US Senate in any future election would likely be "wet" on the issue of Prohibition, he took a vital issue away from them and made his candidacy more attractive to crossover Democrats, such as Irish and German immigrants, who made up large voting blocs in Connecticut.

McLean supported the causes of other immigrant groups, too. For example, he repeatedly introduced petitions in the Senate in 1920 on behalf of constituents calling for recognition of the newly formed Irish Free State. Similarly, in April of 1922, McLean voiced public support for creating a homeland for the Jewish people in Palestine, and received the endorsement of the Connecticut Zionist Club on October 27, 1922, a week before his reelection vote.[65] Club President Reuben Taylor praised McLean' efforts in support of Zionist causes, and urged followers to vote for him in November.[66] By 1922, waves of immigration had changed Connecticut drastically; the Jewish population in Hartford had increased to about 6,500, many having escaped from Russia's pogroms and antisemitic laws.[67]

While these stances helped McLean reach crossover voters like veterans, immigrants, and women, McLean's signature issue in his reelection campaign was tariff reform. Long part of his playbook, protective tariffs appealed to his base: the state's many manufacturers and their workers. With Harding in office, Republicans were determined to increase tariff rates after years of downward revisions under Wilson.

As a member of the Senate Finance Committee, McLean played a

---

65   "McLean for Use of Palestine as Jewish Homeland," *Hartford Daily Courant*, April 29, 1922, 8.

66   "Zionists Working to Elect McLean," *Hartford Daily Courant*, October 28, 1922, 15.

67   Betty N. Hoffman, "Tradition and Transformation Define Hartford's Jewish Community," January 27, 2021, Connecticut History.org, https://connecticuthistory.org/tradition-and-transformation-define-hartfords-jewish-community/, accessed March 12, 2021.

major role in the complex negotiations that led to the signing of the Fordney-McCumber Tariff Act on September 21, 1922, just six weeks before the November elections. In the end, the tariff rates rose to an average of 38 percent for dutiable imports.[68] McLean made sure his state's industries were protected. Six leading Connecticut manufacturers praised McLean's key contribution in the tariff bill in a front-page article in the *Hartford Courant on* November 3, 1922—the Friday before the election. One of them, C. B. Cook, vice president of the Royal Typewriter Co. of Hartford, thanked McLean for his support of Connecticut's manufacturers. The new tariff law will protect the jobs of Connecticut's working men and usher in a new era of prosperity for the state and the nation, Cook declared.[69]

McLean's Democratic opponent for the 1922 Connecticut Senate race was forty-two-year-old Thomas J. Spellacy, twenty-two years younger than McLean. Spellacy was a former US Attorney appointed by Woodrow Wilson and a legal adviser to Assistant Secretary of the Navy Franklin D. Roosevelt. Spellacy was well-connected with both the Connecticut and the national Democratic Party, and he was viewed as a formidable opponent for McLean.

With the election viewed as a dead heat, McLean and Spellacy agreed to one debate on October 24, 1922. McLean relentlessly hammered Spellacy for his opposition to the tariff, pointedly asking him just what rates he would reduce. Would he lower the protective tariff rates on cutlery, clocks, tobacco, wool, or silk? Which of the new tariff rates recently secured for Connecticut's industries were too high or too low? Spellacy weakly replied that he "had not sufficient information," that such questions were for the Tariff Commission to decide. Aghast,

---

68   Edward S. Kaplan, *American Trade Policy, 1923–1995* (Westport, CT: Greenwood Press, 1996), 8–10.

69   "Manufacturers Declare McLean Saved Connecticut Industry," *Hartford Courant,* November 3, 1922, 1

McLean called Spellacy a wolf of free trade in sheep's clothing, whose Senate election spelled doom for Connecticut's workingmen.[70]

McLean was not above the use of an "October surprise," a political maneuver orchestrated on the eve of an election in the hopes of affecting the outcome. A few months before the election, the Republican State Central Committee (and Chairman J. Henry Roraback) released to the press some private letters showing that Spellacy, when the US Attorney for Connecticut, had misused his government expense account to support the presidential aspirations of A. Mitchell Palmer, Attorney General of the United States, Spellacy's boss. During much of 1919 and 1920, Spellacy used not only his work time campaigning for Palmer, but also dispensed jobs at the Department of Justice in return for supporting Palmer.[71] Spellacy considered the release of the correspondence "underhanded work," and said the letters were obtained illegally from his private secretary. McLean defended the action, saying the people of Connecticut are entitled to know if Spellacy wrongly charged up his expenses to pay for a friend's reelection.

In his closing statement at the debate, McLean said he was proud of the record of the Harding administration. Since taking office, McLean declared, Republicans have been busy undoing the mistakes of the Wilson administration, especially rejuvenating the economy and curing unemployment. He reminded his audience that restoring protective tariffs would contribute to the nation's continued prosperity, allowing Connecticut to regain its role as an exporter of manufactured goods.[72]

For his part, Spellacy, characterized McLean as old and out-of-touch with his constituents. Spellacy criticized McLean for "occupying a rocking chair in a Hot Springs, Virginia resort" in the weeks leading

---

70 "Senator McLean Makes Answers to Charges by Spellacy," *Norwich Bulletin*, November 4, 1922, 5.

71 "Bartering for the Presidency," *The Nation*, November 29, 1922, 577–78.

72 "Woman Justified in Telling Everything," *Hartford Courant,* November 3, 1922, 2.

McLean 1922 Senate Campaign Button (from the collection of Dr. Kenneth Florey)

up to the election "when he ought to be appearing before the people of Connecticut." Days later, several newspapers came to McLean's defense, probably to Spellacy's everlasting chagrin. The *Bridgeport Telegram* wrote that Spellacy knew (or should have known) that McLean was at the Hot Springs health spa tending to his wife, who had likely suffered a stroke.[73] The newspaper concluded with this chastisement: "any other husband in a similar predicament could hardly have acted otherwise."[74]

McLean won reelection to his third term in the US Senate on November 7, 1922, receiving fifty-two percent of the vote, a comfortable majority of 22,248 votes. Spellacy received forty-five percent of the total, and the Socialist Party candidate had just under two percent of the vote. These 1922 results were a marked improvement for McLean over his 1916 election to the Senate when he got fifty-percent of the vote, or an 8,000-vote majority.

At the age of sixty-five, McLean was headed back to the Senate for another six-year term.

---

73 "Some Undesirable Features," *The Bridgeport Telegram*, November 2, 1922, 2.

74 "Letters from the People: Mrs. McLean's Illness," *Hartford Daily Courant*, November 5, 1922, 10.

★ CHAPTER ELEVEN ★

CLOSING WITH COOLIDGE

> Calvin Coolidge is honest and economical and careful
> and wise. His tastes and speech when on or off duty
> are clean. He is the kind of man we would like to have
> for our next-door neighbor. Did we ever have a better
> man come into his own in a better way?
>
> *George P. McLean in a speech at the Republican State
> Convention, September 13, 1926[1]*

While McLean was a loyal Republican and likely wanted Harding to run for a second term in 1924, McLean did not turn a blind eye to Harding's weaknesses. As good as Harding's core Cabinet selections were—appointments like Charles Evans Hughes, Andrew Mellon, Herbert Hoover, Henry Wallace, and Charles Dawes—he made just as many poor choices. Reflecting on Harding in 1931, humorist Will Rogers wrote: "Betrayed by friendship is not a bad memorial to leave."[2]

In March 1923, Harding's nominee for comptroller of the currency, James P. McNary appeared before McLean's Banking and Currency Committee for confirmation. After days of intensely grilling McNary

---

1   "Senator Gives Keynote Address," *Hartford Daily Courant*, September 14, 1926, 10.

2   Amity Shlaes, *Coolidge* (New York: Harper, 2013), 257.

about past practices of granting suspicious loans, exorbitant dividend payments, and engaging in currency speculation, McLean announced that he was unalterably opposed to his confirmation. McLean had been pressured by Harding to go along with the appointment. A newspaper noted that this was the first time in McLean's long career that he openly opposed a Republican administration.[3]

McLean had a run-in with another Harding banking appointee, an Ohio friend who sought confirmation for an important post from Mc-Lean's Banking and Currency Committee. Asked after the hearing by a Washington, DC, reporter for his opinion of the man, McLean said the nominee was "an incompetent, inefficient nincompoop who knows less about banking than you do."[4]

Starting around the summer of 1922, the presidency had become an increasing burden for Warren G. Harding. Both Harding and his wife were experiencing serious health problems, and the presidency seemed to have overwhelmed him. Biographer Robert K. Murray describes an incident in early 1923 when an aide found Harding poring over a stack of correspondence, paralyzed at the thought of responding to each letter. Encouraged to delegate the job to others, an exasperated Harding plowed on.[5]

Moreover, in early 1923, the first of his administration's many scandals was made public. On January 29, 1923, Charles Forbes, head of the Veterans Bureau, resigned in anticipation of a Senate investigation. He was eventually indicted and convicted on charges of fraud, conspiracy, and bribery, having stolen an estimated $200 million from the government.[6] Senate investigators would later learn that Veterans

---

3   "McLean Blocks Confirmation," *Hartford Daily Courant*, March 4, 1923, 1.

4   "Harding and the Chicago Banker," *Dayton* (OH) *Daily News*, July 6, 1934, 11.

5   Robert K. Murray, *The Harding Era*, (Minneapolis: University of Minnesota Press, 1969), 417.

6   Rosemary Stevens, *A Time of Scandal: Charles R. Forbes, Warren G. Harding, and the Making of the Veterans Bureau* (Baltimore: Johns Hopkins University Press, 2017), 303.

Bureau officials had even stolen the gold meant for veterans' teeth.[7] Before Forbes resigned, Harding allegedly accosted Forbes in the White House Red Room, shaking his former poker buddy by the neck and shouting: "You yellow rat! You double-crossing bastard!"[8]

To defend himself from the taint of these scandals and retain any chance of reelection, the beleaguered Harding, in June 1923, undertook an arduous, two-month, cross-country speaking tour dubbed the "Voyage of Understanding." His trip included a visit to the territory of Alaska, the first time a president had visited there. It was on this fateful speaking tour that Harding died of a heart attack in San Francisco on August 2, 1923. Harding's death was stunning news, and the nation deeply mourned the loss of the president, who was still popular despite the emerging scandals. An estimated nine million people watched the train that bore his body from San Francisco to Washington.[9] McLean was unable to attend Harding's funeral, and released a brief statement of condolence. [10]

At 2:30 in the morning on August 3, 1923, Vice President Calvin Coolidge received word of Harding's death while visiting his boyhood home in Plymouth Notch, Vermont. By the light of a kerosene lamp, his father, a notary public, administered the oath of office to Coolidge as he placed his hand on the family Bible. For sixty-five-year-old George McLean, after almost four decades in public service, there could not be a better man to fill the role vacated by the death of Warren G. Harding.

McLean met with Coolidge at the White House two days after his first State of the Union address.[11] Coolidge had made it clear that he would stick with most of his predecessor's appointees and policies until

---

7   Shlaes, *Coolidge*, 268.

8   Ibid.

9   John W. Dean, *Warren G. Harding: The American Presidents Series* (New York: Henry Holt, 2004), ii.

10   "He Will Have a High Place in History, McLean Says," *Boston Globe*, August 4, 1923, 11.

11   "President Greets Leaders of Party," *Baltimore Sun,* December 9, 1923, 2.

the next presidential election in November 1924. Coolidge pledged to continue Harding's policies of tax reduction and spending cuts. With McLean a member of both the Finance Committee and Banking and Currency, Coolidge was relying on McLean to help shepherd additional tax reform through the Senate.

Treasury Secretary Andrew Mellon had a new set of ambitious tax reform plans; the Revenue Act of 1921 was just a start. The idea behind Mellon's tax cuts was that if people got to keep more of their money, they would hire others. This had been proven out in the wake of the Revenue Act of 1921—more of the same was needed, Mellon believed. Coolidge and Mellon, however, would encounter stiff resistance to steeply cutting taxes and spending from both Congressional Democrats and Republicans. As historian Benjamin Rader points out, "all of the tax legislation in the 1920's fell short of Mellon's requests; all required compromises between the competing interest groups represented in Congress."[12] In fact, it will be shown that Progressive Era forces did not come to a screeching halt in the 1920s: the progressive graduated income tax survived, and a significant federal government entitlement program emerged in 1924, one backed by George McLean—the soldier's bonus bill would not go away.

Both Coolidge and Mellon were adamantly opposed to any bonus payment for soldiers returning from the Great War. In fact, they decided to couple the idea of tax reduction, popular with Americans, with the defeat of the soldiers' bonus.[13] Both the Mellon tax plan and the soldiers' bonus bill were taken up by Congress in early 1924, heading into the 1924 presidential election in November. Both houses of Congress passed the long-delayed soldier's bonus bill, but Coolidge vetoed

---

12   See Benjamin G. Rader, "Federal Taxation in the 1920s: A Re-examination," *The Historian*, Vol 33, 1971, 415.

13   Anne L. Alstott. and Benjamin Novick, "War, Taxes, and Income Redistribution in the Twenties: The 1924 Veterans' Bonus and the Defeat of the Mellon Plan," *Law & Society: Public Law eJournal* (2006): 376.

it on May 15, 1924, saying "patriotism...bought and paid for is not patriotism." McLean joined with others in Congress and overrode his veto a few days later.

Why did McLean "die on the hill" of the soldier's bonus? Wasn't he a loyal Republican, eager to please his new president? Along with showing appreciation to veterans, the bonus was viewed as a replacement to the corrupt pension system that followed the American Civil War. These pension payments to Northern soldiers and their dependents were enormous in scale and lasted generations. Yale Law School Professor Anne Alcott additionally argues that the 1924 bonus bill foreshadows the G.I. Bill used after World War II: both recognized the economic situation of the returning veteran, and both aimed to help them transition back to civilian life.[14] The ever-friendly *Hartford Courant* spotlighted McLean's character and his commitment to making good on the pledge he had made to his state's veterans in 1921. McLean, the *Courant* wrote, showed this same independence and courage as governor, bucking his own party to lead reform of the Connecticut Assembly. Why should he be any different now?[15]

With the 1924 presidential nominating conventions approaching in June, the Mellon tax plan was in danger of going down in defeat. "Many of the vital provisions of the Mellon proposal have been repudiated," McLean said in a newspaper interview on May 4, 1924.[16] McLean fought in the Finance Committee for a compromise solution. With time running out, the Finance Committee held late-night sessions to salvage the bill. In the end, though, Coolidge and Mellon were unhappy with the final bill. It reduced both normal and surtax rates by roughly 25 percent, about half the reduction that Coolidge had

---

14   Anne L. Alstott and Benjamin Novick "War, Taxes, and Income Redistribution in the Twenties," 379.

15   "McLean," *Hartford Courant*, January 14, 1924, 10.

16   "GOP Senate Leaders Fight to Lower Tax," *Democrat and Chronicle* (Rochester, NY), May 4, 1924, 1.

wanted.[17] Yale's Anne Alstott concludes that the 1924 Revenue Act represented a victory for progressive forces. The Revenue Act of 1924 kept income tax rates higher at the top and lower at the bottom than the Mellon Plan proposed; the new law also included the highest estate tax rates ever enacted, and a new gift tax.[18] Progressives also triumphed with the passage of the bonus bill which resulted in income "redistribution albeit with a patriotic face," in Alstott's words. Moreover, the progressive taxation system prevailed, and its replacement by a national sales tax was once again defeated.

One of the defining political issues of the 1920s was immigration. Beginning in the late nineteenth century, about 350,000 immigrants arrived each year in the United States, and that number had risen significantly throughout the early 1900s, reaching a record-high 1.2 million new arrivals in 1907. In fact, between 1900 and 1915, America welcomed over fifteen million immigrants, more than it had accepted during the previous forty years.[19]

Theodore Roosevelt, who was president during this peak period, viewed immigrants as a needed source of labor for the nation's expanding economy, but he also insisted on their complete assimilation. As president, Roosevelt visited Ellis Island several times, concerned with the medical treatment given there, and even broke through red tape once to help a widowed woman with children pass inspection.[20] The World War significantly slowed immigration: levels fell to just over

---

17 Christina D. Romer, and David H. Romer "A Narrative Analysis of Interwar Tax Changes," unpublished paper, University of California, Berkeley, February 2012, 8, https://back.nber.org/appendix/w17860/A%20Narrative%20Analysis%20of%20Interwar%20Tax%20Changes%20Feb%202012.pdf, accessed December 12, 2020.

18 Anne L. Alstott. and Benjamin Novick, "War, Taxes, and Income Redistribution in the Twenties," 377.

19 Ben J. Wattenberg, *The Statistical History of the United States, From Colonial Times to the Present*, Series B304–330: Immigration-Immigrants By Country: 1820 To 1945 (New York: Basic Books, 1976).

20 Howard Markel, *When Germs Travel* (New York: Pantheon Books, 2004), 100.

100,000 arrivals in 1918.[21] US public opinion toward immigration shifted dramatically after the war. Americans increasingly viewed immigrants with distrust, particularly because some openly embraced communist, socialist, or anarchist ideologies. Politicians from both parties sought ways to restrict immigration and protect the interests of people who were already here.

McLean adopted Theodore Roosevelt's view that immigration and assimilation must go hand-in-hand. In the Senate, McLean advocated for the compulsory education of adult immigrants since children would learn English in the public schools. In 1919, McLean backed a bill which provided remedial education to foreign-born adults between the ages of 16 and 45 who did not speak English. McLean promoted the idea of teaching English to immigrants based on a successful program used in Connecticut.[22] It designated $12 million in federal aid to the states each year for the education of adult immigrants until 1923. The so-called Kenyon measure passed the Senate in January 1920, but was not voted on in the House.[23]

At the conclusion of World War I Congress imposed restrictions on immigration by passing the 1921 Emergency Quota Act, which provided three percent quotas for nationalities in proportion to their presence in the United States in the 1920 census. This act resulted in strict caps on future immigration from Russia, Italy, and other parts of southern Europe, reflecting an element of anti-Catholicism and antisemitism toward Russian Jews. The Emergency Quota Act passed the Senate on May 3, 1921, by a margin of 78–1, but sixteen did not vote.

21 US Bureau of the Census, *Historical Statistics of the United States, Colonial Times to 1970*, Series B304–330: Immigration, 1820–1945, Washington, DC, 1975.

22 "Senator McLean Would Have All Aliens Go to School," *The Meriden* (CT) *Daily Journal*, November 11, 1919, 12.

23 Cyrenus Cole, *A History of the People of Iowa* (Cedar Rapids, IA: The Torch Press, 1921), 529.

McLean was among those sixteen.[24] His abstention may have resulted from his ambivalence about the measure, or his disapproval, or perhaps he sensed that the bill had overwhelming support, so he took the politically expedient course of simply not voting.

McLean took a clear stand on the Immigration Act of 1924, which made permanent what the 1921 Emergency Quota Act had put in place temporarily. The 1924 law not only re-defined the annual quotas that capped the number of immigrants that could come from each country, but it also included a controversial proposal to end Japanese immigration altogether.

With the vote on the bill scheduled for May of 1924, election-year politics came into the picture. Coolidge wanted to win the presidency in his own right in November of 1924, and the immigration issue would influence voters in many "nativist-leaning" states throughout the country. The 1924 Immigration Act contained even more restrictive immigration quotas than the 1921 Emergency Act. These quotas favored continued immigration from western Europe, but limited Italians, Greeks, eastern Europeans, Russians, Poles and Slavs.[25]

In a Senate vote of 69–9, McLean voted against the act, strongly objecting to the Japanese exclusion clause, calling it a "dangerous gratuitous insult" to Japan, a friendly nation with whom the United States desires improved relations and participation at global disarmament talks.[26] A few weeks after the vote, the Japanese Diet (their congress) condemned the action, saying it deeply injured Japan's national pride. The statement by the Diet implied that the "public temper" in Japan might give way to feelings of natural resentment, a thinly-guised

---

24   "TO PASS H. R. 4075, AS AMENDED, WHICH RESTRICTS IMMIGRATION ... -- Senate Vote #21 -- May 3, 1921," GovTrack.us, accessed April 9, 2021, https://www.govtrack.us/congress/votes/67-1/s21.

25   See Henry Pratt Fairchild, "The Immigration Law of 1924," *The Quarterly Journal of Economics* 38, no. 4 (1924): 653–65, accessed March 27, 2021, http://www.jstor.org/stable/1884595.

26   A Bill To Limit The Immigration Of Aliens Into The United States (P. 8568–2), May 15, 1924, GovTrack.us.

warning to the international community.[27] Scholars have concluded that passage of the Japanese Exclusion clause set loose an unhealthy nationalism in Japan with far-reaching consequences.[28]

McLean viewed the 1924 Immigration Act as a harmful action that could endanger the results of the Washington Disarmament conference. It would likely set back years of building up friendly relations with Japan. McLean told his Senate colleagues that officials at the Washington Disarmament Conference had reported to him on the "friendly spirit" of the Japanese participants, and McLean said he feared this vote would derail the talks.[29]

Coolidge's renomination to the presidency in 1924 was far from a sure thing. Many Republican leaders viewed him as an accidental president, not worthy of the office. There had been rumors in early 1922 that Harding might dump him from the ticket in 1924.[30] Harding had rarely consulted with Coolidge, referring to him as "that little fellow from Massachusetts."[31] His taciturn nature and insipid speech-making did not inspire some Republican kingmakers.

Yet, on a number of other considerations, Coolidge was the right man in the right place at the right time. The economy was expanding rapidly in 1924, unemployment was low, and Coolidge's reputation for

---

27 "Japanese Leaders Try to Restrain Peoples' Resentment Over Exclusion," *Hartford Daily Courant*, May 25, 1924, 1.

28 Tadashi Aruga, "Reflections on the History of U.S.-Japanese Relations," *American Studies International* 32, no. 1 (1994): 11, accessed March 27, 2021, https://www.jstor.org/stable/41280813. McLean stated: "I consider the action of the Congress in passing the Japanese exclusion clause a gratuitous insult to a friendly nation that cannot but harm our relations with Japan and endanger the results of the Washington Arms conference. The action of Congress endangers the work of years of building up friendly relations with Japan. McLean told his Senate colleagues that officials at the Washington Disarmament Conference reported on the "friendly spirit" of the Japanese participants, and McLean said he feared this vote would be interpreted as a "dangerous insult."

29 "Exclusion Act Called Insult by McLean," *North Adams* (MA) *Transcript*, May 10, 1924, 9.

30 Kenneth Whyte, *Hoover: An Extraordinary Life in Extraordinary Times* (New York: Alfred A. Knopf, 2019), 296.

31 Robert K. Murray, *The Politics of Normalcy: Governmental Theory and Practice in the Harding-Coolidge Era* (New York: W. W. Norton & Company, 1973), 130.

honesty and moral rectitude was a welcome antidote to the unfolding corruption of the Harding years. Coolidge's persona, like his fiscally conservative policies, were calming and reassuring to the country. In an era of rapid social change and modernization, Coolidge hearkened back to America's agrarian values of honesty, hard work, and traditional morality. At the June 1924 Republican National Convention, in Cleveland, Coolidge won the nomination on the first ballot with 1,065 votes; his only opponent, Senator Robert La Follette, received just 34 votes.

A few weeks later, the Democratic Party held its presidential nominating convention in New York City at Madison Square Garden. In contrast to the unity and discipline exhibited by the Republicans in Cleveland, the Democratic National Convention was a disaster. It lasted from June 24 to July 9, 1924, the longest political convention in US history, and it was one of the wildest and most destructive. After sixteen days of balloting, the Democrats selected John W. Davis on the 103rd ballot, an unpopular compromise candidate. The Democratic Party in 1924 was hopelessly divided: "wets" versus "drys," and Catholics versus fundamentalist Protestants. It was also divided regionally, with many Southern Democrats holding sway. Some party members still held out hope for joining the League of Nations, and others remained vehemently isolationist.

In November, Coolidge won the presidency by a wide margin in a three-way race. Former Republican Robert La Follette ran on the Progressive ticket, winning 16 percent of the popular vote. The Democratic candidate, John W. Davis, a West Virginia lawyer and former ambassador to Great Britain under Wilson, received just 28 percent of the popular vote, and he won only the twelve states of the Old Confederacy. Coolidge won a clear victory, winning almost every state outside of the Solid South.

The President and First Lady with one of their white collies at the White House (source: Getty Images)

McLean and Coolidge shared many professional and personal interests, including fishing and enjoying the outdoors, and they both dabbled as gentleman farmers. Their lives mirrored each other—unassuming New England farm boys, trained as lawyers, who climbed the ladder of local politics to become governors, and then national political figures. There are several good examples of the Coolidge-McLean friendship. President Coolidge loved dogs, beginning each day playing with his white collies, often sharing a strip of bacon or other table scraps with them.[32] On the day that the McLeans visited the White House with their bulldog, Peggy, the president noticed that she was favoring one of her legs. Mrs. McLean explained that the dog had hurt her leg during a recent outing at Washington's Potomac Park, trying to keep up with the McLeans as they motored leisurely through the park.

---

32   "Calvin Coolidge's Dog, Prudence Prim," Presidential Pet Museum (website), accessed January 4, 2020, https://www.presidentialpetmuseum.com/pets/coolidge-prudence-prim/.

Calvin Coolidge Fishing at Trout Pond at McLean's Simsbury estate, 1932
(source: Getty Images)

Coolidge, concerned, insisted that Peggy be taken to Walter Reed Hospital for X-rays. McLean later said that Peggy got well and "returned to thank her benefactor."[33]

In his retirement, Coolidge was a frequent visitor to Simsbury, perfecting his newfound hobby of fly-fishing at McLean's estate. Coolidge drove himself to Simsbury, about a one-hour trip from his home in Northampton, Massachusetts, usually accompanied by his wife, Grace. In 1932, Coolidge, usually reticent, agreed to let a bevy of newspaper reporters and photographers chronicle him fishing at McLean's Trout Pond on opening day of trout season. The pond was stocked with fish, and the former president, wearing a three-piece suit, hat, and fishing waders, caught over a dozen good-sized trout.

A few years earlier, when Coolidge fished there on the opening day of trout season April 17, 1929, he took home sixteen large rainbow trout.

---

33   "Farmer McLean," *The Watertown* (CT) *News*, June 10, 1927, 4.

Reporters later learned that he had been fishing without a license, a misdemeanor in Connecticut. McLean admitted that the former president did not have a license, "but I had one and I didn't think he needed one inasmuch as he was fishing in a private stream." Just to be sure, a few months later, the Connecticut State Legislature passed a law allowing Calvin Coolidge to fish in Connecticut anytime he wanted without a license.[34]

Near the end of 1924, Connecticut's senior US senator and long-time McLean associate, Frank Brandegee, killed himself by inhaling gas on October 14, 1924. Newspaper coverage of Brandegee's death was sensational and filled with wild speculation. One newspaper alleged that Brandegee was a frequent social companion of some of Harding's scandal-ridden "Ohio-gang" associates.[35] Another newspaper reported that Brandegee left debts exceeding $1 million (about $14.8 million in 2020 dollars), and was further distraught that none of his wealthy Connecticut friends would come to his aid.[36] McLean was deeply shaken by Brandegee's death, noting the "torturing shadows" that had come over him in his final months.[37]

McLean and Brandegee had parallel political careers, and had even been roommates in the 1890s in Hartford. As roommates, McLean recalled how they both had big political ambitions, an oddity since they were both essentially very introverted. McLean admired Brandegee's intellect, citing "flashes of genius" that pierced through complex issues with "X-ray precision," but the two men differed over matters of both policy and style. McLean characterized Brandegee as an un-

---

34   "Coolidge Can Now Fish in Full Safety," *Vidette-Messenger of Porter County* (Valparaiso, IN), April 18, 1929, 2.

35   Edward Stillman, *The Roaring Twenties* (New York: American Heritage, 2015), 112.

36   "Brandegee Debts Put at One Million," *The Sentinel* (Carlisle, PA), October 17, 1924, 1.

37   United States. 68th Congress, 2. session, Frank B. Brandegee: Memorial addresses delivered in the Senate and House of Representatives of the United States in Memory of Frank B. Brandegee Late a Senator from Connecticut (Washington, DC: US Government Printing Office, 1925), 5–13.

abashed conservative whose favorite word was "no," like his stance as an Irreconcilable on the League of Nations. McLean said Brandegee "was as free from subtlety as the traditional bass drummer in a Salvation Army band." This characteristic "cost him friends he could and should have kept."[38]

On December 16, 1924, Hiram Bingham III was elected to represent Connecticut in the US Senate to fill the vacancy created by the suicide of Frank Brandegee. Almost two decades younger than McLean, Bingham developed a close, almost father-son relationship with McLean. Bingham had achieved worldwide renown when he "discovered" the largely forgotten Inca city of Machu Picchu in Peru in 1911. It has been suggested that Bingham may have been the person on whom the iconic movie character Indiana Jones is based.[39] A daring explorer/adventurer who became an aviator in 1917, Bingham is credited with significantly advancing training standards and promoting government regulation of the aviation industry. He was a close friend of Charles Lindbergh, who at the age of twenty-five attained world fame by making the first nonstop flight from New York City to Paris in 1927.

The aviation industry was still in its infancy in the 1920s, and most Americans associated airplanes with danger and daring, a perception that inhibited the commercialization of air travel. Leaders of the nascent industry desperately wanted the federal government to oversee aviation by licensing pilots, inspecting aircraft, constructing and operating airports, monitoring airplane manufacturing, and promoting flying to the American people.[40] In March 1928, Charles Lindbergh came to Washington, DC, to boost the public's interest in aviation.

---

38   "McLean Calls Brandegee Truly Great," *The Bridgeport Telegram*, 10.

39   Dan Collyns, "Machu Picchu: What is the legacy of 'Indiana Jones discoverer'?" *BBC News,* July 7, 2011, https://www.bbc.com/news/world-latin-america-14060341, accessed November 11, 2020.

40   McMillan Houston Johnson V, "Taking Off: The Politics and Culture of American Aviation, 1920–1939," PhD diss. (University of Tennessee, 2011), ii.

At the White House, on March 21, 1928, President Coolidge bestowed on Charles Lindbergh the Congressional Medal of Honor in recognition of his transatlantic flight of 1927. The following evening, McLean attended a "stag dinner" at the home of Hiram Bingham, along with guests Charles Lindbergh and Senator Frederick Hale of Maine. Lindbergh had been taking many congressmen and their families on short flights over the city. Relaxing at the table after dinner, McLean and Lindbergh fell into a conversation about flying and Lindbergh made the suggestion that the senator take a trip in the air with him.

"No, thank you," McLean replied.

"I dare you," Lindbergh countered, in front of Bingham and Hale.

"Listen, young man," the seventy-year-old senator from Simsbury replied, "I never took a dare in my life and I'm too old to start now. When can you take me up?"

"Tomorrow," Lindbergh said.

The following morning, with cloudy skies, brisk winds, and temperatures in the mid- thirties, McLean and Bingham met Lindbergh at DC's Bolling Field (about six miles from the Capitol) for McLean's first-ever flight. They flew in a "big Douglas transport biplane," likely a six-passenger Douglas model C-1, and they saw the Capitol, Washington Monument, and other sites from about one thousand feet.

McLean later admitted that he felt a little uneasy during the twenty-minute flight, especially during takeoff. When he deplaned, surrounded by Hiram Bingham, the swashbuckling adventurer, and Charles Lindbergh, the "Lone Eagle," McLean had one final comment for the reporters who had gathered: "I enjoyed it," he said, "but I am not going to allow it to become a habit."[41] Just two days later, overwhelmed with the non-stop public adulation and loss of privacy,

---

41   "Sen. McLean, 70, Dared by Lindbergh, Takes First Flight," *Hartford Daily Courant,* March 23, 1928, 15.

Connecticut Senator Hiram Bingham III (source: Library of Congress, Prints and Photographs Division)

Charles Lindbergh announced that he was retiring from public life. The ten months following his successful transatlantic flight had been grueling and exhausting. "I can't stand it," Lindbergh said. "I'll go out of my mind if people don't stop pushing me."[42]

With new momentum from the 1924 election, Coolidge urged his Secretary of the Treasury, Andrew Mellon, to press for more tax reform, leading to the Revenue Act of 1926, considered Coolidge's and Mellon's crowning achievement. McLean was appointed one of four senators empowered to negotiate the details of the Revenue Act of 1926 with their House counterparts. It lowered the top tax rate again, this time down to twenty-five percent for incomes over $100,000. The bill eliminated the gift tax and reduced the inheritance tax from forty to twenty percent. Personal income taxes were lowered across the board; by 1928, the majority of taxpayers were paying less than one percent of the federal income tax, and wealthy Americans were paying twenty-five percent. The tax cuts were accompanied by reductions in spending and a disciplined effort to pay down the nation's debt. The Revenue Act of 1926 also stopped "tax avoidance" by eliminating many tax shelters.[43]

---

42   "Lindbergh Retiring from Public Appearances," *Hartford Daily Courant*, March 25, 1928, 1.

43   "Tax Policy, Coolidge Style," Calvin Coolidge Presidential Foundation, Inc., website, accessed November 4, 2020, https://www.coolidgefoundation.org/blog/tax-policy-coolidge-style/.

During the sixty-eighth Congress (1923–25), McLean was a member of the prestigious Foreign Relations Committee, one of the original ten standing committees of the Senate. (His other committee memberships were Finance, Territories, and Banking and Currency, where he was chairman.) As a member of the Senate Foreign Relations Committee, McLean helped the Coolidge administration find a way to help America become more involved in international affairs. In a 1926 Senate speech, McLean admitted that he now thought the United States would have been better off as a participating member of the League of Nations (modified with the Lodge reservations, he added). But the League was a closed matter, so McLean joined President Coolidge in advocating the next best thing—US membership in the World Court, an arm of the League of Nations created to provide for the remediation and peaceful resolution of international disputes.[44]

Warren Harding had advocated US participation in the World Court in his 1922 inaugural address. Coolidge firmly endorsed the "law not war" philosophy behind the World Court, and in 1926, he enlisted McLean's help to sell the idea to the Senate. The World Court debate revived many of the same controversies as the League of Nations discussions in 1919. This time McLean would become a target of the Senate's isolationists. On January 13, 1926, McLean made a speech in the Senate, urging World Court membership. America was a leader in world trade and needed to face up to its need to join international organizations, McLean argued. The world needs, and the United States must join, an international tribunal for the settlement of international disputes. While it is not wise for the "American eagle to act like a Shanghai rooster," neither is it right to act like an ostrich with its head in the sand.[45]

---

44   "McLean Cites Prohibition Issue Danger," *Hartford Daily Courant*, September 14, 1926, 10.

45   George P. McLean (CT), "The World Court," *Congressional Record* 67—Senate, January 13, 1926, 1970, https://www.govinfo.gov/content/pkg/GPO-CRECB-1926-pt2-v67/pdf/GPO-CRECB-1926-pt2-v67-12-1.pdf.

While the Senate ultimately approved membership in the World Court on January 27, 1926, it was conditional, loaded down with five major reservations. The same "Irreconcilables" who opposed the League of Nations now demanded veto powers for the United States that would prove to be unacceptable to the World Court.[46] On November 11, 1926, Coolidge, recognizing that a workable compromise was impossible, announced that the United States would not join the World Court.[47] Membership in the Court was considered (and rejected) again in 1929, 1932, and in 1935.[48]

Not long after the failure to join the World Court, Coolidge latched onto an even bolder foreign policy initiative, the Kellogg–Briand Pact, under which the leading nations of the world agreed to renounce war as an instrument of national policy. The pact embodied the anti-war sentiments then embraced by a diverse group of American and international peace organizations. The idea took root in the spring of 1927 when French Foreign Minister Aristide Briand proposed that the United States and France sign a treaty to ban the use of armed conflict to settle disputes between the two nations. Coolidge's Secretary of State Frank B. Kellogg suggested that the pact be broadened, and invited all nations to join them in outlawing war. The Kellogg-Briand Pact was eventually signed by fifteen nations, including Germany, Japan, and Italy, in Paris on August 27, 1928. It would now have to be ratified by the US Senate.

On January 5, 1929, McLean delivered his final speech in the Senate. His subject: the Coolidge-backed Kellogg-Briand treaty outlawing war. It is likely McLean knew this would be his final speech. Now seventy-one years old and in poor health, suffering from angina, he

---

46 Ibid.

47 Andrew Glass, "Senate votes to join World Court, Jan. 27, 1926," *Politico,* January 27, 2016, accessed December 4, 2020, https://www.politico.com/story/2016/01/senate-votes-to-join-world-court-january-27-1926-218063.

48 D. F. Fleming, *The United States and the World Court* (New York: Doubleday, 1945), 38.

had told a group of newspaper editors in 1928 that he would not accept renomination for a fourth Senate term. He looked forward to spending his remaining years in restful retirement.[49]

The Kellogg-Briand treaty was popular with the public, and McLean's Senate colleagues saw it as a largely innocuous proposal—unanimous passage was expected. As a member of the Foreign Relations Committee, McLean was very familiar with the treaty. As he prepared to make his final speech to the Senate, McLean likely took stock of the moment, eyeing the ninety-six individual desks arranged on a tiered semicircular platform facing a raised rostrum. The visitor's gallery overlooks the chamber on four sides. This had been his workplace for the last eighteen years, where he had cast over 2,200 votes, and had spent countless hours studying and debating complex issues that resisted easy resolution. Sixteen years earlier, on January 12, 1913, McLean had made his maiden speech to the Senate. His subject: protecting migratory birds.

As the afternoon sun flooded through the large skylight in the ceiling of the blue-carpeted Senate chamber, McLean rose from his mahogany desk in the second row. The gallery, packed with spectators, including McLean's wife, Juliette, quieted as he put on his spectacles, and paged through his notes. McLean gathered himself as he stood beside his desk, the venerable "Webster Desk," once used by the great orator Daniel Webster of Massachusetts.

"Mr. President," McLean began, "ordinarily I think too much of my time, however valueless it may be, to consume it fighting what is said to be a lost cause. Six weeks ago, I expected to vote for this treaty without comment, but I have changed my mind." He was speaking today to explain why he could not vote for it.[50] McLean's comments "came as a bolt out of the blue," wrote the *San Francisco Examiner*, as the treaty's

---

49   "The Senator from Connecticut," *The Bridgeport Telegram*, October 3, 1927, 18.

50   George P. McLean (CT), "Why I Cannot Vote for the Peace Pact," *Congressional Record* 70-Senate, January 5, 1929, 1189, https://www.govinfo.gov/content/pkg/GPO-CRECB-1929-pt2-v70/pdf/GPO-CRECB-1929-pt2-v70-1-1.pdf

proponents had anticipated an easy victory. McLean then launched into an hour-long scathing attack on the treaty, holding the Senate and gallery in rapt attention.[51]

The treaty, McLean argued, was ineffectual, troublesome, and quite possibly dangerous. "The time has arrived to stop throwing peace paper wads at the dogs of war, expecting that they will injure the dogs or destroy their appetite." McLean compared the treaty to the folly of Prohibition. When will the US Congress learn that it cannot stop men wanting what they want to do? McLean asked. The Eighteenth Amendment abolished the right to make and sell alcohol, but $2 million worth of alcoholic beverages were consumed in Washington, DC, in 1928, according to the *Washington News*, McLean stated. Trying to stop man's "combative instincts" with this treaty is nothing more than a goodwill gesture that will accomplish nothing. Forbidden fruit, McLean stated, is as sweet and popular today as it was in the Garden of Eden. McLean's characterization of the treaty's ineffectual nature was echoed fifty years later by Harvard professor and former US Secretary of State Henry Kissinger, who called the Kellogg-Briand Pact "as irresistible as it was meaningless," while American diplomat and historian George Kennan (1904–2005) described it as "childish, just childish."[52]

McLean then went on to identify a host of dictators in Europe and other threats to world peace, including Russian autocrats determined to destroy economic liberty through world revolution. Russia had an army numbering five million, McLean said. We know how these dictatorships end—nations are dismembered like Austria and Germany were in the last war. We must remember that our forefathers used force to preserve the only kind of peace worth having. It is not time for us to surrender our sovereignty to "misinformed saints or well-informed

---

51   "U.S. Must Depend on Arms, Not Pact, Says McLean," *The San Francisco Examiner,* January 6, 1929, 14.

52   Elizabeth Borgwardt, *A New Deal for the World* (United Kingdom: Harvard University Press, 2007), 67.

sinners. It is our manifest and sacred duty to keep our powder dry and in sufficient quantities."

McLean's central legal objection to the treaty was that it failed to recognize America's right to self-defense and to uphold the "Monroe Doctrine," the historic US policy toward the Western Hemisphere, formulated in 1823 by President James Monroe. That doctrine warned European nations that the United States would not tolerate further colonization or interference with independent governments in the Americas. "If this treaty is ratified," McLean warned, "our neighbors will claim that we have ignored the Monroe Doctrine," and "foreign powers will insist that the League of Nations is to settle disputes which may arise in the Americas."

With his retirement just two months away, McLean's passionate tone and his one-hour "bolt out of the blue" speech was noteworthy. He could have just quietly walked away from the debate and returned to his estate in Simsbury, knowing that the treaty had near-unanimous support. But he didn't. One is reminded of the Dylan Thomas poem, "Do Not Go Gentle Into That Good Night," where the protagonist, sensing life's end, does not respond passively or cynically, but vows to fight on for what is right and true. As Dylan Thomas penned, "Old age should burn and rave at close of day; Rage, rage against the dying of the light."[53] McLean's speech conveyed his underlying frustration with using government power to fix the moral failings of human nature, especially when he equated the Kellogg-Briand treaty outlawing war with the equally futile prohibition of alcohol. He warned Americans of their coming disappointment. If people continue to look to the lawmaker or world treaty for what is right and good, they will be sorely disappointed, McLean concluded soberly.

---

53   Dylan Thomas, "Do Not Go Gentle Into That Good Night," All Poetry, https://allpoetry.com/Do-Not-Go-Gentle-Into-That-Good-Night?page=5, accessed March 12, 2021.

On January 15, 1929, the Kellogg-Briand treaty passed the Senate on 85–1 with nine not voting. McLean was among those not voting.[54] (The only dissenting vote came from Senator John Blaine, a Wisconsin Republican who asserted that treaty ratification would constitute an endorsement of British imperialism.[55])

After his final speech to the Senate on January 4, 1929, McLean returned to his home on Massachusetts Avenue, where he remained for the last two months of his term. Except for a few low-key visits to the Capitol in late February to meet with visitors and constituents, McLean never made another public appearance on the Senate floor. His eighteen-year career in the Senate ended on March 4, 1929, the very day that Herbert Clark Hoover was sworn in as the thirty-first president of the United States, standing on the east portico of the US Capitol, repeating the oath as it was read by Chief Justice William Howard Taft.

After forty-five years in public service, it was time to go home.

54   "Roll Call Vote—Multilateral Peace Treaty," *Congressional Record*—Senate 70, January 15, 1929, 1714, https://www.govinfo.gov/content/pkg/GPO-CRECB-1929-pt2-v70/pdf/GPO-CRECB-1929-pt2-v70-9-1.pdf.

55   "All By Himself: Sen. John J. Blaine," *Green Bay Press-Gazette*, January 16, 1929, 1.

PART THREE

GOING HOME

★ CHAPTER TWELVE ★

COMING FULL CIRCLE

> Always courteous, always kindly, always intelligently
> informed, I regard Senator McLean's retirement as a
> distinct loss to the Senate and to the country.
> *US Senator Carter Glass, a Democrat, on the floor of*
> *the Senate, March 2, 1929*[1]

McLean's speech opposing the Kellogg-Briand Peace Pact on January 5, 1929, was indeed his final appearance in the Senate. Newspaper accounts indicate that he was stricken with a flu-like illness and housebound for most of January and February of 1929. Two days before the date of his retirement (March 4, 1929), Senator Carter Glass, a Democrat from Virginia, often referred to as the "father of the Federal Reserve" banking system, paid tribute to McLean on the floor of the Senate. Glass, a senator from 1920 to 1946, served as secretary of the treasury (1918–1920) under President Woodrow Wilson. Glass said he tried in vain to get McLean to run for a fourth term—odd for a member of the opposite party. Party differences aside, Glass said their association on the Banking and Currency Committee

---

1   "Senator McLean's Retirement," *Hartford Daily Courant*, March 4, 1929, 8.

was based on cooperation and personal respect. McLean was a worthy, public man, whom he would deeply miss.[2]

A more surprising tribute came from a frequent McLean foe, Senator J. Thomas "Cotton Tom" Heflin, a Democrat from Alabama. Born in 1869 in a small Alabama town, Heflin became a lawyer, then entered politics. He dressed like a Southern gentleman, wearing a white linen frock coat with a double-breasted waistcoat, and spats on his shoes.[3] McLean and Heflin often sparred about the Federal Reserve System. Heflin, an outspoken critic of the Fed, was particularly galled whenever the central bank raised the discount rates to member banks, which increased the cost of borrowing, hurting Alabama's farmers. One memorable exchange occurred when McLean refused to yield to the long-winded Heflin. McLean said, while he wanted to be courteous, he didn't care to have Heflin "cool his tea in my saucer this afternoon." Heflin replied to the delight of the Senate that he'd pour his tea on McLean's head when he's through.[4] When Heflin learned of McLean's planned retirement, he was effusive in his praise, saying McLean "is the strongest man intellectually that New England ever sent to the Senate. I think he is one of the greatest Senators who ever sat on the Republican side of the aisle."[5]

McLean remained in Washington, D.C., for a few months after his term expired, waiting for the weather to warm before returning to Simsbury.[6] Juliette was less eager to return to Simsbury. She had always liked the Washington social scene more than her husband, and contin-

2   Carter Glass (VA), "George P. McLean," *Congressional Record 70*—Senate, March 2, 1929, p. 5024, https://www.govinfo.gov/content/pkg/GPO-CRECB-1929-pt5-v70/pdf/GPO-CRECB-1929-pt5-v70-5-1.pdf.

3   "Heflin Suggests People of the South Wear Cotton Exclusively," *The Montgomery* (AL) *Advertiser,* March 17, 1929, 22.

4   "Hot Debate in Senate," *The Twin-City Daily Sentinel* (Winston-Salem, NC), January 12, 1922, 10.

5   "Brainiest Senator" *Berkshire* (MA) *Eagle,* April 28, 1928, 8.

6   "McLean to Retire to Large Farm," *Meriden* (CT) *Record,* March 11, 1929, 15.

ued hosting friends and social events right up to the end. As a senator's wife, she opened up their Massachusetts Avenue home to visitors every Thursday afternoon, as regularly noted in the local society pages. Her last activity in the city, on February 24, 1929, was to co-sponsor a lecture by the exiled Russian czar, Grand Duke Alexander. The scion of Russia's former ruling family lectured on the "religion of love and the theory of spiritual democracy" as a method of "fighting the Communists and Bolsheviks who have taken over his country."[7] Among those in attendance were Vice President Charles G. Dawes and his wife.

Shakespeare is believed to have originated the expression "to come full circle" in *King Lear* (Act 5, Scene 3) when he wrote "The wheel is come full circle." It means that after a lifetime of change and growth, things often return us to our starting point. We may wander this way or that, for years even, but in the end, we may find ourselves back where we began, complete, whole. Coming full circle brings us to a unique vantage point: a place of closure and healing, a chance to celebrate, a time to experience gratitude and affirmation and to reflect upon key moments and the people who helped us along the way.

Such an experience occurred for McLean on June 14, 1929, when Trinity College in Hartford awarded him an honorary doctorate of laws. Almost fifty years earlier, McLean, then age twenty-two, his ambitions unfulfilled as a cub reporter at the *Hartford Post,* took a job as a bookkeeper at Trinity College, making $300 a year. After two years at the college, his ambitions unsatisfied, McLean left to study law and enter a life in politics. Others receiving honorary degrees with him at Trinity that day were two peers he knew well, both former Coolidge Cabinet members—Secretary of State Frank B. Kellogg and Treasury Secretary Andrew W. Mellon.

Five months after McLean received his honorary doctorate, the stock

---

7   "Many Festivities for Grand Duke Alexander," *Evening Star* (Washington, DC), February 25, 1929, 14.

market crashed. On October 29, 1929, investors traded some 16 million shares on the New York Stock Exchange in a single day. Billions of dollars were lost, wiping out thousands of investors. How bad was the fall in stock prices? General Motors stock went from $73 a share to $8; US Steel fell from $262 a share to $22. The president of the Union Cigar company shot and killed himself after seeing his company stock fall from $113 to $4 a share.[8] Billionaire John D. Rockefeller's fortune fell by four-fifths; songwriter Irving Berlin lost $5 million, virtually his entire net worth, as did Groucho and Harpo Marx, whose losses were even worse since they, like many others, had been buying stocks on credit.

Decades later, McLean's nephews and great-nephews would speculate that since Uncle George was heavily invested in the stock market, he must have taken a beating in the crash, left mainly with his real estate holdings. In 1913, McLean disclosed to a Senate investigating panel that he indeed owned stocks, including shares in the National Biscuit Company and 300 shares of General Electric stock.[9] (300 shares of GE had a value of around $42,000 in 1913, or $1.1 million in 2021 dollars).[10] There is evidence, however, that the McLeans were not entirely wiped out by the crash, since he and Juliette traveled extensively in their retirement. For instance, they spent the winter of 1931 at the elegant Whitehall Hotel in Palm Beach, Florida, and they made frequent trips to visit Juliette's cousin, Mr. and Mrs. Joseph Ensign, at their beach house in Weekapaug, Rhode Island. In her widowhood, Juliette bought her own summer home in Weekapaug near the Ensigns.[11]

While McLean's finances were probably diminished severely because of the stock market collapse, an even bigger concern after retiring was

---

8   "The Great Depression," Minnesota Libraries Publishing Project, https://mlpp.pressbooks.pub/ushistory2/chapter/great-depression/, accessed November 2, 2020.

9   "McLean Owns Electric Stock," *Carbondale Free Press* (Carbondale, IL), June 4, 1913, 1.

10   "New York Stock Market," *Boston Globe*, October 14, 1913, 11.

11   "Mrs. George P. McLean," *Hartford Daily Courant*, August 16, 1942, 17.

his health. On April 19, 1930, he underwent an operation for an un-named ailment at a New York hospital.[12] Periodic updates to the press over the next two months suggested that he was improving but re-mained hospitalized. While the nature of his ailment is unknown, two months in the hospital suggests a serious medical problem.

In a far-reaching sense, the stock market crash of 1929 and the Great Depression had long-lasting consequences for McLean and his Re-publican peers. Many historians blame Harding and Coolidge for the Great Depression, and have relegated them and their colleagues to the "ash heap of history." The dominant historical narrative of the Great Depression originated in the 1950s when historians like Arthur M. Schlesinger, Jr. argued that Franklin D. Roosevelt's New Deal policies were a much-needed antidote to the do-nothing, *laissez-faire* approach of the Republicans of the 1920s. These historians largely dismiss Re-publican governance in the decade of the 1920s, seeing it as little more than a period of irresponsibility and ineptitude.

But historian Thomas Tacoma in *Calvin Coolidge and the Great De-pression: A New Assessment* takes a very different view. Tacoma asserts that Coolidge deserves little if any of the blame assigned to him for the Depression.[13] A closer examination of the record reveals that President Coolidge was keenly aware of the dangers facing the economy and the stock market. He recognized the warnings sounded by leading econ-omists like Harvard's William Z. Ripley, who wrote in 1926 that lax state incorporation laws were fueling speculative stock trading practic-es. And Coolidge shared the prevailing view that the independent (and newly created) Federal Reserve Board, not the White House, should oversee the nation's financial markets.[14]

---

12   "Former Senator McLean to Undergo Operation," *Hartford Daily Courant*, April 20, 1930, 11.

13   Thomas Tacoma, "Calvin Coolidge and the Great Depression: A New Assessment," *The Independent Review* 24, no. 3 (Winter 2019/20): 361–80.

14   Ibid., 371.

Historian Amity Shlaes further challenges the idea that the prosperous 1920s are to blame for the Great Depression. In her book *The Forgotten Man: A New History of the Great Depression*, Shlaes asserts that business activity is inherently cyclical, and economic expansions last about fifty-eight months, followed by contractions that last about eleven months. The real question about the Great Depression, Shlaes says, is not what caused it, but why it lasted so long. She argues that federal intervention between 1929 and 1940 unnecessarily deepened and prolonged the Depression, largely because of Herbert Hoover's errors (like raising taxes, signing the Smoot-Hawley Tariff Act, and advocating wage increases businesses could ill afford); and Franklin Roosevelt's experimental approach to fixing the economy. Taken together, it was those ill-advised moves that combined to make the Depression "Great."[15]

By mid-summer of 1930, McLean had recuperated from his operation and returned to Simsbury. One of his greatest passions in retirement was managing his herd of Guernsey cows. He acquired his first Guernsey in 1918, and steadily increased the herd through acquisition and breeding. On May 22, 1929, he paid a record $9,100 for a Guernsey bull (about $136,000 in 2020 dollars). The milk from Holly Farms was sold in bulk to distributors in Hartford, door-to-door locally, and to their biggest account, the Ethel Walker School in Simsbury, a college preparatory day and boarding school for girls.

Why did McLean love Guernseys? The reddish-brown cows are famous for the "golden" color of their milk, resulting from a high concentration of solids, both protein and fat, creating a high cream and butter content. The breed reached its peak in the United States at nearly 2 million head in 1920. Today, there are only around 14,000 Guernseys,

---

15   Amity Shlaes, *The Forgotten Man: A New History of the Great Depression* (New York: Harper Collins Publishers, 2008).

supplanted by the much more productive Holstein breed.[16] The dairy farm was McLean's greatest joy during his retirement. Ever hopeful for the birth of a best-in-show cow, McLean found managing his Guernsey herd as "thrilling as a horse race."[17] He occasionally welcomed newspaper reporters to visit Holly Farm. McLean was an animated host, chatting about the idiosyncrasies of individual cows and bulls, showing off his well-ventilated, spick-and-span barns, and offering his guests cool glasses of fresh milk or a bowl of rich ice cream.[18]

That dairy farming was McLean's "greatest joy" in retirement is another example of his life having come full circle. In a widely retold story about his youth, McLean had emphatically declared that he disliked farming, its endless tedium, scratchy hand-made clothing, and its backbreaking exertions.[19] Like many ambitious children, McLean was so eager to grow up and conquer the world that he viewed his youth with impatience and resentment. But now, in retirement, having seen the world, and interacted with some its most powerful decision-makers, having debated questions of war and peace, studied and legislated complex issues relating to taxation, banking, and conservation, McLean found joy and peace in simple things—a walk in the woods, the birth of a calf, a clean barn, watching his herdsmen milk his cows, and seeing the good, clean "golden Guernsey" milk poured into ten-gallon, steel milk cans, and loaded onto wagons for distribution to the citizens of Simsbury.

McLean was just as voracious a reader in retirement as he had been throughout his life. One visitor described his study at Holly House. At one end, a fire burned in a fireplace. There were books everywhere,

---

16 Janet Vorwald Dohner, *The Encyclopedia of Historic and Endangered Livestock and Poultry Breeds* (New Haven: Yale University Press, 2001), 275.

17 Ibid., 1.

18 "Farmer McLean," *The Watertown* (CT) *News*, June 10, 1927, 4.

19 Mary McLean Daniells, "George Payne McLean and His Family" (unpublished manuscript, c. 1971), 16, author's collection.

piled on his desk, on the fireplace mantle, and a heap of periodicals on a daybed. A few of McLean's favorites included apologetics by G. K. Chesterton, the essays of Ralph Waldo Emerson and Charles Lamb, and James Bryce's *The American Commonwealth,* a classic work in political science and economy. McLean could go through four or five newspapers with astonishing rapidity, noted a friend.[20] He also had a particular interest in British literature, and would often read Shakespeare aloud.[21]

One of McLean's grand-nephews recalls seeing his philosophically minded "Uncle George" reading Alfred North Whitehead's *Process and Reality* on his porch in 1931.[22] Published in 1929, *Process and Reality* is Whitehead's *magnum opus,* considered one of the most influential philosophical texts of the twentieth century. Reading such a book in retirement at age seventy-two shows that McLean never stopped searching for truth or shied away from intellectual challenges. A reviewer in 1930 wrote that *Process and Reality* was not hammock reading but a challenging philosophical treatise on life's deepest questions.[23]

Whitehead's process philosophy is based on the notion that everything is in a "process of becoming," rather than static or fixed. Perhaps McLean was attracted to Whitehead's basic view that everything changes from moment to moment, that all things flow, that one must resist the idea of clinging to fixed truths. As a political reformer, McLean battled with the traditionalists who wanted to keep the "town system" of representation, and he fought with those who supported the legislature's pardoning power that dated back to Connecticut's seventeenth-century origins. While these ideas were good at the start,

---

20   "Governor McLean at His Home," *Hartford Daily Courant,* January 18, 1911, 13.

21   William K. Hutchinson, "Hobbies of the Great: George P. McLean," *The Herald-Press* (Saint Joseph, MI), August 12, 1925, 4.

22   Dana McLean Greeley speaking at 1984 McLean family reunion in Simsbury (unpublished audio recording).

23   "Books: Process and Reality," *Minneapolis Star,* January 4, 1930, 27.

by the nineteenth century both these ways of doing things needed to be reformed to free them from the taint of political corruption.

In mid-March 1931, on his way north from wintering in Georgia, McLean attended the 1931 Progressive Conference in Washington, DC. The goal of the conference was to formulate a progressive legislative agenda to combat the nation's ever-deepening economic depression. Over one-hundred state and national political leaders attended the conference, along with leaders of industry, labor, education, and academia. The nonpartisan conference of progressive leaders was chaired by US senator George Norris, a Republican from Nebraska.[24] Norris, a Republican, made it clear that he would not support President Hoover in the upcoming 1932 presidential election.[25] In fact, Norris would eventually support the Democratic candidate, Franklin D. Roosevelt, for the presidency in 1932.

The conference was held on the Senate floor to a packed gallery, including former senator McLean. How surprised he must have been to hear the conference endorse an idea that he had championed years before. It was one of the conference's final recommendations—to create legislation that would require cabinet members and federal department heads to appear before Congress and submit to questioning.[26] McLean had introduced this same proposal to the Senate four times: in 1917, 1919, 1922, and again in 1925.[27] Such a questioning period of the cabinet is a feature of most parliamentary systems; the prime minister of Great Britain regularly appears before the House of Commons.[28] In fact, cabinet questioning had been an acceptable practice in the US

24 "Nation's Leaders Called to Arms," *Spokesman-Review* (Spokane, WA), March 3, 1931, 1.

25 "Norris Sees Need of a Roosevelt," *Hartford Daily Courant*, March 13, 1931, 8.

26 "Progressive to Adopt Program At Closing Session," *New Castle News* (New Castle, PA), March 12, 1931, 6.

27 "Wants Congress to Boss Cabinet," *Sandusky* (OH) *Star-Journal,* July 5, 1919, 1.

28 Mathew Glassman, "A Parliamentary-Style Question Period," *Congressional Research Service,* March 5, 2009, https://fas.org/sgp/crs/misc/RL34599.pdf.

Congress in the early nineteenth century, but it fell out of favor over concerns about the separation of powers.

McLean generally kept a low profile on political issues during his retirement, preferring to focus on his dairy farming and his beloved estate, which he called the "reserve."[29] Among his most valued household staff and farmhands was the estate caretaker, Amos E. George, a member of Connecticut's Pequot tribe. He worked as McLean's caretaker for a total of thirty-eight years. Amos was born on the Pequot Indian reservation in Ledyard, Connecticut, in 1882, when only a few dozen Pequots remained, living in extreme poverty.

The sad history of the Pequot tribe is an all-too familiar story. At first, the Pequots peacefully coexisted with the puritan settlers, but as the European population grew, cooperation descended into conflict over land ownership and hunting practices. In 1637, Captain John Mason led a band of armed English settlers in a "defensive attack" on the Pequot village in Mystic, Connecticut, slaughtering all but a handful of its inhabitants.[30] It is hard to imagine that George McLean, a thoughtful student of Connecticut history, did not know about Mason's war with the Pequot tribe. Especially since one of McLean's campaign biographies boasts that his mother was a descendant of both Captain John Mason and William Bradford.[31]

Amos George's duties on the estate were varied. He blazed and maintained a system of trails through the hundreds of acres of McLean's woodlands, and built shelters, including the warming cabin near Trout Pond. He raised quail and Ruffed grouse, which were later released to stock the reserve. Amos George also patrolled the grounds and arrested

---

29   "Farmer McLean," *Watertown* (CT) *News,* June 11, 1927, 1.

30   Michael Freeman, "Puritans and Pequots: The Question of Genocide," *The New England Quarterly* 68, no. 2 (1995): 278–93, accessed March 8, 2021, doi:10.2307/366259.

31   William Harrison Taylor, *Taylor's Legislative History and Souvenir of Connecticut, Vol III,* (Putnam CT: William Taylor, 1901), 12, https://www.cga.ct.gov/hco/books/Taylors_Legislative_History_Souvenir_CT_1901_Vol_III.pdf.

poachers. His exploits as a hunter were occasionally noted in the *Hartford Courant*, like the time he trapped a twenty-five-pound wildcat or his captures of many otters and foxes.

He retired as caretaker in 1947 at age sixty, but continued to live at a house he'd built on the estate. In a 1956 interview, Amos George reminisced about leading hunting and fishing expeditions on the grounds for Senator McLean and guests like William Howard Taft and Calvin Coolidge. He looked for a moment at a photograph of a younger version of himself fishing with Coolidge, and he said wistfully, "I'll be here till I die."[32] McLean's respect and affection for Amos E. George is reflected in his 1931 will. He left his former caretaker an outright bequest of $5,000 plus an annual income of $1,200, and he provided $600 per year for his wife, Cora, in the event of Amos' death.[33]

On Memorial Day of 1932, McLean was part of a dedication ceremony in Simsbury for the newly completed Eno Memorial Hall, a Classical Revival brick-and-stone structure, two stories high, that would serve the town as a courthouse, city hall, and public auditorium. The dedication ceremony included many of McLean's friends and associates. One was his fellow conservationist Gifford Pinchot, now governor of Pennsylvania. At this last public appearance on Memorial Day in 1932, McLean reminisced about his boyhood chores, how they taught him self-reliance.[34] He next read a few telegrams from benefactors who were unable to attend in person, reporting that even with "the drop in securities," the donors had managed to fulfill their obligations and make the building a reality.[35] Turning to the Memorial Day portion of the ceremony, McLean scanned his audience of thousands lining

---

32   "Connecticut's Indians," *Hartford Daily Courant*, January 22, 1956, 88.

33   Last Will and Testament of George P. McLean, September 1, 1931, housed at McLean Care Archives.

34   "Self-Reliance is Urged by McLean," *Hartford Daily Courant*, May 31, 1932, 12.

35   Ibid., 1.

Hopmeadow Street, noting with a touch of sadness that there were no surviving members of the Grand Army of the Republic left in Simsbury.

Civil War soldiers were the fixtures and heroes of McLean's youth. Sixty-seven years earlier, at age seven, he had celebrated the triumphant end of the Civil War in these same Simsbury streets, blowing a tin horn to his utmost with his youthful lungs amidst the sound of church bells, steam whistles, and throngs of celebrating people. During that celebration, an old gentleman driving an old wagon passed by at a furious pace, obliged to stop after his hat blew off. McLean never forgot the exultant look in the old man's face when McLean handed him his lost hat. "Don't stop blowing your horn!" the old man had instructed him.[36]

McLean, now seventy-four, was no longer that high-spirited seven-year-old; now he had become "the old gentleman." The world had changed dramatically and in countless ways over his lifetime. He now lived in a modern world that he could not have imagined at age seven. On this Memorial Day of 1932, with Harding's postwar disarmament treaties in shambles, and defiant military dictatorships on the rise in Japan, Germany, and Italy, McLean concluded his brief remarks with a warning to his listeners. "War is a crime," he said, "but it doesn't make any difference if it's a mouse, a mastodon, or a man; if he doesn't put up his fists and defend himself, out he goes. The race that cannot stand up goes down."[37]

On Monday, June 6, 1932, six days after presiding at the dedication of the Eno Memorial Hall, McLean, seated at his breakfast table, told grand-nephew George McLean Milne and others present that he wasn't

---

36   "Connecticut Soldiers: How Their Memory Was Honored Yesterday," *Hartford Daily Courant*, May 31, 1890, 6.

37   "McLean Speaks at Simsbury Dedication," *Hartford Daily Courant*, May 31, 1932, 12.

feeling well.[38] That week had been exceptionally hot in Simsbury, with temperatures over ninety degrees. "He excused himself and went upstairs," Milne later recalled. Milne thought the hot weather may have gotten the better of his uncle. George P. McLean died at four o'clock that afternoon from a heart attack.

While McLean's health had been declining for several years, the news came as a shock to his family, friends, and thousands of constituents and associates in Connecticut, New England, and Washington, DC. Former President Coolidge phoned Juliette to extend his condolences, and telegrams streamed in from friends and colleagues, including President Herbert Hoover. Funeral services were held two days later at the Simsbury Congregational Church, where the pulpit had once been occupied by McLean's grandfather, Allen, and where McLean maintained a lifetime membership. The funeral services were said to be puritan in their simplicity, conducted by McLean's pastor, the Reverend Edwin Knox Mitchell, and assisted by Dana McLean Greeley, McLean's twenty-four-year-old grand-nephew, who was a seminarian at Harvard Divinity School.

The two men read selections from the scriptures and three poems, and then a male quartet sang two hymns.[39] The poems are unnamed, but could well have been authored by one of the Romantic poets he so loved, like Burns, Kingsley, or Whittier.[40] Similarly, the two hymns were not identified; one could have been "Amazing Grace," a favorite of McLean's mother, Mary Payne McLean.[41] The church's seating capacity of 500 was vastly exceeded by people standing in the side aisles, and many others gathered in the vestibule and outside the church. Former President Calvin Coolidge was an honorary pallbearer; he was not

---

38   "George P. McLean Made A Difference Then and Now," *Hartford Courant,* June 16, 1996, 123.

39   "Final Rites Tribute to Ex-Senator," *Hartford Daily Courant,* June 9, 1932, 1.

40   "Golden Jubilee of Dr. Parker," *Hartford Daily Courant,* January 12, 1910, 10.

41   George McLean Milne, letter to the author, March 24, 1998.

present, though his wife Grace was there. The actual pallbearers were drawn from McLean's household staff, including driver Frank Passini, caretaker Amos George, gardener Thomas Joyce, and herdsman Harry Costello. Businesses in Simsbury closed during the time of the funeral; so did most state offices.

McLean's Last Will and Testament reflects his love and concern for his wife, Juliette, his extended family, his household and estate staff, his community, and his deep reverence for nature. His estate was valued at $1.8 million, about $31 million in 2020 dollars.[42] He left more than $400,000 to family members and associates, including $25,000 to each of his nephews and nieces, and $10,000 each to his many grand-nephews and grand-nieces. Similar amounts were bequeathed to members of his household staff, not insignificant gifts considering that in 1932 the Great Depression was in full swing.

McLean's meticulously written will provided for the care of sick and elderly women in several significant ways. First, he set aside $20,000 for the Simsbury Visiting Nurses Association in memory of his sisters Hannah and Sarah. Second, he set up a trust fund such that when it reached $10 million, 20 percent of the money would be used to construct a facility to care for the indigent or sick mothers, widows and other state residents needing medical help. This facility would be established in honor of his mother, Mary Payne McLean, and his aunt Sarah Abernethy. In many ways, the McLean Home is a forerunner of today's assisted living residences. It was envisioned in an era before Social Security and Medicare when, for the most part, women didn't have the means to live independently in their old age. The McLean Home opened in 1971, and it is still operating today.[43]

Community groups provided for in his will included $60,000 each

---

42   "George P. McLean Made A Difference Then and Now," *Hartford Courant*, June 16, 1996, 123.

43   "McLean Care Assisted Living," https://mcleancare.org/about-us/.

for Hartford Hospital, established in 1854, and St. Francis Hospital, the largest Catholic hospital in New England; $30,000 for his home church, First Church of Christ in Simsbury; $10,000 for the construction of St. Mary's Catholic Church in Simsbury; and $5,000 each to the Connecticut School for the Blind and the Connecticut Audubon Society. His will established "The McLean Fund," which continues to this day, spending about $800,000 annually on the public and charitable purposes set forth in his will.[44]

The centerpiece of his will was the creation of the McLean Game Refuge, a 3,000-acre nature preserve of meadows and forests that McLean feared would be lost to development and resource exploitation. In subsequent years, more land has been donated or purchased so now the Game Refuge occupies over 4,400 acres (6.9 square miles). McLean wrote in his will that the Game Refuge would be "a place where some of the things God made may be seen by those who love them as I love them and may find in them the peace of mind and body that I have found." It now consists of over twenty miles of hiking trails and hosts around 20,000 visitors per year.

Juliette McLean was sixty-eight years old when her husband died, and she lived another eighteen years. She spent winters in the South; the Vanderbilt Bon Air Hotel in Augusta, Georgia, was her favorite winter retreat. Other winters she traveled to the Mountain Lake Club in Lake Wales, Florida. The Mountain Lake Club features over 1,400 acres of parklike property designed by landscape architect Frederick Law Olmsted, and it's now listed on the National Historic Register. For parts of each summer, she often visited with the Eno and Ensign families in Weekapaug, a part of the town of Westerly on the Rhode Island shore. On at least one occasion, she wintered in Tucson, Arizona.

While in Simsbury, she was active in social and civic affairs with

---

44 "McLean Fund," e-filed 990-series IRS filings, https://www.open990.org/org/066026241/mclean-fund/.

her sister, Nellie Eno, supporting such groups as the Hartford Garden Club, the Daughters of the American Revolution, the American Red Cross, and the Simsbury Visiting Nurses Association. Juliette also oversaw the household staff at Holly House, the operations of Holly Farms Dairy, and the McLean Game Refuge. The *Hartford Courant* reported that she frequently hosted bridge parties during her widowhood. Juliette may have agreed with Warren Buffett, who once said "Bridge is such a sensational game that I wouldn't mind being in jail if I had three cellmates who were decent players."[45]

Juliette died in 1950 at Hartford Hospital at eighty-six. Her funeral was held at Holly House, where she had been living, the home that her husband designed and built in 1896. After her death, the house sat unused until 1956, when it was sold and converted into a convalescent home.

At the conclusion of a biography, it is customary to conclude by reflecting on the subject's significance and achievements. What can we learn from McLean's life and legacy? One of McLean's greatest strengths as a leader was his focus on finding pragmatic solutions to tough political challenges. During the Progressive Era, long-neglected social and economic problems could no longer be ignored. Each political party had vastly different solutions, slowed by stubborn defenders of the status quo who resisted change of any kind. Given this volatile mixture of factionalism, extremism, and inertia, the role of centrists and moderates in breaking the logjam of inaction cannot be overlooked or minimized. George P. McLean was one of those moderate, centrist leaders who was willing to set aside partisan and ideological differences in the name of the greater good. He wasn't in the political center all the time, but he was willing to come to the center and meet people with opposing views to find solutions to intractable problems.

---

45 "Warren Buffett," on Jeff Tang's Bridgebum website, https://www.bridgebum.com/warren_buffett.php.

Many important legislative accomplishments in American history were forged through bipartisan compromises, like Dwight Eisenhower's Federal Aid Highway Act in 1956, Lyndon Johnson's civil rights bills of the 1960s, and Richard Nixon's creation of the Environmental Protection Agency in 1970. All of these achievements were made possible by Democratic moderates and Republican moderates who set aside their partisan and ideological differences to get something done. McLean's Migratory Bird Treaty Act, his greatest achievement, is an example of a significant bipartisan legislative success. It was a landmark victory for conservation, replacing decades of ineffective efforts to protect birds from extinction at the state and local levels with sweeping federal legislation, culminating in a series of international treaties.

McLean was the "change agent"—the catalyst—in Congress on behalf of saving migratory birds. Over a seven-year period, he guided Congress through a complex legislative process resulting in the Migratory Bird Treaty Act in 1918. McLean learned through bitter past experiences that leading change is never easy—change agents inevitably face hostile criticism from opponents wedded to the status quo. He initiated action by making compelling speeches about the plight of birds to get the Senate's (and the public's) attention. He then enlisted the help of Audubon Society leaders, naturalists, hunters, business leaders, and other critical allies to build the case for change. Ever the prosecuting attorney, he used facts, legal tactics, and persuasion to craft legislative solutions. With passage of the Weeks-McLean bill in 1913, he generated an important short-term win, knowing that it might be struck down on states-rights grounds by the courts. He built on the success of Weeks-McLean by extending his vision to protect migratory birds through international treaties. Most importantly, McLean forged a critical partnership with the leader of the other political party, President Woodrow Wilson. Passage of the 1918 Migratory Bird Treaty Act, along with his setting aside thousands of acres for the future McLean

Game Reserve, demonstrates that McLean was one of the Progressive Era's leading conservationists.

Another enduring legacy of the Migratory Bird Treaty Act is its longevity. While the original purpose of the MBTA was to regulate over-hunting of migratory birds for the hat trade, in recent decades, regulators have broadened its interpretation and began prosecuting the "incidental take" of protected birds. For instance, the largest fine stemming from the MBTA was the Exxon-Valdez oil spill in 1989, resulting in the deaths of an estimated 250,000 birds. Exxon pled guilty to violations of the MBTA and a US District Court fined Exxon $150 million, the largest fine ever levied for an environmental crime.[46] In September 2021, the US Fish and Wildlife Service overturned an earlier policy, issued in the Trump administration's final days, that said the Migratory Bird Treaty Act only applied when companies or individuals killed birds on purpose. Conservation groups welcomed these new rulings, calling them a major step toward stemming the dramatic loss of more than one in four North American birds over the past half century.[47]

Having thoroughly researched the life of George P. McLean, this book ends with some questions in light of his life and legacy. To paraphrase a song title by American folk singer Pete Seeger, "Where have all the moderates gone?" We live in an era of political polarization marked by extremism and intolerance. It is difficult for our political leaders to even have civil dialogues and engage in the negotiations and compromises that are so necessary for conflict resolution and good governance. The current divide has been decades in the making. Undoubtedly, news coverage and social media have contributed to the echo chamber that fuels extremism. Low voter turnout and partisan fund-raising practices

---

46   Christopher Chesne, "Un-Pheasant Consequences: The Migratory Bird Treaty Act and the Trump Administration," *LSU Journal of Energy Law and Resources*, February 2019, 497.

47   Andy McGlashen, "Biden Administration Restores Migratory Bird Treaty Act Protections," *Audubon Magazine*, September 29, 2021, https://www.audubon.org/news/biden-administration-restores-migratory-bird-treaty-act-protections.

further favor extremists, giving them a disproportionate voice in controlling the outcomes of elections. What is the end-result of extremism? The nation rightly recoiled in horror at scenes of rioting and chaos in the US Capitol on January 6, 2021. The Capitol riot is a clear lesson in where extremism ultimately takes us: destruction, chaos, and anarchy. Maybe this tragic event will serve as a needed wake-up call for centrists and moderates in America. Did our nation finally hit bottom with the Capitol riots? Do Americans really want extremism and polarization? Are there no realistic alternatives to rigid partisanship? Will a new generation of political leaders emerge who will return to moderation and turn away from the extremism of their parents and grandparents?

In 2018, George P. McLean's name was once again in the public eye, appearing on Twitter and internet searches, information media unimaginable in McLean's lifetime. During the one-hundredth anniversary of the Migratory Bird Treaty Act of 1918, many conservation officials praised McLean's efforts on behalf of bird conservation at public ceremonies marking the occasion. It is interesting that during his lifetime, McLean himself never boasted about his achievement on behalf of migratory birds. For example, he never mentioned it when running for reelection, nor did he highlight it in his campaign advertising. If anything, he occasionally took flak from his opponents for his outsized interest in birds at the expense of what they considered to be more important issues. One of his few public comments came in a 1915 newspaper interview: "It has been my dream that the people of the United States would realize the importance of our birds before it is too late, and I am proud to say that progress has been made in that direction."[48]

Dozens of news articles on the MBTA appeared in 2018 with headlines like "The Migratory Bird Treaty Act Is 100 Years Old!" and "A

---

48   "Senator McLean Shoots Birds but Only with Camera," *Hartford Daily Courant*, December 19, 1915, 20.

Century of Saving Birds," and "Making the Migratory Bird Treaty Work: A Centennial Assessment." In an interview in January of 2018, Paul Schmidt, chief conservation officer of Ducks Unlimited and a former US Fish and Wildlife official, called the Migratory Bird Treaty Act "one of the greatest conservation achievements of the 20th century."[49] Schmidt praised McLean and the bill's co-sponsor, US Representative John W. Weeks, for their vision and determination to see the legislation through. Reflecting upon the significance of the 1918 Migratory Bird Treaty Act, the National Audubon Society said: "The Migratory Bird Treaty Act, signed into law in 1918, is among the oldest wildlife protection laws on the books. In the years since its enactment, the MBTA has saved millions, if not billions, of birds."[50]

Saving the lives of billions of God's most beautiful creatures—now that's a legacy to treasure.

---

49   Paul Schmidt, "The Migratory Bird Treaty Centennial," Ducks Unlimited press release, n.d., https://www.ducks.org/conservation/public-policy/the-migratory-bird-treaty-centennial?poe=s econdlevelmostrecent.

50   "The Migratory Bird Treaty Act, Explained," National Audubon Society press release, January 26, 2018, https://perma.cc/Y8SZ-LRR9.

★ EPILOGUE ★

The 2015 hit musical "Hamilton" ends with Alexander Hamilton's tragic death in a duel, followed by his going over to the "other side," where he's reunited with the people he loves—his friend, John Laurens; his mentor, George Washington; his son, Phillip; and his mother, Rachael Fawcett. The musical raises the question of whether it's possible we all will someday reunite with the ones we love. The evangelist Billy Graham once said that was one of the questions people ask him most often: "Will we recognize our loved ones in heaven?" ("Yes" was Graham's reply.)

So, would I like to meet my great- great- uncle George P. McLean on the "other side"? Resoundingly, yes, I would. Researching and writing his story occupied large portions of my time for over three years. Yet, after all the research, thinking, and writing, I have more questions than answers, and only a fragmentary impression of the man.

What is it that interests me so much about him? I realize that he lived the type of life I yearned for in my youth. One of my earliest memories is watching the 1964 Democratic presidential nominating convention on a black-and-white television, clipboard in hand, tracking the proceedings with rapt attention and a sharp pencil. By studying McLean's life, I have vicariously experienced that dream of living a political life. I have come to know the eight US presidents McLean knew; I now understand the clash of political ideas he understood; and I appreciate the perseverance under pressure, and the skill and dedication he possessed to pass useful legislation, illustrated best by the Migratory Bird Treaty Act, his crowning achievement.

What will it be like, then, meeting him on the "other side"?

It would be nice to start at the Augusta National Golf Course, dressed comfortably in our golf togs on a sunny, early May morning, with temperatures heading for eighty degrees. The smell of freshly mown grass and azaleas will linger in the soft breeze. We will hit every shot squarely, effortlessly, flawlessly, making the greens in regulation, scoring birdies, pars, and an occasional eagle.

On the back nine, we'll be joined by a different US president he knew, beginning on the tenth with Benjamin Harrison, the man who appointed McLean as US Attorney for Connecticut in 1892. Then William McKinley will join us on the eleventh hole, and we'll discuss how he broadened the base of the Republican Party and inspired many presidents who followed him. Theodore Roosevelt will play the twelfth with us; it will be amazing just to behold his aura and energy. I will be content to simply listen and watch the two interact.

On the thirteenth hole, we'll tee off with William Howard Taft. I will take full measure of this likable man, listening expectantly for the sound of his laughter (a mix between a pig's squeal and a girlish giggle, or so I gather). When Woodrow Wilson joins us on fourteen, I want to ask how the two erstwhile foes, McLean, a Republican, and Wilson, a Democrat, managed to work together so effectively on protecting migratory birds. Harding will join us on fifteen—is he at all like Ronald Reagan, as I imagine him to be? Or is he more like Harry Truman, both poker-playing "men of the people"?

Meeting McLean's friend Calvin Coolidge on the sixteenth hole could be the highlight. I will listen closely to their voices and accents—in what ways are their Yankee dialects similar and different? (Hopefully, Coolidge will talk.) Herbert Hoover will join us on the seventeenth hole—the "Wonder Boy," said to be one of the most capable men ever to occupy the Oval Office.[1]

I would like to be surprised on the eighteenth hole. Maybe we'll be joined by Hiram Bingham (who seems like Indiana Jones) or Charles Lindbergh or Andrew Mellon or Mark Twain. Or McLean's brother, John B. McLean, the well-liked, peripatetic educator and "man for all seasons." Or maybe one of McLean's mentors will show up, like Orsamus Fyler, Morgan Bulkeley, or J. Henry Roraback. It will be the most exciting and rewarding round of golf that I've ever played.

After golfing, we'll relax with cigars and play bridge flawlessly with Juliette McLean, bidding and making slams, playing no-trump contracts with absolute control and ease. We'll have a variety of bridge partners—Franklin and Eleanor Roosevelt, Herbert Hoover, and Warren Harding. Then we'll tool around McLean's estate in his Rolls-Royce, and I'll meet chauffeur Frank Passini, and caretaker Amos George, and visit the Guernsey cows. Many of my cousins and uncles will join us in the barn for a bowl of homemade ice cream – people like William Roger Greeley, Roland, Hannah and Phil, Dana and Deb, my mother and father.

Later we'll fish in Trout Pond and swap stories around the stove in the little cabin there. And in the early evening, I'll meet McLean's mother, Mary and his father, Dudley, and they'll tell us stories about him as a boy and what it was like to watch him and his siblings grow up. McLean's father and I will play the flute over the sound of crickets as the golden sun blankets the hills that border the beautiful McLean estate in Simsbury.

We'll all eat together in the dining room at Holly House, where I'll meet the household staff, and then we'll repair to the library and talk about books. We'll easily discuss Whitehead's *Process and Reality*, deep-

---

1   Kenneth Whyte, *Hoover: An Extraordinary Life in Extraordinary Times* (New York: Alfred A. Knopf, 2017).

ening our understanding, paragraph by paragraph. Maybe he'll read his favorite excerpts from Shakespeare's plays, or a favorite poem or two. Then we'll sip bourbon by the fireplace from Waterford decanters, clinking glasses after making a toast to the Eighteenth and Twenty-first Amendments to the US Constitution.

We'll go over my book chapter by chapter, feeling the warmth of the fireplace, his two Wirehaired Pointing Griffon dogs, Cassius and Caesar, snoozing at our feet. He'll show me what I got right and what I missed, and in the end, it will all make sense. I'm going to tell him how much I appreciated his looking after his sister Hannah when she was widowed with three young children, one of whom was my grandfather. I'll thank him for financing my grandfather's (his nephew's) education at Harvard Medical School. And for leaving him and his other nephews and nieces $400,000 each in his will, a gift received during the depths of the Great Depression that no doubt came in handy.

What I really want to say is that it's more than the money that I appreciate—it's his care and concern for family, for setting an example, for showing a seriousness of purpose about right and wrong, for setting the bar high, for being philosophically-minded about government, conservation, theology, the law, and Guernsey cows.

The following morning, rested, nourished, and fortified by rich, strong coffee, we'll go birding in the woods surrounding the estate. On the path, we'll be hailed enthusiastically by Theodore Roosevelt, who will help us find the most elusive birds on our life lists. Eventually the birding party will include all those who helped McLean with the Migratory Bird Treaty Act: Hornaday, Pearson, Job, Woodrow Wilson and his family, and John James Audubon himself.

A Carolina Parakeet will land unafraid on my outstretched index finger. We'll see clouds of passenger pigeons that nearly blot out the sun, and maybe an Ivory-billed Woodpecker, Heath Hen, or Great Auk or two. We will truly experience the wish McLean recorded in his will, that the refuge being a holy place, where the things God made may be seen, and a sanctuary for the soul, a place to find peace of mind and body.

In the midst of all this peace and solitude, however, we will be joined by an ever-increasing number of people, beginning with our family, then moving out to our friends, and then connecting to the multitudes, *ad infinitum.* At last, we, the "two-thirds recluses," will be connected with the infinite and our souls will be filled with the love of God.

One thing we will not talk about is nervous prostration. It will no longer exist. God will have wiped away all the tears from our eyes, and there will be no more death, nor sorrow, nor crying, nor pain. All of that will be gone forever. For the old conditions and the former order of things will have passed away.

New ways, new days.

★ BIBLIOGRAPHY ★

MANUSCRIPTS

Albert H. Walker Papers. New York Public Library Manuscripts and Archives Division.

Board of Pardons records. Connecticut State Archives, Hartford, Connecticut.

Connecticut Governor records. Correspondence, 1811–1933. Connecticut State Archives, Hartford, CT.

E.W. Nelson Papers. Smithsonian Institution Archives, Washington, DC.

Francis Maxwell Autograph Collection. Connecticut Historical Society, Hartford, CT.

George Bird Grinnell papers. The Huntington Library, San Marino, CA.

Henry C. Robinson Papers, Yale University, New Haven, CT.

Herbert Hoover Papers. Herbert Hoover Presidential Library-Museum, West Branch, Iowa

William Howard Taft papers. Library of Congress, Manuscript Division, Washington, DC.

Mark Twain Project Online. University of California Los Angeles.

O.R. Fyler Papers. Torrington (CT) Historical Society, Torrington, CT.

Papers Relating to George P. McLean. McLean Care Archives, Simsbury, CT.

The Last Will and Testament of George P. McLean, September 1, 1931. McLean Care Archives, Simsbury, CT.

Theodore Roosevelt Collection. Harvard College Library, Cambridge, MA.

Theodore Roosevelt Digital Library at Dickinson State University, Dickinson, ND.

BOOKS

Bates, Gordon. *The Connecticut Prison Association and the Search for Reformatory Justice, 1875–2015.* Middletown, CT: Wesleyan University Press, 2017.

Beers, Clifford. *A Mind That Found Itself.* New York: Longmans, Green and Co., 1905.

Blake, Silas Leroy. *The Separates: The Strict Congregationalists of New England.* Boston: Pilgrim Press, 1902.

Borgwardt, Elizabeth. *A New Deal for the World.* Cambridge, MA: Harvard University Press, 2007.

Brands, H.W. *American Colossus: The Triumph of Capitalism, 1865–1900.* New York: Doubleday, 2010.

Brooks, David. *The Second Mountain: The Quest for a Moral Life.* New York: Random House, 2019.

Cannadine, David. *Mellon: An American Life.* New York: Knopf, 2006.

Chambers, John W. *The Eagle and the Dove: The American Peace Movement and United States Foreign Policy, 1900–1922.* Syracuse University Press, 1991.

Cole, Cyrenus. *A History of the People of Iowa.* Cedar Rapids, IA: The Torch Press, 1921.

"Connecticut Notes." *The New Hartford Tribune,* August 26, 1892, 2.

Coolidge, Louis A. *An Old-Fashioned Senator: Orville H. Platt of Connecticut.* New York: G.P. Putnam's Sons, 1910.

Crapol, Edward P. *James G. Blaine: Architect of Empire.* Wilmington, DE: Scholarly Resources, 2000.

Cronan, Michael. *James A. Reed: Legendary Lawyer; Marplot in the United States Senate.* Bloomington, IN: iUniverse Books, 2018.

Dahill, Edwin McNeill, Jr. "Connecticut's J. Henry Roraback." PhD diss., Columbia University, 1971.

Dean, John W. *Warren G. Harding: The American Presidents Series.* New York: Henry Holt, 2004.

Dehler, Gregory. *The Most Defiant Devil: William T. Hornaday.* Charlottesville: University of Virginia Press, 2013.

Dohner, Janet Vorwald. *The Encyclopedia of Historic and Endangered Livestock and Poultry Breeds.* New Haven: Yale University Press, 2001.

Dorsey, Kurkpatrick. *The Dawn of Conservation Diplomacy: U.S.-Canadian Wildlife Protection Treaties in the Progressive Era.* Seattle: University of Washington Press, 1998.

Ellsworth, Grant. *The Senator from Simsbury.* West Hartford, CT: Fenwick Productions, 2001.

Ellsworth, John E. *Simsbury: Being a Brief Historical Sketch of Ancient and Modern Simsbury, 1642–1935.* Simsbury, CT: Simsbury Committee for the Tercentenary, 1935.

Evensen, Bruce J. *Journalism and the American Experience.* New York: Routledge, 2018.

Fleming, D.F. *The United States and the World Court.* New York: Doubleday, 1945.

Gould, Lewis. *Four Hats in the Ring: The 1912 Election and the Birth of Modern American Politics.* Lawrence, Kansas: University Press of Kansas, 2008.

———. *Grand Old Party: A History of the Republicans.* New York: Oxford University Press, 2015.

———. *The William Howard Taft Presidency.* Lawrence: University Press of Kansas, 2009.

Grob, Gerald N. *Mental Illness and American Society, 1875–1940.* Princeton, NJ: Princeton University Press, 2019.

Grosvenor, Charles H. *William McKinley, His Life and Work.* Washington, DC: The Continental Assembly, 1901.

Hardy, Mary McLean. *A Brief History of the Ancestry and Posterity of Allan MacLean*. New York: Marquand, 1905.

Hayward, John. *The New England Gazetteer: Containing Descriptions of All the States*. Concord, NH: I. Boyd and W. White, 1839.

Heath, Frederick Morrison. "Politics and Steady Habits: Issues and Elections in Connecticut, 1894–1914." PhD diss., Columbia University, 1965.

Hicks, Ratcliffe, and Gardiner, Cornelius, eds. "The Johnson Trial." *Speeches and Public Correspondence of Ratcliffe Hicks*. United States: The University Press, 1896.

Hornaday, William T. *Our Vanishing Wildlife: Its Extermination and Preservation*. New York: Scribners, 1913.

Job, Herbert K. *Propagation of Wild Birds*. Garden City, NY: Doubleday, 1915.

Johnson, McMillan Houston. *Taking Off: The Politics and Culture of American Aviation, 1920–1939*. PhD diss., University of Tennessee, 2011.

Kaplan, Edward S. *American Trade Policy, 1923–1995*. Westport, CT: Greenwood Press, 1996.

Kaplan, Justin. *Mr. Clemens and Mark Twain*. New York: Simon & Schuster, 1966.

Larned, Ellen D. *History of Windham County, Connecticut*. Worcester, MA: Charles Hamilton, 1874.

Markel, Howard. *When Germs Travel*. New York: Pantheon Books, 2004.

McGerr, Michael. *A Fierce Discontent: The Rise and Fall of the Progressive Movement in America, 1870–1920*. New York: Free Press, 2003.

McLean, George P. *The Plumage And The Tariff Extermination Of Useful Birds For Their Plumage A Grave Economic Blunder Speech Of Hon. George P. McLean In The Senate Of The United States*. Washington, DC: US Government Printing Office, 1913.

———. "Speech of His Excellency, George P. McLean, Governor of Connecticut" ("Connecticut and the Puritan"). In *Ninety-Sixth Anniversary Celebration of the New England Society in the City of New York*. New York: William Green Co., 1901.

Mee, Charles L., Jr. *The Ohio Gang: The World of Warren G. Harding*. New York: M. Evans and Co., 1981.

Milkis, Sidney. *Theodore Roosevelt, the Progressive Party, and the Transformation of American Democracy*. Lawrence: University Press of Kansas, 2009.

Montgomery, M. *Anne of Green Gables*. New York: Bantam Books, 1976.

Moriarity, Audrey. *Pinehurst: Golf, History, and the Good Life*. Ann Arbor, MI: Sports Media Group, 2005.

Morris, Edmund. *The Rise of Theodore Roosevelt*. New York: Coward, McCann & Geoghegan, 1979.

———. *Theodore Rex*. New York: Random House, 2001.

Murphy, Kevin. *Crowbar Governor: The Life and Times of Morgan Gardner Bulkeley.* Middletown, CT: Wesleyan University Press, 2010.

Murray, Robert K. *The Harding Era.* Minneapolis: University of Minnesota Press, 1969.

————. *The Politics of Normalcy: Governmental Theory and Practice in the Harding-Coolidge Era.* New York: W. W. Norton & Company, 1973.

Nichols, Carole. *Votes and More for Women: Suffrage and After in Connecticut.* New York: Haworth Press, 1983.

O'Neill, Jessie H. *The Golden Ghetto: The Psychology of Affluence.* Center City, MN: Hazelden Publishing, 1996.

O'Toole, Patricia. *The Moralist: Woodrow Wilson and the World He Made.* New York: Simon & Schuster, 2018.

Ogden, Brent D. *Railroad-Highway Grade Crossing Handbook.* Washington, DC: Federal Highway Administration, Office of Safety Design, August 2007.

Paine, Henry D. *Paine Family Records: A Journal of Genealogical and Biographical Information*, Volume 2. Albany: J. Munsell, 1883.

Pearson, Thomas Gilbert. *Adventures in bird protection; an autobiography.* New York: D. Appleton-Century, 1937.

Price, Jennifer. *Flight Maps: Adventures with Nature in Modern America.* New York: Basic Books, 1999.

Randall, Willard S. *Alexander Hamilton: A Life.* New York: HarperCollins, 2003.

Ratner, Sidney. *Taxation and Democracy in America.* New York: Wiley, 1967.

Rose, Gary L. *Connecticut Government and Politics: An Introduction.* Fairfield, CT: Sacred Heart University Press, 2007.

Roy, Mark J. "Land Grant Status Acquired After 'Yale-Storrs Controversy,'" *UConn Today,* University of Connecticut Communications Department, September 26, 2012, https://today.uconn.edu/2012/09/land-grant-status-acquired-after-yale-storrs-controversy/.

Sanders, C. W. *Sanders' School Speaker: A Comprehensive Course of Instruction in the Principles of Oratory; with Numerous Exercises for Practice in Declamation.* New York: Ivison & Phinney, 1857.

Schriftgiesser, Karl. *This Was Normalcy.* New York: Oriole Editions, 1948.

Shlaes, Amity. *Coolidge.* New York: Harper, 2013.

————. *The Forgotten Man: A New History of the Great Depression.* New York: Harper Collins Publishers, 2008.

Sinclair, Alexander Maclean. *The Clan Gillean.* Charlottetown, Canada: Hazard and Moore, 1899.

Statistical History of the United States, from Colonial Times to the Present. Series B 304–330: Immigration-Immigrants by Country: 1820 to 1945. New York: Basic Books, 1976.

Stephenson, George M. *The Puritan Heritage.* New York: MacMillan Co., 1952.

Stevens, Rosemary. *A Time of Scandal: Charles R. Forbes, Warren G. Harding, and the Making of the Veterans Bureau.* Baltimore: Johns Hopkins University Press, 2017.

Stillman, Edward. *The Roaring Twenties.* New York: American Heritage, 2015.

Taylor, Dorceta E. *The Rise of the American Conservation Movement: Power, Privilege, and Environmental Protection.* Durham: Duke University Press, 2016.

Taylor, William Harrison. *Taylor's Legislative History and Souvenir of Connecticut, Vol III.* Putnam CT: William Taylor, 1901.

Uhler, John William. "Yellowstone National Park Visitor Statistics." Yellowstone Up Close and Personal, https://www.yellowstone.co/stats.htm.

Wahlgren, Mark. *Party Games: Getting, Keeping, and Using Power in Gilded Age Politics.* Chapel Hill: University of North Carolina Press, 2004.

Ward, Susan Hayes. *The History of the Broadway Tabernacle Church.* New York: The Trow Print, 1901.

Warshauer, Matthew. *Connecticut in the American Civil War: Slavery, Sacrifice, and Survival.* Middletown, CT: Wesleyan University Press, 2011.

West, Robert Craig. *Banking Reform and the Federal Reserve.* Ithaca: Cornell University Press, 1977.

Whittlesey, Lee H. *Storytelling in Yellowstone: Horse and Buggy Tour Guides.* Albuquerque: University of New Mexico Press, 2007.

Whyte, Kenneth. *Hoover: An Extraordinary Life in Extraordinary Times.* New York: Alfred A. Knopf, 2017.

Williams, Richard. *Realigning America: McKinley, Bryan, and the Remarkable Election of 1896.* Lawrence: University Press of Kansas, 2010.

Wilson, John. *Church and State in American History.* New York: Routledge, 2019.

"Yale-Storrs Controversy." *New York Times*, September 25, 1895, 4.

ARTICLES

Albert, Richard. "The Progressive Era of Constitutional Amendment." *Revista de Investigações Constitucionais*, no. 3 (2015).

Alstott, Anne L., and Novick, Ben. "War, Taxes, and Income Redistribution in the Twenties: The 1924 Veterans' Bonus and the Defeat of the Mellon Plan." *Law & Society: Public Law Journal* 59 (2006).

"America's Worst Vice Presidents." *Time*, August 21, 2008, https://time.com/4314491/americas-worst-vice-presidents/.

Andrews, Champe S. "The Importance of the Enforcement of Law." *The Annals of the American Academy of Political and Social Science* 34, no. 1 (1909).

Armstrong, Ken. "The Suspect, the Prosecutor, and the Unlikely Bond They Forged." *Smithsonian*, January 2017.

Aruga, Tadashi. "Reflections on the History of U.S.-Japanese Relations." *American Studies International* 32, no. 1 (1994): 8–16. https://www.jstor.org/stable/41280813.

Beasley, Vanessa B. "Engendering Democratic Change: How Three U.S. Presidents Discussed Female Suffrage." *Rhetoric and Public Affairs* 5, no. 1 (Spring 2002): 79–103. https://www.jstor.org/stable/41939718.

Benedict, Michael Les. "Constitutional Politics in the Gilded Age." *The Journal of the Gilded Age and Progressive Era* 9, no. 1 (2010): 7–35. doi:10.1017/S1537781400003777.

Buzwell, Greg. "Man is not truly one, but truly two: duality in Robert Louis Stevenson's *Strange Case of Dr. Jekyll and Mr. Hyde.*" *British Library Newsletter*, May 15, 2014.

Bybee, Jay S. "Ulysses at the Mast: Democracy, Federalism, and the Sirens' Song of the Seventeenth Amendment." *Scholarly Works*, 1997. https://scholars.law.unlv.edu/facpub/350/.

Canon, David T. "Committee Hierarchy and Assignments in the U.S. Senate, 1789–1946." Paper delivered at the Norman Thomas Conference on Senate Exceptionalism, Vanderbilt University, October 21–23, 1999.

Chapman, Frank M. "Birds and Bonnets." *Forest and Stream* 26, no. 5 (February 25, 1886).

Clark, Charles Hopkins. "The Charter Oak City." *Scribner's Monthly* XIII, no. 1 (November 1876).

Collyns, Dan. "Machu Picchu: What is the legacy of 'Indiana Jones discoverer?'" *BBC Newsletter*, July 7, 2011.

Countryman, William A. "Connecticut's position in the Manufacturing World." *Connecticut Magazine* 7 (1902).

Daniels, Doris Groshen. "Theodore Roosevelt and Gender Roles." *Presidential Studies Quarterly* 26, no. 3 (Summer 1996): 648–65. https://www.jstor.org/stable/27551623.

"Diagnosing depression: What is the difference between a recession and a depression?" *The Economist*, December 30, 2008, https://www.economist.com/finance-andeconomics/2008/12/30/diagnosing-depression.

Diamond, Stephen A. "Who Were the Alienists?" *Psychology Today*, January 26, 2018.

Duffy, Patrick. "Pilgrims of the Air." *Dublin Review of Books*, January 1, 2015.

Easton, Barbara. "Industrialization and Femininity: A Case Study of Nineteenth Century New England." *Social Problems* 23, no. 4 (1976): 389–401. https://www.jstor.org/stable/799850.

Entzminger, Betina. "Fin de Siècle Anxieties and Cave Endings: Mark Twain's A Connecticut Yankee in King Arthur's Court." *Mark Twain Journal* 55, no. 1/2 (Spring/Fall 2017): 100–112. https://www.jstor.org/stable/44504997.

Fairchild, Henry Pratt. "The Immigration Law of 1924." *The Quarterly Journal of Economics* 38, no. 4 (August 1924): 653–65. https://www.jstor.org/stable/1884595.

———. "The Literacy Test and Its Making." *The Quarterly Journal of Economics* 31, no. 3 (May 1917): 447–60. doi:10.2307/1883384.

Freeman, Michael. "Puritans and Pequots: The Question of Genocide." *The New England Quarterly* 68, no. 2 (June 1995): 278–93. https://www.jstor.org/stable/366259.

Gladden, George. "Federal Protection for Migratory Birds." *Outing Magazine* LXII, no. 3 (April 1913).

Glass, Andrew. "Senate Votes to Join World Court, Jan. 27, 1926." *Politico*, January 27, 2016.

Gonzalez, Jonathan. "Home Guard Patrols Helped in Connecticut During WWI." *Southern Connecticut State University Journalism blog*, November 2018.

Goodheart, Lawrence, B. "Rethinking Mental Retardation: Education and Eugenics in Connecticut, 1818–1917." *Journal of the History of Medicine and Allied Sciences* 59, no. 1 (2004): 90–111. doi:10.1093/jhmas/jrg043.

Haight, R. J. (Rufus J.). "Literature Received." *The Modern Cemetery, The Association of American Cemetery Superintendents* 3, no. 7 (September 1893).

Hallahan, Frances, and Lathrop, Eleanor. "Wilderness in Suburbia: The Management Dilemma." Yale School of Forestry and Environmental Studies, 1981.

Harper, George. "Scar't of Him." *Harper's Weekly* LIV, no. 2819 (December 31, 1910).

Henretta, James A. "Charles Evans Hughes and the Strange Death of Liberal America." *Law and History Review* 24, no. 1 (2006): 115–71. doi:10.1017/S0738248000002285.

Hovenkamp, Herbert. "Regulatory Conflict in the Gilded Age: Federalism and the Railroad Problem." *The Yale Law Journal* 97, no. 6 (May 1988): 1017–72. https://www.jstor.org/stable/796340.

Istre, Logan Stag. "Theodore Roosevelt and the Case for a Popular Constitution." *American Affairs* IV, no. 3 (Fall 2020).

Janick, Herbert. "Senator Frank B. Brandegee and the Election of 1920." *The Historian* 35, no. 3, (May 1973): 434–51. https://www.jstor.org/stable/24443018.

"J. Henry Roraback: Yankee Boss." *Time*, vol. 29, no. 22, May 31, 1937.

Job, Herbert K. "Ducks and the Senator." *Outing Magazine* 69 (October 1916).

Johnson, Roger T. "Historical Beginnings . . . The Federal Reserve." Boston: Public and Community Affairs Department, Federal Reserve Bank of Boston, February 2010.

Jones, Mark, and Albert, Nancy O. "Women's Suffrage: Setting the Watch Fires of Liberty." *Connecticut Explored*, Fall 2005.

Korzi, Michael J. "Our Chief Magistrate and His Powers: A Reconsideration of William Howard Taf"'s 'Whig' Theory of Presidential Leadership." *Presidential Studies Quarterly* 33, no. 2 (2003): 305–24. doi:10.1111/j.1741-5705.2003.tb00031.x.

Kraig, Robert Alexander. "The 1912 Election and the Rhetorical Foundations of the Liberal State." *Rhetoric and Public Affairs* 3, no. 3 (2000): 363–95. https://www.jstor.org/stable/41940243.

Lautenschlager, Karl. "The Submarine in Naval Warfare, 1901–2001." *International Security* 11, no. 3 (1986): 94–140. doi:10.1162/isec.11.3.94.

Lehrman, Robert. "Seriously, the Gridiron Club dinner matters." *The Hill*, March 6, 2016.

Lofgren, Charles A. "Missouri v. Holland in Historical Perspective." *The Supreme Court Review* (1975): 77–122. https://www.jstor.org/stable/3108809.

Maga, Timothy P. "Prelude to War? The United States, Japan, and the Yap Crisis, 1918–22." *Diplomatic History* 9, no. 3 (1985): 215–31. https://www.jstor.org/stable/24911662.

McDaniel, Carl, and Gowdy, John M. "Markets and biodiversity loss: some case studies and policy considerations." *International Journal of Social Economics* 25, no. 10 (January 1998): 1454–65.

Mennell, S. J. "Prohibition: A Sociological View." *Journal of American Studies* 3, no. 2 (1969): 195–75. doi:10.1017/S0021875800008100.

Merchant, Carolyn. "Women of the Progressive Conservation Movement: 1900–1916." *Environmental Review* 8, no. 1 (1984). doi:10.2307/3984521.

Miller, Gary, and Norman Schofield. "Activists and Partisan Realignment in the United States." *The American Political Science Review* 97, no. 2 (2003): 245–60. doi:10.1017/S0003055403000650.

Miller, Joe C. "Never A Fight of Woman Against Man: What Textbooks Don't Say about Women's Suffrage." *The History Teacher* 48, no. 3 (May 2015): 437–82.

Minichiello, J. Kent. "The Audubon Movement: Its Origins, Its Conservation Context, and Its Initial Accomplishments." *Journal of the Washington Academy of Sciences* 90, no. 2 (Summer 2004): 33. https://www.jstor.org/stable/24531344.

Moline, Brian J. "Early American Legal Education." *Washburn Law Journal* 42, no. 4 (Summer 2004): 775–802.

Moore, John A. "The Original Supply Siders: Warren Harding and Calvin Coolidge." *The Independent Review* 18, no. 4 (2014): 597–618. https://www.jstor.org/stable/24563172.

Murnane, Susan. "Selling Scientific Taxation: The Treasury Departments Campaign for Tax Reform in the 1920s." *Law & Social Inquiry* 29, no. 4 (2004): 819–56. https://www.jstor.org/stable/4092770.

Murphy, John. "'Back to the Constitution': Theodore Roosevelt, William Howard Taft and Republican Party Division 1910–1912." *Irish Journal of American Studies* 4 (1995): 109–26. https://www.jstor.org/stable/30003333.

Nelson, Dean E. "Civil War: Connecticut Arms the Union." *Connecticut Explored*, Spring 2011.

"Obituary for Hannah McLean Greeley, 1848–1906." *Proceedings of Lexington Historical Society and Papers* 4 (1906).

Palmer, Niall A. "The Veterans' Bonus and the Evolving Presidency of Warren G. Harding." *Presidential Studies Quarterly* 38, no. 1 (2008).

Pavord, Andrew C. "The Gamble for Power: Theodore Roosevelt's Decision to Run for the Presidency in 1912." *Presidential Studies Quarterly* 26, no. 3 (1996): 39–60. https://www.jstor.org/stable/27552303.

Pecquet, Gary M., and Thies, Clifford F. "Reputation Overrides Record: How Warren G. Harding Mistakenly Became the 'Worst' President of the United States." *The Independent Review* 21, no. 1 (2016): 29–45. https://www.jstor.org/stable/43999675.

Peskin, Allan. "Who Were the Stalwarts? Who Were Their Rivals? Republican Factions in the Gilded Age." *Political Science Quarterly* 99, no. 4 (1984): 703–16. https://www.jstor.org/stable/2150708.

Pinta, Emil R. "Examining Harry Thaw's "Brainstorm" Defense: APA and ANA Presidents as Expert Witnesses in a 1907 Trial." *Psychiatric Quarterly* 79, no. 2 (July 2008): 83–89. doi:10.1007/s11126-007-9054-y.

Primm, James Neal. "A Foregone Conclusion: The Founding of the Federal Reserve Bank of St. Louis." *Federal Reserve Bank Review*, 1989.

Rader, Benjamin G. "Federal Taxation in the 1920s: A Re-Examination." *The Historian*, 1971.

Reed, Lawrence W. "Andrew Mellon: The Best Treasury Secretary in US History." *Foundation for Economic Education Review*, May 26, 2016.

Robenalt, James D. "If we weren't so obsessed with Warren G. Harding's sex life, we'd realize he was a pretty good president." *Washington Post*, August 13, 2015, https://www. washingtonpost.com/posteverything/wp/2015/08/13/if-we-werent-so-obsessed-with-warren-g-hardings-sex-life-wed-realize-he-was-a-pretty-good-president/.

Ross, William G. "Constitutional Issues Involving the Controversy over American Membership in the League of Nations, 1918–1920." *The American Journal of Legal History* 53, no. 1 (2013): 1–88. doi:10.1093/ajlh/53.1.1.

Rozan, Kristina. "Detailed Discussion on the Migratory Bird Treaty Act." *Michigan State University College of Law Review*. East Lansing, MI: Animal Legal & Historical Center, 2014.

Sammis, Frederick. "Around the World Wireless." *Popular Mechanics*, September 1912.

Schleicher, David N. "The Seventeenth Amendment." *National Constitution Center*, January 5, 2020.

"Senator McLean's Report." *The Lancet-clinic* 112, no. 9 (August 29, 1914).

"Senator McLean Champions Women in Civil Service." *The Labor Journal*, December 12, 1919.

Sinclair, Iain. "An introduction to The War of the Worlds." *British Library Newsletter*, May 15, 2014.

Tacoma, Thomas. "Calvin Coolidge and the Great Depression: A New Assessment." *The Independent Review* 24, no. 3 (Winter 2019/20): 361–80. https://www.jstor.org/stable/45238861.

Thorndike, Joseph J. "Was Andrew Mellon Really the Supply Sider That Conservatives Like to Believe?" *Tax Analysts Inc.*, March 24, 2003.

Toms, Jonathan. "The Mental Hygiene Movement and the Trapdoor in Measurements of Intellect." *Journal of Intellect Disabilities Research* 54, no. s1 (April 2010): 16–27. doi:10.1111/j.1365-2788.2009.01234.x.

"Treason in the Senate." *Washington Post*, June 28, 1906, 4.

Vose Clement E. "State Against Nation: The Case of Missouri vs. Holland." *Prologue: The Journal of the National Archives* (Spring 1984).

"What Was the Worst Year in History?" *The Atlantic*, December 2013.

Wicker, Elmus R. "A Reconsideration of Federal Reserve Policy during the 1920–1921 Depression." *The Journal of Economic History* 26, no. 2 (June 1966): 223–38. https://www.jstor.org/stable/2116229.

Wills, Matthew. "A Really Contested Convention: The 1924 Democratic 'Klanbake.'" *JSTOR Daily*, May 11, 2016.

Wojtowicz, Robert. "Lewis Mumford: The Architectural Critic as Historian." *Studies in the History of Art* 35 (1990): 237–49. https://www.jstor.org/stable/42620520.

Wolfensberger, Don. "Woodrow Wilson, Congress and Anti-Immigrant Sentiment in America." Woodrow Wilson International Center for Scholars, March 12, 2007.

Woodward, Walter W. "The German Invasion of Connecticut." *Connecticut Explored*, Spring 2017.

Yeh, Puong Fei. "The Role of the Zimmermann Telegram in Spurring America's Entry into the First World War." *American Intelligence Journal* 32, no. 1 (2015). https://www.jstor.org/stable/26202105.

Zacks, Richard. "The Nineteenth-Century Start-Ups That Cost Mark Twain His Fortune." *Time*, April 19, 2016, https://time.com/4297572/mark-twain-bad-business/.

GOVERNMENT DOCUMENTS

49 Cong. Rec. H4799 (daily ed. Mar. 3, 1913) (statement of Rep. Mondell).

49 Cong. Rec. S1487 (daily ed. Jan. 14, 1913) (statement of Sen. McLean).

49 Cong. Rec. S1870 (daily ed. Jan. 22, 1913) (statement of Sen. McLean).

49 Cong. Rec. S4149 (daily ed. Feb. 27, 1913) (statement of Sen. Jorgenson).

49 Cong. Rec. S4149 (daily ed. Feb. 27, 1913) (statement of Sen. Bryan).

51 Cong. Rec. S545 (daily ed. Dec. 9, 1913) (statement of Sen. McLean).

51 Cong. Rec. S8449 (daily ed. May 12, 1914) (statement of Sen. McLean).

55 Cong. Rec. S4399 (daily ed. June 27, 1917) (statement of Sen. Reed).

55 Cong. Rec. S4400 (daily ed. June 27, 1917) (statement of Sen. McLean).

59 Cong. Rec. S3734 (daily ed. Mar. 3, 1920) (statement of Sen. McLean).

59 Cong. Rec. S6451 (daily ed. May 3, 1920) (statement of Sen. McLean).

61 Cong. Rec. S6091-93 (daily ed. Oct. 7, 192) (statement of Sen. McLean).

67 Cong. Rec. S1970 (daily ed. Jan. 13, 1926) (statement of Sen. McLean).

70 Cong. Rec. S1189 (daily ed. Jan 5, 1929) (statement of Sen. McLean).

70 Cong. Rec. S1714 (daily ed. Jan. 15, 1929) (Roll Call Vote—Multilateral Peace Treaty).

70 Cong. Rec. S5024 (daily ed. March 2, 1929) (statement of Sen. Glass).

Gibson, Campbell, and Kay Jung. 2002. Historical census statistics on population totals by race, 1790 to 1990, and by Hispanic origin, 1970 to 1990, for the United States, regions, divisions, and states. Washington, DC: US Census Bureau.

Public Documents of the State of Connecticut. Vol. I, "Message of His Excellency George P. McLean to the Connecticut General Assembly, January 1901." Hartford: Order of the General Assembly, 1901. https://babel.hathitrust.org/cgi/pt?id=ucw.ark:/13960/t6c25xs8s&view=1up&seq=13&skin=2021&q1=mclean.

US Census Bureau. "Connecticut, Hartford, Simsbury, District 0237, 'George P. McLean.'" Washington, DC: US Government Printing Office, 1910.

US Census Bureau. Census of Population and Housing (CPH-2-8). "Connecticut: Table 1." Washington, DC: US Government Printing Office, 2010.

US Census Bureau. Census of Manufactures. Vol. 8. "Table 1: Connecticut Comparative Summary, 1850 to 1900." Washington, DC: Government Printing Office, 1900. https://www2.census.gov/library/publications/decennial/1900/volume-8/volume-8-p2.pdf.

United States. 68th Congress, 2nd session. *Frank B. Brandegee: Memorial addresses delivered in the Senate and House of Representatives of the United States in Memory of Frank B. Brandegee Late a Senator from Connecticut.* Washington: US Government Printing Office, 1925.

United States. Department of Justice. *The United States Attorneys' Manual*, April 2018.

NEWSPAPERS

Baltimore Sun
Berkshire (MA) *Eagle*
Boston Evening Transcript
Boston Globe
Bridgeport (CT) *Post*
Bridgeport Telegram
Bridgeport Times
Buffalo (NY) *Review*
Burlington Free Press (Burlington, VT)
Carbondale Free Press (Carbondale, IL)
Cincinnati Enquirer
Daily Inter-Ocean (Chicago)
Daily Tribune (Wisconsin Rapids, WI)
Dayton Daily News (Dayton, OH)
Edmonton Journal (Canada)
Evening Star (Washington, DC)
Evening Sun (Baltimore)
Green Bay Press-Gazette
Hartford (CT) *Daily Courant*
Herald-Press (Saint Joseph, MI)
Kansas City Times
Meriden (CT) *Record*
Meriden Daily Republican
Meriden Journal (Meriden, CT)
Montgomery Advertiser (Montgomery, AL)
Morning News (Wilmington, DE)
Naugatuck (CT) *Daily News*
Nebraska State Journal
New Castle News (New Castle, PA)
New Hartford (CT) *Tribune*
New Haven Journal-Courier
New Haven Morning-Journal Courier
New York Times
New York Tribune

Norwich (CT) *Bulletin*
Oakland (CA) *Tribune*
Pittsburgh (PA) *Post-Gazette*
Record-Journal (Meriden, CT)
Salt Lake (UT) *Tribune*
San Francisco Examiner
Sandusky Star-Journal (Sandusky, OH)
Spokesman-Review (Spokane, WA)
St. Joseph News-Press (MO)
Standard Union (Brooklyn, NY)
Star Tribune (Minneapolis, MN)
Star-Gazette (Elmira, NY)
Sun (New York)
Times-Democrat (New Orleans, Louisiana)
Times-Tribune (PA)
Topeka (KS) *Daily Capital*
Twin-City Daily Sentinel (Winston-Salem, NC)
Washington (DC) *Herald*
Washington Post
Washington (DC) *Times*
Watertown (CT) *News*
Wichita Beacon (KS)
Worker's Chronicle (Pittsburg, KS)

★ INDEX ★

★ COLOPHON ★

Editor
Alexandra Hoff

Designer
Eric C. Wilder

Production
Marnie Soom

Printer
More Vang
Alexandria, Virginia

This book was made possible, in part,
through the generosity of More Vang.

Paper
70# Uncoated Cougar Natural